*The Book of the Heart*

# The
# BOOK
## of the
# HEART

Eric Jager

The University of Chicago Press

Chicago & London

ERIC JAGER is associate professor of English at the University of California, Los Angeles. He is the author of *The Tempter's Voice: Language and the Fall in Medieval Literature* (1993).

The University of Chicago Press, Chicago 60637
The University of Chicago Press, Ltd., London
© 2000 by The University of Chicago
All rights reserved. Published 2000
Printed in the United States of America

09 08 07 06 05 04 03 02 01 00          1 2 3 4 5
ISBN: 0-226-39116-7 (CLOTH)

Library of Congress Cataloging-in-Publication Data
Jager, Eric, 1957–
    The book of the heart / Eric Jager.
        p.   cm.
    Includes bibliographical references and index.
    ISBN 0-226-39116-7 (alk. paper)
        1. Literature—History and criticism.    2. Heart in literature.    3. Literature, Medieval—History and criticism.    4. Heart—Religious aspects—Christianity.    I. Title.
    PN56.H374 J34 2000
    700'.415—dc21                                                    99-047258

*To Peg o' my heart*

perqu'es vertatz e sembla be
qu'ins e·l cor port, dona, vostra faisso
que·m chastia qu'ieu no vir ma razo

# Contents

# Illustrations

# *Acknowledgments*

First, I am grateful to those who read and commented on this book in manuscript form. Besides the two anonymous readers for the press who critiqued the entire book, a number of friends and colleagues kindly donated time to examining individual chapters: James Bednarz, Jesse Gellrich, Henry A. Kelly, William Kolbrener, and Kenneth Reinhard. Further improvements I owe to Alan Thomas, Executive Editor; Randolph Petilos, Assistant Editor; Erin DeWitt, Manuscript Editor; and the superb staff at the University of Chicago Press. Any errors or oversights are, of course, my own.

For crucial help in the project's early stages, I am indebted to two former Columbia University colleagues, Howard Bloch and David Damrosch, who glimpsed some of this book's possibilities even before I did. And for suggestions about specific points, I am grateful to many others who gave me the benefit of their varied expertise: Michael J. B. Allen, A. R. Braunmuller, Douglas Brooks, Caroline Bynum, Consuelo Dutschke, John Fleming, Lowell Gallagher, Tobias Gittes, Curtis Gruenler, Jeffrey Hamburger, Katherine Hayles, Gordon Kipling, V. A. Kolve, Jayne Lewis, Claire McEachern, Stephen Nichols, David Rahmel, Jane Rosenthal, Richard Rouse, Eve Sanders, James Shapiro, Debora Shuger, Jocelyn Penny Small, Ted Tayler, Mark Vessey, Robert Watson, Winthrop Wetherbee, and Joan Williamson.

Several fine research assistants at Columbia and UCLA helped me in gathering research sources and tracking down elusive library items: Jessica Brantley, James Cain, Thomas Hill, Andrey Slivka, and especially Marlene Villalobos Hennessy and Victoria Simmons. The professional staffs of many research libraries, museums, and archives also provided crucial assistance during on-site research visits or via correspondence: Maryan Ainsworth and Veronique Sintobin of the Metropolitan Museum of Art; Inga Dupont of the Pierpont Morgan Library; Lorne Campbell and Margaret Daly of the National Gallery, London; Christopher Coleman of the University Research Library at UCLA; David Bruce Whiteman and Stephen Tabor of the William Andrews Clark Memorial Library in Los Angeles; and Alison Jasonides of Art Resource, New York.

In its early stages, this project also received valuable responses at conferences and invited lectures. For the chance to present my work in progress, I am grateful to Columbia University, Duke University, Louisiana State University, Washington University in St. Louis, the UCLA Friends of English (including Annie Reynoso), the Metropolitan Museum of Art (especially Stella Paul), the Modern Language Association, and the Medieval Academy of America. A preliminary version of this study appeared in *Speculum*, to whose editor, Luke Wenger, I am indebted for several useful suggestions at the time, and now for permission to reproduce part of that (much revised) material.

This project was also supported by institutional gifts in the form of sabbatical leave and research funding. A full year of freedom from teaching responsibilities was provided by the combined generosity of the American Council of Learned Societies and UCLA's Department of English, to whose former and current chairs, Eric Sundquist and Thomas Wortham, I am much indebted. Funds for travel and research were provided by the UCLA Academic Senate and greatly expedited by Doris Wang. Photography permissions were generously paid for by the UCLA Friends of English.

Above all, I am grateful to my wife, Peg Eby-Jager, who helped me at many a turn with her expertise as a research librarian, and without whose moral support, enthusiasm, and love this book never could have been written. As a book of the heart in more ways than one, it is dedicated to her.

# *Note on Translations*

Wherever possible I have used standard translations such as the Loeb Classical Library, sometimes with minor stylistic alterations (e.g., "your" for "thy," or "honor" for "honour"), but with all substantive changes indicated in the notes. Scriptural passages are from the Revised Standard Version, unless otherwise noted. Translations for which no source is indicated in the notes or bibliography are my own.

# Introduction

Today we often describe our lives and ourselves in terms of the visual and electronic media that dominate our culture. Picturing the mind as a computer, we casually talk of mental "software," "hard-wired" personality traits, and even people who are "missing a chip." Or treating mental life as a movie, we experience events in "slow motion," "replay" our memories, or offer our "take" on things. These are more than just popular expressions of the Information (or Entertainment) Age. The computer in particular has become the dominant scientific model of the mind (or brain) and is likely to remain as such until well into the twenty-first century.

Yet even as we model ourselves on the latest technology, we continue to use another, much older metaphor of selfhood that is based on what until quite recently was the world's most powerful communication medium—namely, the written word. Hardly a day passes without our referring to someone's "character," or to our own "impressions," to "reading" another person's mind, or to making a "mental note." Less common today but still familiar are various references to the "book" of the self, such as "turning over a new leaf" or "taking a leaf out of (someone else's) book." "In *my* book . . . ," people still say in reference to their ideas or opinions (though now many are more likely to invoke what is "on my screen"). Book metaphors have even been co-opted by other media, as with "clichéd" characters—a printing term adapted to film—and "scripted" emotion or behavior, which started as a book ("manuscript"), then went to the movies (as "script"), afterward entered therapy (as "scripted"), and finally settled in popular speech. What all of these expressions have in common is the metaphor of the self as a *text,* a metaphor that goes back to the beginnings of Western literacy, when the idea of the textual self was born.

This book examines the history and significance of this metaphor during its long and now diminishing life in Western culture. Like words in general, metaphors often undergo historical changes of form and meaning, and the self-text metaphor is no exception. Both its imagery (or "vehicle") and its conceptual content (or "tenor") have changed substantially over time. As the written word has taken various material forms over the centuries, so the self or psyche has been successively likened to the ancient scroll or the writing tablet, the medieval manuscript codex, and the modern printed book. And as cultural changes have entailed different moral, religious, or philosophical conceptions of the human being, so the textual self has been variously defined in terms of the ancient (Neoplatonic) "soul," the medieval (Christian) "heart," and the modern (secular) "brain."

Although I trace the self-text metaphor from antiquity to modernity, I devote most of my attention, as my title suggests, to the medieval millennium during which this metaphor, as a book of the heart created in the image of the manuscript codex, reached the height of its ideological power and poetic expression. The period from roughly 400 C.E. to 1500, or from the ascendancy of the codex in the late Roman Empire to the advent of the printed book during the late Middle Ages, saw not only the full flowering of the book of the heart as a literary trope, but also its transformation into a pictorial image and even a tangible artifact.

Medieval culture constructed key aspects of inward experience, from knowledge and memory to pious devotion and sensual passion, in terms of the manuscript codex and the related tropes of reading, writing, erasure, and interpretation. For example, romances tell of lovers' hearts inscribed with signs of the beloved, and saints' legends celebrate martyrs whose hearts received marks of special divine favor. Clergy are instructed to let their inner scribe copy God's commands onto the pages of their hearts, and ordinary believers pray for Christ to write the memory of his Passion in their "heart books." In the realm of visual art, authors are portrayed holding a heart and a pen, and some late medieval paintings depict the sitter as a scribe or reader holding a heart-shaped manuscript codex. Medieval artisans also produced actual books in this shape, examples of which are still preserved in European archives.

The book of the heart is a quintessentially medieval trope in that it combines the central symbol of medieval textual culture, the manuscript codex, with a psychology and anthropology that were centered on the heart rather than the head. Since ancient times the heart was the traditional seat of human emotion, and although Galen (129– c. 199 C.E.) established perception and cognition as functions of the brain, the emotions remained localized in the heart (*kardia*). Aristotle, whose direct influence was renewed after the twelfth century in the West, associated the heart with the vital functions, emotions, and sensation. And Scripture, a preeminent authority, equated the heart with the innermost self, including conscience, memory, and volition. In addition, classical Latin commonly used the heart (*cor*) as a synonym for thought, memory, mind, soul, and spirit, as well as for the seat of intelligence, volition, character, and the emotions—a semantic range inherited by patristic Latin and the medieval Romance languages. Especially important were the medieval forms of what eventually became our word "record" (from Latin *cor*), which linked the heart with memory as well as with writing and books.[1]

Besides its attributed physical and psychological functions, the heart was centrally located in the body and hence was regarded as "the vital center of being, seat of understanding, memory, and the passions, a sort of microcosm of the self."[2] As Jacques Le Goff has shown, the heart's physical centrality also lent itself to political metaphor in the Middle Ages: as the heart was the "king" of the body, so the king was the "heart" of the body politic.[3] For example, although the twelfth-century philosopher Bernard Silvester associates intellect with the brain, he treats the heart as the source of vitality for the brain and the other organs—"the animating spark of the body, nurse of its life, the creative principle and harmonizing bond of the senses; the central link in the human structure, the terminus of the veins, root of the nerves, and controller of the arteries, mainstay of our nature, king, governor, creator."[4] Despite the modern "migration of the body's perceived center from the heart up to the head," heart-centered psychology and heart symbolism have left many traces in our language.[5] We still speak of losing heart, taking heart, heartache, courage, and cordiality. Besides its moral and emotional significance, the heart remains a cognitive term as well, as when we refer to learning things "by heart," a relic of the medieval link between the heart and memory.

Equally central to medieval culture was the manuscript codex—as a valuable object, a vehicle of knowledge, and a polyvalent symbol. Ancestor of the book as we know it, the manuscript codex replaced the scroll (or roll) in late antiquity, largely as a result of Christian preference for this format, and by the fourth century it was already an established symbol in Christian art. About the same time, it also became linked to individual spirituality and the inward life, as exemplified by Augustine's famous conversion story in the *Confessions,* where he opens a scriptural codex and reads a passage there that in turn "opens" his heart to God's grace.

The codex enjoyed increasing prestige during the Middle Ages, not only as the primary form of the written word, but also as a preeminent symbol of truth, order, and totality. On the model of Scripture, a self-contained textual order, the manuscript codex was variously used to symbolize God, nature, history, and the human self. Monks and scholars were fond of book metaphors and reveled in elaborate accounts of the inner scribe and the interior scriptorium, where the parchment of the heart was smoothed, ruled, inscribed, checked for errors, studied, and glossed—allegories for various moral and psychological functions. As a distinctly *scribal* metaphor, the book of the heart often took on personal and even bodily qualities associated with the hand-copied codex. At the same time, this metaphor came to represent an interiority, a private sphere of reflection and feeling, made possible by the emerging practice of silent reading. As a result, the book of the heart increasingly came to be identified with the unique individual.

By the twelfth century, the availability of paper, rising literacy rates, the growth of vernacular literatures, and other social and material changes were bringing books out of the cloisters and schools, the privileged sphere of learned Latinity, into the lives of a larger reading public. Along with books and writing materials came textual metaphors that encouraged this new lay audience, including women in particular, to adopt mental habits associated with literacy and even to reimagine themselves in its terms. As the manuscript book became a more common object in people's external lives, it also became a favored symbol for the hidden human subject, as reflected by an explosion of self-text metaphors in popular literature and art, from the love lyric and the romance to the saint's legend and the morality play, from murals in churches to private devotional art. By the late Middle Ages, the book of the heart had become a familiar metaphor to clerics and laypeople, men and women, alike.

༄༅༄༅༄༅

The metaphor of interior writing has attracted scholarly and critical notice for nearly fifty years now. In his famous chapter "The Book as Symbol," Ernst Robert Curtius surveyed medieval heart-text tropes and placed them within a broader metaphorics of writing that goes back to antiquity.[6] More recently, Jacques Derrida marked the crucial role of interior writing in Western sign theory since Plato, declaring that "a history of this metaphor" had yet to be written.[7] Since Derrida's pronouncement, a number of scholars have explored the crucial place of interior writing in such areas as medieval poetics, the idea of the book, the art of memory, and affective piety. For example, Eugene Vance has analyzed the "poetics of the law" that informs Augustine's *Confessions,* showing how Paul's dialectic of letter and spirit, of the stone tablets of the law and the fleshly "tablets of the heart," shapes Augustine's narrative of the self. Jesse Gellrich has analyzed the medieval idea of the book as a cultural paradigm whose numerous textual tropes for God, nature, history, and the self inform medieval theology and poetic fiction alike. Mary Carruthers has explored the medieval "book of memory," including the metaphor of interior writing and the association of memory with the heart. And Jeffrey Hamburger has recently illuminated the heart's central importance—sometimes as a "text"—in late medieval piety.[8]

Despite this attention, however, the book of the heart has not been studied in depth as a key metaphor of medieval selfhood or as a reflection of the culture at large. One reason for the comparative neglect of this metaphor is that much of its history lies across and even *between* disciplines, including biblical and patristic studies, theology, popular religion, various national literatures, art history, and the history of the book. In particular, medieval literary scholars have largely ignored pictorial (and manuscript) versions of the heart-book metaphor, while art historians have scanted the metaphor's many literary precedents. Although I am no expert in many areas touched upon by this study, since my own training lies in medieval literary texts (mainly English), I here attempt a more integrated history of the book of the heart, aiming to show how its various forms and multiple uses are often intimately linked and offer important clues to the nature of medieval selfhood.

The fact that medieval culture commonly represented the human subject in terms of the manuscript book raises questions of various kinds. Some of these questions relate to origins and sources. For example, where does Western tradition begin to define the self in terms of authorial, readerly, and textual functions? Why was the heart originally associated with textuality, and how was this association developed by medieval culture? How does the medieval book of the heart incorporate (or depart from) its various literary precedents, from the Platonic writing in the soul and the biblical tablet of the heart, to the writing on the body evoked by classical and also early Christian poets?

Other questions deal with the relation of ideology or theory to the material conditions of literary culture. For example, how did ideas about the heart-as-text take shape from the physical forms and institutions of literacy, including the often overlapping roles of author, scribe, and reader; the separate inner and outer disciplines of silent and vocal reading; and the many widely recognized analogies between the human body and the manuscript corpus made of parchment—that is, dried and cured animal skin stripped of its flesh? There is also the question of which features of the codex, as the dominant form of the medieval book, may have inspired comparisons to the heart or the inner self: its container-like shape; its capacity to be opened or closed; its bifoliated or diptychal format (which it shares with the stylized pictorial heart); or, in the later Middle Ages, its diminishing size and increasing portability as an often personal, private possession.

Still other questions relate to issues that have occupied academic scholarship for some time now and that have refreshed and reshaped the field of medieval studies. Contemporary studies of the medieval body often center on the genitals, a focus that seems to owe more to modern (e.g., psychoanalytic) preconceptions than to the body images of medieval medical, political, and theological discourse, which often (as quoted earlier from Bernard Silvester) designate the subject's psychosomatic center as the "heart." Yet the book of the heart clearly relates to gender and sexuality, or "sexual poetics" in Carolyn Dinshaw's apt phrase.⁹ For example, if medieval reading and writing are based on a paradigm of male inscription and female receptivity, does the book of the heart ever assume a gendered character, and, if so, exactly how? In what ways does the body-as-text affect medieval representations of the self-as-text, and sexuality-as-textuality? How does erotic writing on the heart contest or subvert the theology of writing, the Christian grammatology, that dominated the Middle Ages? Or does it actually validate and reinforce it? And, not least of all, how do male and female saints with divine inscriptions on their hearts figure in the medieval dialectic of logos and eros, spirit and flesh?

I am especially interested in the contradictions and paradoxes inherent in the book of the heart as a crux for medieval anxieties about writing and truth, language and desire, identity and the body. One of my main concerns is how the "fleshliness" inherent in the book of the heart increasingly asserts itself during the Middle Ages, not only in more and more graphic accounts of inscribed hearts, but also in a process of development that turns this originally literary trope into a visual image and even a manuscript artifact that is *doubly* (as both book and heart) a literary "corpus." The book of the heart also acquires a corporeal specificity as it becomes identified with the sensual experience of the lover, the physical remains of the saint, the devotional feelings of the pious layperson, or the painted likeness of the bourgeois patron. But in the process of achieving the "fleshly" potential that it inherited from a Christian theology of writing (especially Paul's "fleshly tablets of the heart"), the book of the heart also reduced itself to a paradox: namely, "interior writing" rendered in an outward, physical form. The story of this trope thus exposes a cluster of contradictions at the heart of medieval culture, including the necessary but negotiable distinctions between text and self, letter and spirit, word and flesh.

❧❧❧❧❧❧

To trace the medieval relation of self and text, heart and book, is also to examine the origins of the modern individual. For some time now, a persistent issue of literary and cultural study has been the question of when, where, and under what circumstances the modern self (or "subject") was born. To follow the debates over whether this being made its first appearance in Petrarch's sonnets, on Shakespeare's stage, or yet another place, is like receiving frequently updated news bulletins to the effect that one fine day, in 1359 (with the *Canzoniere*) or 1603 (*Hamlet*), the Western self awoke from its medieval slumbers, looked into the mirror of modernity, and recognized its own reflection. The whole controversy depends, of course, on what exactly is meant by the "self" and what precisely are the criteria of "modernity." In many cases, "modernity" and "selfhood" turn out to be largely honorary titles conferred on whatever a certain critic happens to admire or approve of.[10]

In this book I do not propose an answer to the finally impossible question of just when or where the medieval self gave way to a modern one. But I do suggest that a key Western metaphor of selfhood goes back to a time long before Petrarch or Shakespeare supposedly invented our idea of ourselves, and that it continued to operate powerfully until well after the traditional break between the Middle Ages and early modernity (c. 1500). This metaphor originally portrayed the individual's life as a narrative that is "written" in the "books" of both personal memory and divine omniscience. It first appears in classical antiquity and early biblical literature, both of which may have derived it from an ultimately Egyptian source. The classical and biblical notions of memory or conscience as an interior "writing" came together in early Christian theology, which evoked for the first time a book of the heart containing a moral record of the life of the unique individual. This inner book could be read (and even revised) in pursuit of self-understanding, but it remained under divine purview, and it would be "opened" for a final and very public reading at the Last Judgment. Medieval writers in turn gave the book of the heart a wider but still largely moral-theological content, although besides divine laws, a personal moral record, or devotional feelings, it was also imagined (by secular poets) as a transcript of sensual passion. The book of the heart containing a personal narrative written and studied by the individual himself, but still placed under divine authority and interpretation, is epitomized by the late medieval painting reproduced as figure 11 in this book, which locates the reader (and scribe) of the heart within the precincts of the Church.

If the history of the self-book metaphor exhibits a crucial change between the Middle Ages and modernity, it is not mainly with the printing revolution, although this did transform the format of the inner book in significant ways; or with the Protestant Reformation,

which further individualized the inner book yet preserved its moral-
theological function; but with the empiricist psychology of the seventeenth and eighteenth centuries, which exchanged the book of the heart
for a book of the brain. The book of the brain—which appears in
Shakespeare and may be a more telling sign of his modernity than his
much-touted "self-conscious" characters—was the last of three main
historical configurations of the textual self. The earliest of these was
the Platonic "writing in the soul," which defined the (rational) soul as
a noncorporeal human essence; the second was the medieval book of
the heart, which invoked a biblical (and specifically Christian) anthropology where the heart occupied a liminal, psychosomatic zone and
where the self was not wholly reducible to either spirit or flesh. By contrast with its predecessors, the book of the brain was conceived in secular, autonomous, and radically materialist terms. Instead of innate ideas
or eternal moral truths, it contained merely transient feelings or ephem-
eral sensations. Furthermore, it abandoned all relation to a divine or
heavenly original, so that "personal identity" (in Locke's phrase) now
rested wholly on minute (but still mysterious) "impressions" on the
brain. Accordingly, the human individual who long had been the protagonist of a divinely supervised narrative now became the sole author,
reader, and exegete of his own interior "book"—a truly modern self.
But during the last half-century or so, even this modern book of the
self has been rapidly losing ground to personal metaphors drawn from
new technologies. If psychology tends to follow technology, as I con-
tend in the final chapter of this study, what we are witnessing in the
steady replacement of book metaphors by tropes of the machine and
the screen is the advent of a new, post-textual conception of the self.

## Chapter One

# ORIGINS

*ccording to some students of early literacy, writing was a crucial precondition for the very idea of the self. Selfhood, in this view, resulted from the invention of writing—specifically, alphabetic literacy—because writing first enabled the idea of a person to be separated from language.[1] In oral culture, language always takes the form of speech, a living voice, and hence is inextricable from audible words. A spoken exchange leaves no tangible product, such as a written transcript. But as writing technology turned speech into a visual and semipermanent object and "as language became separated visually from the person who uttered it, so also the person, the source of the language, came into sharper focus and the concept of selfhood was born."[2]

Such claims may oversimplify the case. But whether or not the self was born with writing, the concept of the self seems to have evolved with the extension of writing *metaphors* to the realm of psychology. Indeed, if actual writing provided a basis for separating the self from language, metaphorical writing reunited and identified the self with an interiorized text. At the same time, and equally important, the metaphor of interior writing helped to "naturalize" the notion of self-astext, although resistance to this metaphor also marks early Western commentary on literacy and its cultural effects.

This chapter surveys some of the oldest and most formative literature of Western culture, in an attempt to answer three main questions: What are the origins of the metaphor of the inner person or self as a kind of "text"? How did this textual self come to be associated principally with the "heart"? And how did the heart come to be imagined specifically as a "book"? The chapter begins with classical antiquity, tracing how the metaphor of interior writing evolved in connection with memory, ethics, and knowledge from early Greece to imperial Rome. It then turns to the other principal source of Western tradition, the Bible, showing how an interior writing located specifically in the "heart" was used to represent a moral being defined in relation to the Jewish Law and the Christian Gospel. The last section deals with how the Church Fathers combined the classical and scriptural traditions in formulating, for the first time, a book of the heart that represented an eternal and unique moral person.

## Classical Antiquity

Classical literature offers the most continuous and detailed record of the early self-text metaphor. The Greek poets frequently pictured memory, experience, and other aspects of the interior person as a written "tablet" or "scroll," giving this metaphor an important place in ethical and religious thought. In so doing, they often relied on a somatic psychology that identified interior writing with the chest or pectoral region. The Greek philosophers, beginning with Plato, adopted the metaphor of interior writing but reduced its corporeal connotations by using it to portray the rational mind or soul, which they regarded as the essence of the human being. The Roman moralists and rhetoricians, who in turn inherited this metaphor from Greek sources, revised it further to fit their ethical and educational ideals, where the tablet or scroll of the mind took on an increasingly individual aspect.

### THE GREEK POETS

The metaphor of interior writing is absent from the earliest Greek poetry. However, Homer's sole mention of writing, the "folded tablet" in which a mythical hero carries his own death warrant, links writing to concealment as well as to death or destiny, themes that eventually became linked to *interior* writing as well.[3] The metaphor of interior writing first occurs in the lyric poetry, drama, and philosophy of fifth-century Greece, when literacy itself was spreading in urban centers, most notably Athens. Pindar, apparently the first classical author to use this metaphor, employs it to represent memory in an ode (c. 474 B.C.E.) that invokes the Muse to celebrate a victorious athlete's name: "Tell me where it is written in my heart!"[4]

The fifth-century drama helped popularize this rather esoteric trope among a larger, more diverse audience, not all of whom could read but who were nonetheless learning to appreciate the political and symbolic uses of writing.[5] The drama sometimes likens interior writing to a scroll, the principal format for lengthy texts, or "books," in ancient Greece.[6] However, in the drama and elsewhere, interior writing usually takes the form of a writing tablet (*deltos*), the standard medium for notes, drafts, and other shorter writings. Thus Aeschylus has Prometheus urge Io to write the itinerary of his wanderings on "the recording tablets of your mind."[7]

Aeschylus illustrates the typical shape of interior writing as well as its usual applications. Here, as in Pindar, interior writing represents memory, although it also signifies the fate or destiny of a specific individual. A thematic association between inner writing and personal destiny pervades the *Oresteia,* where this metaphor is a kind of leitmotif. In the first play, the Chorus admits its misgivings to the returning Agamemnon: "In ugly style you were written in my heart."[8] The second play deepens the writing metaphor's association with memory, destiny, and even the idea of personal narrative, as Electra urges Orestes, "Hear my tale and grave it on your heart."[9] Finally, in the *Eumenides,* the Chorus proclaims at the outset that Hades, the god of death and the underworld who calls all mortals to account, "surveys all things with his recording mind"—where "recording" (*deltographo*) alludes again to tablets.[10] As a prelude to the great tribunal that closes the trilogy, this metaphor portrays omniscient divine retribution in terms of human record-keeping, much like the biblical "books" of judgment that would shape the Judeo-Christian book of the heart.

English translations of these passages (such as the Loeb Classical Library editions cited here) typically locate interior writing in the "heart" (or "mind").[11] But none of the quoted examples actually refers to *kēr* or *kardia*, the usual Greek words for "heart" in both its physical and psychological senses. Instead, like many other examples that might be cited, they associate interior writing with the *phrenes*—a term often rendered as "midriff" or "diaphragm" (on the basis of later usage) but that originally meant the "lungs."[12] As early as Homer, who refers to "where the *phrenes* shut in the dense heart," the lungs are clearly pictured as a surrounding enclosure for the other organ.[13] And as late as Aeschylus, "*phrenes* appears still to mean 'lungs.'"[14]

Like many other ancients, the Greeks viewed the chest or breast as the seat of physical life and consciousness. The lungs in particular contained the *thymos*, "the vital principle that thinks and feels and prompts to action."[15] The lungs were also linked with speech, and "the belief that thoughts are words and words are breath ... would lead to the belief that the organs of breath, the lungs, are the organs of mind. This conception of words would be natural, inevitable among men unfamiliar with writing. . . . These words or thoughts are kept in the lungs."[16] Long after the introduction of writing, the *phrenes* were still considered not just the physical source of spoken words, but also of the thought, will, or intention behind them. For Idomeneus (c. 300 B.C.E.), a sincere speech comes "from the *phrenes*," much as we might say "from the heart."[17] The metaphor of "writing on the *phrenes*" thus may represent the process of oral culture adapting to the emergent culture of writing. It may have been a way of imagining the chest or lungs, the traditional source of speech, as a repository for the newly written word as well. One classical scholar has even suggested that the "tablet of memory" in the ancient drama reflects the practical need of actors to memorize their lines, to internalize the script.[18]

As late as the fifth century B.C.E., Greek literature preserves an archaic somatic psychology that does not conceptualize an integral psyche but attributes one function to the lungs, another to the liver, a third to the heart, and so on.[19] The heart (*kardia*) was important in ancient Greek psychology; from Homer on, it is commonly the seat of feeling and passion, and Aristotle and Hippocrates associate it with sensory perception as well.[20] Classical Latin links memory to the heart (*recordari*, "to recall," from *re* + *cordis*, "heart"), but Greek and Latin authors almost never associate the heart with interior writing.[21] Given the anatomy of the chest organs and the Greek perception of the lungs as a kind of enclosure for the heart (as in the Homeric quotation above), the *phrenes* may sometimes be used metonymically for the heart. And, as a psychological term, the *phrenes* can denote simply "mind" or "memory" (as in a later application, "phrenology," which is specific to the head). However, a reference to something "written on the *phrenes*," even in figurative use, retains its specific anatomical connotation. And writing on the heart, as such, did not emerge as a trope, let alone as a literary commonplace, until Judeo-Christian culture, with a radically heart-centered anthropology based on Scripture, made its mark on the larger Mediterranean scene.

## THE PHILOSOPHERS

By the end of the fifth century B.C.E., new forms of written discourse—including the scientific history of Thucydides and the philosophical dialogues of Plato—went beyond the dramatists' use of documents and tablets as "models for authoritative memory" to offer writing as a more comprehensive model for the inner self.[22] By contrast with the poets, Plato (c. 429–347 B.C.E.) held to a more unitary conception of the person as an immortal soul that is separable from the body and characterized by reason.[23] Plato's student Aristotle, although differing from his master on key points, furthered the notion of the rational soul as the essential person. Living in an age of increased literacy, the philosophers often resorted to writing metaphors in their ethics, psychology, and epistemology. But they associated interior writing not with the *phrenes*, but rather with the *psychē* (soul) or *nous* (mind), perhaps in part because during the fourth century B.C.E. the term *phrenes* underwent "a shift in meaning from the lungs to the diaphragm or midriff."[24]

Plato treats the textual soul at length in connection with how men of differing mentalities learn and retain knowledge. For example, Socrates likens "the heart of the soul" to the wax imprinted by a signet ring, terms that play on the similarity of the Greek words for "heart" and "wax."[25] But here "heart" denotes a figurative part of the immaterial soul (*psychē*), not a part of the body. Moreover, Plato is arguing that knowledge does *not* consist of sense impressions in the memory but derives instead from the innate Forms or Ideas already present in the soul, to which all such corporeal impressions must be fitted.[26]

Aristotle likewise employs the signet-ring analogy, but to illustrate his contrasting view that all knowledge originates with sense impressions. Aristotle's assimilation of knowledge to writing, and of the mind to a linear space, is evident in his treatise *On Memory and Recollection:* "Suppose one were thinking of a series, which may be represented by the letters ABCDEFGH; if one does not recall what is wanted at A, yet one does at E; for from that point it is possible to travel in either direction, that is either towards D or towards F."[27] The shaping force of alphabetic literacy (and its linearity) on psychological theory could hardly be clearer. In his treatise *On the Soul,* Aristotle even likens the mind directly to a writing tablet: "What the mind [*nous*] thinks, must be in it, in the same sense as letters are on a tablet which bears no actual writing."[28] The blank tablet, or tabula rasa, reappears in patristic and medieval scholastic writings and eventually became a commonplace of modern psychology, from Locke to the behaviorists.

Although both philosophers imply a textual concept of the soul, Aristotle's empiricist tabula rasa contrasts sharply with Plato's idealist writing metaphors, the most famous of which appears in the *Phaedrus.* In a myth about the origins of writing, Socrates tells how King Thamus of Egypt refused the gift of letters offered by the god Theuth on the grounds that it would weaken the minds of those who use it: "Their trust in writing, produced by external characters which are no part of themselves, will discourage the use of their own memory within them." When Phaedrus asks what sort of word (*logos*) a person should therefore keep within himself, Socrates replies: "The word which is written with intelligence in the soul [*psychē*] of the learner, which is able to defend itself and knows to whom it should speak, and before whom to be silent."[29]

One of the ironies in this passage is that just after describing letters as alien to humans ("external characters which are no part of themselves"), Socrates tropes these foreign objects into an image of the enlightened soul, which he pictures in terms of the very medium that allegedly threatens to rob it of memory, knowledge, and truth. Plato thus posits a textual soul, a self defined in terms of writing, even as he seems to censure script itself. The passage captures a cultural moment when writing was still so new and literacy yet so restricted that a textual notion of the psyche could actually seem alien, unnatural, even unlikely to take hold (notwithstanding the testimony of the drama). Poised on the cusp of literacy, Plato's ironic "writing in the soul" may be meant as a prophylactic against an identification between soul and text that is already taking place, a reaction to the advent of "abstract and depersonalized systems of representation, disembedded from any particular social relationship."[30] If so, however, Plato's verbal irony is subsumed by the historical irony that his deliberately alien metaphor eventually came to be seen as so "natural" that today it is held up as a symbol of the essentially human against threatening modern technologies like the computer.

As Jacques Derrida points out in an influential reading of this dialogue, Plato's "writing in the soul" identifies the human subject with a presence that is *prior* to literal (external, material) writing, which it denigrates as a mere sign or trace of that prior presence, as something alien, fallen, and exterior to the self.[31] In other words, metaphorical writing (presumably a by-product of literal writing) assumes the status of "original" writing and reduces literal writing to a mere Platonic shadow or copy of itself. But Plato's attack on writing "fails in a peculiar way because, even as he tries to distinguish speech from writing, Plato needs to describe the former in terms of concepts and metaphors drawn from the latter."[32] By the same token, Plato seems compelled to describe the human subject of language in textual (rather than oral or vocal) terms. Plato's text-based concepts and metaphors emphasize that whether or not the self was actually born of writing, it soon became almost unimaginable without writing metaphors.

While the *Phaedrus* suggests the importance of writing metaphors to Western ontology, other passages in Plato point to ideas about the textual soul that were equally important to theology and ethics. The notion of permanent marks on the soul is crucial to Plato's teaching on the afterlife, for example. In the *Gorgias,* he asserts that after the immortal soul is stripped of the body, everything within it becomes manifest—"its natural characteristics and the experiences which a man's soul has encountered through occupations of various kinds," including "the marks branded on the soul by every evil deed."[33] And the myth of Er in the concluding book of *The Republic* portrays the souls of the dead, good and bad alike, being judged and wearing signs or tokens (*semeia*) "of all that had befallen them."[34] The notion of an individual's deeds permanently marked on the soul also appears in Stoic philosophy, and it parallels the biblical idea of sins recorded on the heart and destined to be revealed at a divine tribunal.[35]

As Greek learning spread to Rome, textual metaphors for the mind became a fixture among Latin authors as well. The heart is a rich locus of thought, feeling, and memory in Latin literature, and poets picture the heart wounded by the "arrows" of passion.[36] But explicit textual metaphors in Latin literature are almost wholly restricted to the mind (*mens, animus*) or the specific faculty of memory (*memoria*). The cultural imprint of these metaphors is clearest in Roman rhetorical treatises, which repeatedly compare the mind to a text when they discuss the art of memory, considered as a branch of oratory. The basic metaphor is summed up in the Pseudo-Ciceronian *Rhetorica ad Herennium,* a handbook widely known throughout the Middle Ages: "The memory places are very much like wax tablets or papyrus, the images like the letters, the arrangement and disposition of the images like the script, and the delivery is like the reading."[37]

Although the handbook mentions "images," the rhetoricians often refer to mental "impressions" (*impressiones*), in keeping with the basic metaphor of a wax writing tablet filled with notes or drafts. Indeed, the Latin vocabulary of the writing tablet (and signet ring) is the ultimate source of our psychological term "impression," from the fact that the pointed end of the writing stylus left semipermanent marks in the soft wax. Quintilian (c. 35–100 C.E.) illustrates this usage and also suggests the extent to which professional rhetoricians, at least, pictured the mind in terms of writing media. Quintilian's educational program urges that each boy be set to copy down morally instructive aphorisms so that he will remember them even as an old man, "and the impression made upon his unformed mind will contribute to the formation of his character."[38] Here the writing on the mind has both a mnemonic and an ethical dimension. Although Quintilian's term for "character" (*mores*) is not a writing metaphor, his description of the ethical self is shaped by the very instruments of elite literacy: the physical act of transcription prompts the memory, enabling the mind or soul to receive interior "impressions" that correspond to external letters on the writing tablet. The pedagogical subject is thus formed, in both practice and theory, by the texts that he reads, copies, memorizes, and ultimately recollects from his tabular mind.

If the rhetoricians' textual metaphors sound technical or even forced, this is because they were mainly meant to inculcate the art of memory for the specific purpose of giving speeches. But educated Romans of the late Republic and early Empire seem to have fallen naturally into such metaphors when speaking of their thoughts, feelings, or interior life. Cicero writes to his friend Atticus, "My plans have all been unfolded to you in previous letters," where to "unfold" (*explicare*) implies the mind's resemblance to a scroll.[39] In an even more overt scroll metaphor, Cicero refers elsewhere to how one might "unroll [*evolvere*] the idea of a good man which lies wrapped up [*complicatam*] in his own mind. . . ."[40] And Seneca, a contemporary of Quintilian, writes in a very personal vein, "I feel that I have suffered the fate of a book whose rolls have stuck together by disuse; my mind needs to be unfolded [*explicandus*], and whatever has been stored away there ought to be examined from time to time, so that it may be ready for use when occasion demands."[41]

Latin authors also applied other terms for turning or unrolling a scroll in order to read it, such as *revolvere*, to mental operations.[42] As mentioned earlier, the scroll appears as a psychological trope in the Greek drama, but these Latin examples elaborate the mind's similarity to a lengthy text whose contents cannot be read without being "unrolled." Seneca's metaphor in particular emphasizes the mind's secret or private nature, the fact that it is closed off from others, and, until moments of recollection, even from oneself. Scroll metaphors as applied to psychology would persist even in the age of the codex, as some medieval authors invoked the older book format to emphasize certain qualities of the mind, soul—or heart. Scroll metaphors still live on in the English words "implicit" and "explicit," and also (as shown by one of the Ciceronian examples above) in the related word "complicated," a term that has become all but indispensable for discussing the modern psyche.

## Scripture

By contrast with classical literature, the Bible associates interior writing almost exclusively with the heart.[43] The heart's key role in Scripture (where the term occurs more than a thousand times) and the specific notion of writing on the heart may ultimately reflect ancient Egyptian

sources, where the heart had a central role and was associated with memorial "writing" as early as about 1300 B.C.E.[44] In the Old Testament,
"heart" (Hebrew *lev, levav*) denotes many aspects of interior life, especially understanding, conscience, memory, and volition. The inscribed
heart, usually figured as a "tablet," typically designates the internalized
Law. Hellenistic Jewish scholars altered the original Hebraic trope to a
more spiritual (Platonic) "writing in the soul." But Christian authors,
beginning with the apostle Paul, seized upon the inscribed "heart" in
general, and the "tablet of the heart" in particular, as arch-metaphors
for divine law, conscience, and the incarnated Gospel. Besides insisting
on the heart as a site of divine inscription, the New Testament deep-
ened the Hebraic notion of a divine judgment that would reveal the
secrets of the heart, and it elaborated the inherited imagery of "opened
books" as symbols of personal revelation.

## THE LAW IN THE HEART

The Old Testament tablet of the heart represents human recollection,
understanding, or obedience in relation to God's law. The tablet of the
heart may have been modeled on the clay tablets used in the Near East
from very early times, or the writing boards of ivory and wood that
superseded them.[45] But it most likely alludes to the original stone tablets of the Mosaic Law—a connection that Paul would make explicit
by associating the inward and outward tablets, respectively, with Ezekiel's distinction between the "heart of stone" and the "heart of flesh."[46]
In the Hebrew Scriptures, the same word (*luach*) is used for both the
internal and the external tablets. Most important, both the stone tablets and the tablet of the heart contain the Law.

A law written on the heart appears in some of the earliest biblical
texts. In Deuteronomy, dating from no later than the seventh century
B.C.E., God says to the Israelites: "These words which I command you
this day shall be upon your heart" (6.6).[47] The book of Proverbs, in a
section dating from the fourth or third century B.C.E., specifies a tablet
of the heart containing the Law: "My son, do not forget my teaching,
but let your heart keep my commandments. . . . Bind them about your
neck, write them on the tablet of your heart" (3.1, 3); and, "Keep my
commandments and live. . . . Bind them on your fingers, write them on
the tablet of your heart" (7.2, 3). Here "writing" on the tablet of the

heart represents the internalized Law, as further symbolized by reference to phylacteries or *tefillin*, small boxes containing Scriptures and attached to the body during worship. Significantly, the individual is depicted as a scribe who records the Law within himself, where the act of inscription signifies memory and obedience.

A passage from Jeremiah (c. 600 B.C.E.) also refers to writing on the heart but depicts God himself in the role of scribe: "This is the covenant which I will make with the house of Israel after those days, says the Lord: I will put my law within them, and I will write it upon their hearts . . ." (31.33). Closer in time to the Mosaic dispensation, this passage seems to be modeled even more directly on the stone tablets "written with the finger of God" (Deut. 9.10).[48] Another passage in Jeremiah offers a different account of the writing on the heart and how it gets written there: "The sin of Judah is written with a pen of iron; with a point of diamond it is engraved on the tablet of their heart . . ." (17.1). Here the interior text is not a divine law but rather a record of human sin (although no scribe, divine or human, is specified). Jeremiah thus introduces the important idea that the tablet of the heart is not limited in its content to divine laws, commands, or ideals. It can also contain a record of human actions, where "the sin of Judah" suggests history, narrative, and particularity—the indicative mood of human will rather than the imperative mood of divine command. As such, the tablet of the heart is still a record of collective, rather than individual, deeds. But in its other occurrences, the Hebraic trope has a distinctly individual form—"the tablet of *your* heart," where "*your*" represents the second-person singular (KJV, "the tablet of *thine* heart").

The Septuagint, the Greek Old Testament produced by Hellenistic Jews and later used by Christians as well, rendered the Hebrew word for "heart" (*lev*) as Greek *kardia*, thus preserving the imagery of the "tablet of the heart."[49] But if the trope survived the translators, it did not always survive interpreters such as Philo of Alexandria (c. 30 B.C.E.–45 C.E.), a Hellenistic Jewish scholar dedicated to synthesizing the Law of Moses with Greek philosophy. Philo held to a Platonic rather than a Hebraic anthropology and avoided using "heart" in the extended biblical sense that includes memory, conscience, or other rational functions, reserving it for the passions or emotions alone.[50] Philo acknowledges the letter of the biblical text, "The law tells us that we must set the rules of justice in the heart [*kardia*] . . . ," but he instead associates the interiorized Law with the phylacteries worn on the head, which, as a Platonist, he regards as the seat of reason: "These best of all lessons must be impressed upon our lordliest part."[51] Philo treats the "unwritten laws" of custom similarly, observing that these are "not inscribed on monuments nor on leaves of paper which the moth destroys, but on the souls of those who are partners in the same citizenship," where "soul" ( *psychē*) has its Platonic sense.[52]

But if Philo adapted the tablet of the heart to a Platonic ideal, he also portrayed the textual soul in terms of age and sex differences that suggest a more individualized self. An infant, unlike an adult, says Philo, "possesses only the simplest elements of soul, a soul which closely resembles smooth wax and has not yet received any impression of good or evil, for such marks as it appears to receive are smoothed over and confused by its fluidity."[53] What we would call developmental psychology—the mental changes relative to age and experience—are here represented in terms of a "mark" or "impression" (*kharakter*) in the malleable "wax" of the soul. Philo's use of the term *kharakter* for an interior writing having an ethical significance ("any impression of good or evil") is an early example of what became our word "character" in its modern moral sense.[54]

Philo likewise compares the soul of a newly wed virgin to "a sheet of wax levelled to show clearly the lessons to be inscribed upon it," whereas that of a previously married woman is "rather like one roughened by the imprints already scored upon it, which resist effacement" or "confuse them with their own indentations."[55] Apart from its sexual overtones, this passage looks ahead to the more individualized interior writing evoked by Christian authors, including the patristic model of religious conversion as an erasure and rewriting of the inner tablet. Although he was a Hellenistic Jew who gave the tablet of the heart a Platonic gloss, Philo anticipates the Christian sense of the soul (or heart) as a unique and detailed record of personal experience.

## "A LETTER FROM CHRIST"

If Philo found the tablet of the heart too fleshly for the Platonized Law, Saint Paul found it perfectly suited to the incarnated Gospel. Paul epitomizes the biblical "mystique of the heart" that countered the Platonic and Neoplatonic tendency "to limit the heart's psychic role to the affections and to eliminate the metaphorical uses of the word *kardia* abundantly introduced into Greek by the Septuagint and the New Testament."[56] Paul, unlike Philo, embraced the Hebraic notion of man as a fleshly being whose "heart" (*kardia*) "denotes the center of the person as a rational, emotional and volitional being"—the "hidden core of the self."[57] Yet, in a radical revision of his Jewish heritage, Paul reduced the Mosaic Law to a "figure" or "foreshadowing" of the Gospel as revealed in the historical person of Christ. Accordingly, for Paul, the tablet of the heart contained not only an internalized Law, but also the Christian revelation as incarnated in each believer.

A hallmark of Paul's teaching that helped transform Christianity from a small Jewish sect into a world religion was his stress on the universality of the Gospel, addressed to Jew and Gentile alike. Accordingly, with Paul, writing on the heart likewise assumes a universal meaning. In addition to taking the Hebraic trope beyond the boundaries of traditional Judaism, Paul gave it a new and highly suggestive relation to conscience, sin, and divine judgment.[58] As he states in his Epistle to the Romans, the Law was specially revealed to the Jews, but the Gentiles, too, "show that what the law requires is written on their hearts, while their conscience also bears witness and their conflicting thoughts accuse or perhaps excuse them on that day when, according to my gospel, God judges the secrets of men by Christ Jesus" (2.15–16).

As we have already seen, the Old Testament tablet of the heart usually relates to God's law, but in one instance (Jer. 17.1) it contains instead a record of collective sin ("the sin of Judah"). Paul similarly links the inner law with an awareness of sin or guilt—"conscience." Paul's phrasing suggests a more individual recognition of sin, although he does not formulate this awareness in textual terms; the thoughts that "accuse" and "bear witness" suggest a forensic, not a scribal, metaphor. Still, Paul closely aligns the inscribed heart with the convictions of conscience as well as with what he calls the "secrets of men"—a phrase that patristic commentators on this passage freely exchange with another Pauline formula, the "secrets of [the] heart."[59] In this, Paul anticipates the frequent conjunction of heart and conscience in later writers, especially under the metaphor of a "book" containing *both* a record of divine ideals and an account of individual sins.

Paul's debt to (and revision of) Jewish tradition is even more explicit in his famous discussion of the letter and the spirit, where he

evokes a *tablet* of the heart: "You yourselves are our letter of recommen-
dation, written on your hearts, to be known and read by all men; and
you show that you are a letter from Christ delivered by us, written not
with ink but with the Spirit of the living God, not on tablets of stone
but on tablets of human hearts" (2 Cor. 3.2–3).[60] There is a touch of
self-conscious irony here as Paul frames the metaphorical "letter from
Christ" within his own (literal) letter to the Corinthians. But the most
pointed contrast between internal and external script concerns the
Gospel embodied in "tablets of human hearts" and the Law written on
"tablets of stone," as emphasized a few verses later by reference to the
Law "carved in letters on stone" (2 Cor. 3.7).

Whereas the Hebrew Scriptures treated the law written on the heart
as identical with the external Law, Paul uses the *formal* difference between the tablets of stone and flesh to signify a profound difference of
*content* as well—namely, the difference between "letter" and "spirit," or
the Law that convicts humans of sin (Rom. 7.7) and the Gospel's saving
grace. Paul's contrast between inward and outward writing recalls
Plato's censure upon external writing as inferior to the "writing in the
soul."[61] In structural terms, Paul repeats Plato's "reversal" of priority
between literal and metaphorical script. In substance, however, Paul's
trope is very *un*-Platonic. Whereas Philo had transformed the original
Hebraic trope into a writing on the "soul," Paul follows the heart-
based terminology preserved in the Septuagint. Indeed, this passage
actually refers to the heart as a physical organ, albeit figuratively.[62]

Paul even enhances the bodily aspect of the Hebraic trope by ex-
panding it to "tablets of *human* hearts," or "*fleshly* hearts" (translating
Greek *sarkinais*). Paul often uses "the flesh" as a synecdoche for the sinful impulses of the body.[63] But here the "fleshly" heart inscribed with
the Gospel evidently represents the whole person, both what Paul repeatedly calls the "inmost self" (e.g., Rom. 7.22) and the outward or
bodily self. Since the heart is primarily a physical organ, writing on the
heart has a bodily aspect that is consistent with both the Hebraic notion of man as a psycho-physical self and the Christian idea of the incarnated Word.

In a development that was crucial for the future book of the heart,
the Pauline tablet of the heart retained its fleshly aspect in the Latin
Bible, where *cor* (heart) is a similarly psychosomatic term.[64] Jerome's
Vulgate, which gradually became the standard version in the Western

Church after about 400 c.e., refers in 2 Corinthians 3.3 to a letter from
Christ written in "fleshly tablets of the heart" (*tabulis cordis carnalibus*). In
its Latin form, Paul's metaphor even inspired later writers to exploit
the similarity of the term *cor* (heart) to *caro* (flesh) and *corpus* (body).
Although not quite accurate to the original Greek, the Latin formula
would echo centuries later in the influential Douay-Rheims version as
"fleshly tables of the heart" and even in the (Greek-based) Authorized
Version as "fleshy tables of the heart." [65] Thus Paul endowed writing
on the heart with a heightened fleshliness that would haunt the metaphor throughout its long career.

## THE OPENED BOOKS

Other important biblical sources for the later book of the heart were
the heavenly "writings" associated with sin and judgment, with human
secrets and divine revelation. [66] Divine books containing records of human deeds are common in ancient traditions, including the Egyptian
*Book of the Dead* and the Greek "Tablets of Zeus." [67] In Judeo-Christian
tradition, the notion that God not only observes human sin but records
it in writing is probably as old as the written Law itself, since God tells
Moses that sinners will be "blot[ted] out of my book" (Exod. 32.33).
The Psalmist similarly suggests that God keeps a moral account when
he prays, "Blot out my transgressions," and the idea continues in New
Testament references to "sins ... blotted out," a "canceled ... bond,"
and the like. [68]

Sometimes the moral account is not a book kept by God but instead
a record in the human heart. Jeremiah, as we have seen, depicts the collective sin of Judah as written on the tablet of the heart. In a more
individualized vein, the Psalmist links the "blotting out" of sins to the
cleansing of the heart: "Blot out my iniquities. Create in me a clean
heart" (Ps. 51.9–10). Since ink was erased from papyrus by either blotting or washing, this imagery assimilates (although it does not equate)
the heart with a written record. Equally important, it exhibits the
Judeo-Christian nexus between sin, writing, and filth or uncleanliness
(ancient ink was made of sooty carbon), a nexus that reappears in the
Christian book of the heart. [69]

On a larger scale, entire "books" of divine record appear in biblical
apocalyptic texts. An early example occurs in Daniel's vision of a divine

Judge surrounded by the myriads of his heavenly court as "the books were opened" (7.10). The actual content of these books—which are imagined, of course, as scrolls—is not specified, although their being unrolled represents a process of "interpretation" (7.16). Similar books reappear in the well-known judgment scene of Saint John's Revelation (c. 90–95 C.E.): "And I saw the dead, great and small, standing before the throne, and books were opened. Also another book was opened, which is the book of life. And the dead were judged by what was written in the books, by what they had done" (Rev. 20.12). Despite some ambiguity about the number and nature of the books indicated, there is a clear link between the books being publicly opened to reveal what is written in them and the lives or deeds of those present. The multiple books mentioned here (and in Daniel) prompted some later authors (and artists) to assume that each individual would be represented at the Judgment by a *separate* book, each book representing an individual's "heart."

Many apocryphal works not included in the scriptural canon but often known to patristic writers give a more detailed account of the divine books of judgment and their contents.[70] One of the most vivid accounts appears in the *Testament of Abraham* (c. 100 C.E.), in which Adam's son Abel presides over an immense book attended by two angels "holding papyrus and ink and pen. . . . The one on the right recorded righteous deeds, while the one on the left [recorded] sins." When a soul appears, the judge commands, "Open for me this book and find for me the sins of this soul. . . ."[71] An important detail here is that the book contains a record of *both* good and evil deeds, a feature often shared by the later book of the heart.

Although Scripture never refers to a "book" of the heart, only a "tablet," at least once it juxtaposes a divine book with the inscribed human heart: "In the roll of the book it is written of me, I delight to do thy will, O my God; thy law is within my heart" (Ps. 40.7–8). This passage hints that "the writing in the heart may be translated into the book of life. . . ."[72] The apocryphal text known as *Second Enoch* suggests even more clearly that God (or his prophet) transcribes sins from the human heart into a heavenly book: "See how I have written down all the deeds of every person before the creation, and I am writing down what is done among all persons forever. And no one can contradict my handwriting; because the Lord sees all the evil thoughts of mankind, how vain they are, where they lie in the treasuries of the heart."[73] But since the date of this work is uncertain, it offers only a hint rather than direct evidence as to how the heart came to be pictured as a book.

## Patristic Allegories

During the early Christian centuries, the tablet of the heart evolved into a full-blown book of the heart in the writings of the Church Fathers, who were heirs to both Scripture and the Graeco-Roman classics. The Fathers accomplished this metamorphosis largely by means of allegory—that is, by taking one thing in Scripture as a sign or symbol of another. Allegory, a mode of interpretation derived largely from classical sources, enabled the tablet of the heart, the secrets of the heart, the opened books of judgment, and many other disparate and apparently unrelated scriptural passages to be woven together into something quite new.

One type of patristic allegory, "typology," treated Old Testament persons or events as foreshadowings (or "types") of persons or events in the New Testament. Paul had employed typology in adapting the metaphor of the inscribed heart from the Law to the Gospel, and patristic writers extended it to the whole span of history, from the divine law written in Adam's heart to the individual secrets of the heart revealed at the Last Judgment. The impact of typology was reinforced by another kind of allegory that eventually came to be known as "tropology." Tropology, whose application to Scripture began with Philo, took external objects or events in the biblical narrative as signs of inward moral or spiritual truths applicable to each individual. It enabled patristic exegetes to equate the opened books of judgment, for example, with opened hearts.[74]

Allegory, while widely practiced among early Christian exegetes, was especially in vogue at Alexandria, where secular Greek scholars had originated many of the interpretive methods eventually adopted by Christians. Alexandria was home to Philo and, two centuries later, to Origen, a prolific Christian allegorist who may have invented the book of the heart. Philo and Origen, in turn, became models—in both interpretive method and content—for Ambrose, bishop of Milan and a leading fourth-century exegete who refined the book of the heart and passed it on to his most famous protégé, Augustine of Hippo.

## THE CORRECTED HEART

While the book of the heart evolved mainly in the work of Christian allegorists, its general development can be glimpsed in a wide variety of patristic writers during the third and fourth centuries who adapted the metaphor of writing on the heart to various practical and theoretical uses. On the simplest level, the Church Fathers used the inscribed heart to represent the learning, recollection, or understanding of God's word. For example, John Chrysostom (c. 347–407) warned wealthy book owners not to prize the material form of Scripture over its spiritual content and to be sure to "write" God's word within themselves: "The Scriptures were not given us for this only, that we might have them in books, but that we might engrave them on our hearts."[75] Patristic authors applied similar metaphors of reading and writing even to the blind. The early Church historian Eusebius (c. 260–c. 339) reports that John of Egypt "had written whole books of the Divine Scriptures 'not in tables of stone,' as the divine apostle says, neither on skins of animals, nor on paper which moths and time destroy, but truly 'in fleshy tables of the heart.'" John would then "read" aloud from these "tablets." When Eusebius first heard John reciting Scripture in a large congregation, he thought he was reading from a book, until he approached and saw that "he was using only the eyes of his mind. . . ."[76] Here a man blinded after years of literacy is still imagined as "reading" a memory text "written" on the heart.

The letters of Jerome, in the late fourth century, exhibit many variations on Paul's tablet of the heart, as if to claim sanction from the founding father of the Christian epistle. Jerome cautions Eustochium, a regular female correspondent, "Rend not the letter written on your heart," and he chides a monk for having failed to write him: "You have not merely blurred but erased the writing of that epistle which, as the apostle tells us, is written in the hearts of Christians."[77] Jerome employs a similar trope when he urges new Christians to commit Scripture to their hearts like students learning to write: "Write in your heart, like children learning their ABCs, carving the curved letters with trembling hand in the tablet, and learning by concentration to write correctly. . . ."[78]

More telling than such commonplaces are the metaphors that patristic authors use to describe the crucial experiences of religious life, especially the trauma of conversion and the pains of spiritual renewal. The textualized heart appears in early Christian monastic writings, especially in the East, where ascetic practices included daily introspection for signs of one's spiritual condition. This examination of the heart, what the Greek Fathers called *cardiognosis*, was especially characteristic of the fourth-century Desert Fathers, whose eremitical life and comparative lack of books forced an alternative to the focus on scriptural exegesis in urban Christian communities.[79] As Peter Brown describes it, "the monk's own heart was the new book," and this new book required its own "infinitely skilled exegesis. . . ."[80]

For Basil of Caesarea (c. 329–379), the heart of the aspiring monk is like a wax writing tablet that must be erased before it can hold the fresh script of the new converted self. The monk's heart, says Basil, must be ready to receive "the impressions produced there by divine instruction. And this disposition follows the unlearning of worldly teachings which previously held possession of the heart." To unlearn is to erase: "Just as it is not possible to write in wax without first smoothing down the letters already engraved upon it, so it is impossible to impart the divine teachings to the soul without first removing from it the conceptions arising from worldly experiences."[81] Here conversion or reform is figured not by washing or blotting ink, but by "smoothing" the wax with the rounded end of the stylus. Basil's trope recalls Philo's comparison of the souls of married women to roughened wax tablets that retain the traces of earlier writing. Religious conversion, like remarriage, requires erasing the previous writing that represents ingrained habit—what Philo, turning a scribal term to ethical and psychological use, had called acquired "character."[82]

The booklike heart of early Christian asceticism may reflect the outlook of those who wrote the spiritual guides and histories rather than that of their often less-learned subjects. But bookish terms pervade accounts of the inner life with amazing regularity.[83] For example, an early history of monasticism compiled by Rufinus (c. 400) borrows the technical language of the scribe to portray how the monk is supposed to examine his own heart: "Withdrawing into himself, he says, 'How shall

I warn others and yet deceive myself? Or how shall I correct [*corrigo*] others, and not correct [*emendo*] myself?'"[84] John Cassian (360–435) uses the same terminology to recommend the spiritual benefits of reading Scripture. Unless we combat evil impulses, he says, we shall lose our free will along with "the habit of correcting ourselves," and we can "emend" the thoughts in our hearts by reading and meditating on Scripture.[85] Some early monastic authors even exploited the resemblance between the Greek words *kardia* (heart) and *chartes* (papyrus) to evoke the interior space of spiritual writing, as when Nilus of Ancyra (d. c. 430) refers to a believer "writing a prayer on the opened sheet of his own heart."[86] Medieval monks and scholars would similarly exploit and allegorize technical terms and concepts in their more elaborate accounts of the inscribed, examined, and corrected book of the heart.

A few patristic authors recommended that monks keep actual written records of their spiritual lives—transcripts from the heart, as it were. For example, the influential *Life of Saint Anthony*, written by Athanasius around 350, recommends a daily journal for the purpose of moral self-examination. In a speech to fellow ascetics, Anthony cites Paul's reference to the day when God will judge the "secrets of men" (Rom. 2.16) and goes on to urge the monks to record their own secrets in writing: "Let each one of us note and record our actions and the stirrings of our souls as though we were going to give an account to each other. . . . Let this record replace the eyes of our fellow ascetics, so that, blushing as much to write as to be seen, we might never be absorbed by evil things."[87] Such spiritual diaries were apparently rare in patristic times; not until some two centuries later does John Climacus record that he saw monks carrying in their belts small books in which they wrote down their good and evil thoughts each day.[88] But this example is important because it suggests a belief that the inner person can actually be represented in writing and that writing is a valuable means of self-discovery.

## ORIGEN OF ALEXANDRIA

By the middle of the third century, Origen (185?–?254 C.E.) had already incorporated the same Pauline reference to the "secrets of men," along with other scriptural passages, into an interior book. The idea that each person's good or evil actions leave a unique internal record in the form of "writing" that will be revealed at the Last Judgment is a frequent theme in Origen, who is one of the earliest patristic authors to figure the secrets of the heart expressly as a book.[89]

Origen sometimes pictures the inner moral self as a simple writing tablet. For example, in a gloss on Romans 2.14–16, he writes, "Whenever we have good or evil thoughts, traces of good or evil are left on our hearts like letters or marks in wax. Present now in the secret part of our breast, these will be revealed on that day by none other than he who alone knows the secrets of men."[90] But the wax writing tablet—typically used in antiquity for notes, drafts, and other ephemera—does not suggest the permanence that a parchment or papyrus book does.

Later in his Romans commentary, Origen varies the tablet of the heart with the metaphor of an interior scroll. Explaining Paul's remark that "each of us shall give account of himself to God" (Rom. 14.12), Origen cites Daniel's reference to "opened books," which he allegorizes in turn as books of the heart:

> Our heart shall be made known to all rational creatures, and all hidden things revealed. . . . And these things shall be read by all rational creatures as though they were inscribed books or incised tablets containing an account of all our thoughts and actions. This is what I believe is indicated where Daniel says, "And books were opened" (7.10). These books are now rolled up and hidden in the heart, containing written records of our deeds and marked, so to speak, with the reproofs of conscience, and still known to no one but God. But these books of our soul or tablets of our heart [*libri animae nostrae, vel hae cordis nostri paginae*] shall be opened before the throne. . . .[91]

Like Origen's gloss on the heart as a wax tablet, this passage was originally written in Greek toward the middle of the third century but survives only in an early-fifth-century Latin translation by Rufinus. As such, it is very likely one of the oldest patristic glosses on the heart as a book.

Although the gloss refers expressly to "books" (*libri*) rolled up "in the heart" (*in corde*), it equivocates about the precise format of this interior writing, mentioning also "tablets." These variations may have been introduced by the translator, or they may have been original to the lost

Greek text. Reasons for varying the traditional "tablet" of the heart
with a "book" may have included the relative impermanence and limited textual capacity of the tablet. Scratch marks in wax were not as
durable as inked parchment or papyrus; and although it was common
in antiquity to attach several pairs of tablets together, the resulting wax
notebook still could contain only a small amount of text.[92] In addition,
the idea of an interior record of an entire life—what Origen calls "an
account of all our thoughts and actions"—may have recommended the
"book," with its larger capacity, as a more suitable image. In any case,
it is important to stress that Origen imagines the interior book not in
the still relatively new format of the parchment (or papyrus) codex, but
in terms of the far more prevalent and ancient format of the scroll that
is "rolled up" (*involutus*). The codex was already well established among
Christians in the middle of the third century, but its dominance as a
symbol or metaphor was at least a century away.[93]

On the psychological side, Origen's gloss seems to imply a separate
interior book for each person, although it refers to the heart in an
impersonal or collective manner: *cor, cor nostrum*—"the heart," "our
heart." (Origen's gloss also varies between "heart" and "soul," although
"heart" predominates.) Despite his Neoplatonic belief that the individual's ultimate destiny was to merge with the divine Oneness, Origen
held that during the earthly life each person was a distinct and unique
being.[94] Indeed, for Origen, a person's "heart" was as characteristic as
his face or his handwriting: "Just as faces differ from each other, so do
the hearts of men.... Similarly, one can recognize from certain signs,
certain traits, the hand that has authored a text...."[95] The graphologi-
cal analogy expressly likens the individuality of the psyche to that of a
person's script. As such, it recalls Philo's notion of the soul's specific
"character," even as it anticipates more elaborate medieval accounts of
the individual's book of the heart.

Origen also emphasizes another theme that reappears in many later
commentaries on the book of the heart: the moment when the book
will be opened and its secrets revealed to the gathered hosts of heaven.
Tens of thousands of angels and heavenly servants, he says, "shall see
these things and read [*legent*] them, and our sins, which now we are
ashamed to tell even one person, shall then be witnessed by the count-
less hosts of heavenly virtue."[96] Here the book of the heart almost
seems to surpass Scripture itself as an object of reading and revelation,

as a text of obscure meanings that are finally made manifest. On a personal level, this passage reflects its author's proclivities as an Alexandrian allegorist ("Origen thought of himself, above all, as an exegete").[97] On a cultural one, it inaugurates a tradition that recreated persons, divine and human alike, in the image of textual metaphors.

## AMBROSE OF MILAN

Saint Ambrose (339–397), one of the four Latin Doctors of the Church, had a firsthand familiarity with the writings of Greek Fathers such as Origen and Basil (as well as Philo), and it was probably he who carried the book of the heart into Latin theology and exegesis. His Greek and Latin learning, his knowledge of both Scripture and the classics, superbly equipped Ambrose for the work of cultural synthesis, and his position as the politically powerful bishop of Milan (373–397) gave his writings great influence. One of his foremost achievements was to collect, combine, and allegorize biblical writing metaphors to create a coherent theology of writing, a Christian grammatology. As part of this effort, Ambrose refined the metaphors of the inscribed and legible heart that were already central to patristic notions of selfhood. One major result was a complex "book of the heart" derived from multiple scriptural passages and representing a secret inner self with a very individual stamp.

Ambrose treats the inscribed heart as a secret, hidden place, using Paul's tablet of the heart to suggest the concealed quality of the "inner man": "If the letter of the Apostle is written in the Spirit, what hinders us from believing that the Law of God was written not with ink, but with the Spirit of God, which certainly does not stain but enlightens the secret places of our heart and mind?" In the same passage, Ambrose equates the Christian heart renewed by God's writing with an essential psychological unity: "If your faith fails, the tablet of your heart is broken. The coherence of your soul is lessened if you do not believe the unity of Godhead in the Trinity."[98] Although Ambrose, like Origen, evokes the inscribed and hidden heart in collective terms (*cor nostrum*), he also gives it a more individual aspect as "the tablet of *your* heart" (*tabula cordis tui*).

Ambrose emphasizes this individuality by picturing a private self characterized by the "secrets of the heart," a Pauline phrase that Am-

brose often uses to designate the interior person. It is a key idea in
an undated letter to Irenaeus where Ambrose outlines the influential
theology of writing that he would bequeath to Augustine and the
Middle Ages. Ambrose extends Paul's notion of a natural law written
in the hearts of the Gentiles (Rom. 2.15) to the full span of human
history, from Creation to Judgment, asserting that God first wrote this
law in Adam's heart, where it was "corrupted and blotted out" by the
Fall, thus necessitating the external Law of Moses.[99] Yet the writing on
the heart is not limited to an internal law partly "erased" by sin and
then corrected by reference to the external tablets of the Law. According to Ambrose, the heart also contains a personal record of sins
that will be opened at the Last Judgment: "That which has always been
apparent to the Lord will be clearly revealed on the Day of Judgment,
when the secrets of the heart, which were thought to be hidden, will
be called to an account."[100] By substituting the "secrets of the heart"
for Paul's original phrasing ("the secrets of men"), Ambrose intensifies
the picture of the heart as a record of hidden things.

Elsewhere, in a commentary on the Psalms, Ambrose portrays the
"secrets of the heart" expressly as a book to be opened at the Last Judgment, citing as his authority the familiar passage about the "opened
books" in Daniel (7.10):

> What are these opened books, if not our consciences, which, like
> books, contain the long story of our sins . . . ? Wherefore is it
> said, "And books were opened"? Certainly he does not speak of
> books written with ink but with the filth and stains of sin and
> shame. The book of your conscience shall be opened; the book
> of your heart [*liber cordis tui*] shall be opened; our guilt shall be
> read aloud.[101]

If Origen had mainly interiorized Daniel's trope, Ambrose emphatically individualized it, a crucial step in the evolution of the heart-book
metaphor. Besides introducing the compact formula, *liber cordis* (apparently modeled on *tabula cordis*), Ambrose gave it a very individual stamp
by virtue of grammatical person and number. Instead of the plural
"books" (*libri*) in Origen's gloss, Ambrose specifies a singular "book"
(*liber*), and instead of a first-person plural pronoun (*noster,* "our") he

uses a second-person singular form, thus creating the "book of your heart" (*liber cordis tui*). Latin *tui* (genitive of *tuus*), equivalent to the early English "familiar" forms "thy" and "thine," suggests a unique and separate inner book for each person. The reformulated trope—either as a generalized "book of the heart" or one individualized by personal pronouns and the like—was to have a very long life in subsequent centuries.

Ambrose further accents the inner book's individuality by implying that each person shares in its authorship, at least insofar as he "erases" the grace of God from his own heart and "writes" there instead his own sins:

> If you have lived righteously, [God's] writing shall remain. See that you do not remove the grace of the Holy Spirit; see that you do not erase it and write with the ink of your evil deeds, lest the Day of Judgment should come and the Judge say: "Let the books be read aloud, let the tablets of his deeds be declaimed." And lest he say to you: "It was I who wrote your tablets; why did you erase my letters? And it was I who recorded my gifts; why did you erase these and write your own dishonor?"

Again the familiar second-person pronoun (*tu, tuus,* etc.) dominates this passage, especially the direct warnings not to erase good, or write evil, in the book of one's heart.[102] Jointly authored by God and the individual, this inward text has evolved far beyond Paul's exclusively divine tablet of the heart.

Ambrose, like Origen, locates his more individualized book of the heart squarely within the late antique book culture of orally delivered texts: "Our sin shall be read aloud" (*recitabitur*). Vocal reading was typical in the late fourth century—although Ambrose himself occasions a famous counterexample, in Augustine's account of the bishop's private reading—and it would remain so until the rise of silent reading in the Middle Ages, which accompanied a radical redefinition of the book as a primarily visual rather than an oral (and aural) text.[103] For early Christians accustomed to texts without word division and with minimal punctuation, sounding the words aloud was the first step in the process of interpretation. Accordingly, to read the book of the heart aloud at the Judgment, to turn hitherto secret writing into public utterance for a vast heavenly audience, suggested the idea of profound personal revelation.

But whereas Origen had clearly evoked a scroll-like book of the heart, Ambrose leaves some ambiguity about the format of the inner book. In the late fourth century, "book" (*liber*) could still mean either a scroll or a codex, and the figurative "ink" (*atramentum*) mentioned by Ambrose could likewise point to a book of either format.[104] Ambrose wrote near the close of the fourth century, about 150 years after Origen, and would have witnessed the growing use of the codex book among Christians. It is even possible that he imagined the book of the heart as a codex, although the continuing use of scrolls in his time, and the inertial pull of scroll-book metaphors in the Bible, makes it equally likely that he instead imagined it as an inner scroll—a book "rolled up" in the heart, to recall Origen's phrase.[105] However, it is clear from the writings of Ambrose's most famous student and most important successor, Saint Augustine, that by the beginning of the fifth century, the book of the heart was beginning to assume not only a more "human" and individual quality, but also what is to us moderns a more familiar shape, as we shall see in the next chapter.

*Chapter Two*

# AUGUSTINE

᭡᭡᭡᭡᭡᭡᭡᭡᭡᭡᭡᭡᭡᭡᭡᭡᭡᭡᭡᭡᭡᭡᭡᭡᭡᭡᭡᭡᭡᭡᭡᭡᭡᭡᭡᭡᭡᭡᭡᭡

*T*he book of the heart as it appeared in the writings of early Christian thinkers such as Origen and Ambrose was developed further by Augustine of Hippo (354–430), the most influential theologian and exegete of all the Church Fathers. Augustine extended the range and subtlety of patristic textual metaphors as part of a comprehensive theory of the written word that was the first of its kind.[1] For his seminal work on language and sign theory, Augustine is said to have "inaugurated what we may call the semiological consciousness of the Christian West."[2] He also inaugurated a specifically *textual* consciousness, one that saw in the book (*liber*) a structural pattern for the entire created universe. As Augustine put it in one of his sermons, the cosmos is as legible as Scripture itself: "The very countenance of creation is a great book. Behold, examine, and read this book from top to bottom."[3] Augustine applied his textual model broadly beyond the physical world, comparing the progression of time to the successive syllables of a psalm, the course of history to a divinely composed poem, and even God himself to a heavenly book studied by the angels.[4] And nowhere did Augustine employ this textual model of things more insistently and imaginatively than with respect to humans.

To Augustine, humans resembled a text in many ways. For example, the animal skins that originally clothed their bodies (Gen. 3.21) are of a piece with Scripture, likewise written on cured animal hides.[5] And body and soul are analogous to the visible "letter" and the invisible "sense" of a text.[6] But it was above all the inner person to which Augustine gave a textual shape. What has come to be called "interiority" was largely "discovered" by Augustine, who emphasized not so much the (Platonic) distinction between body and soul as the (Pauline) difference between the inner and outer person.[7] For Augustine, the inner person and interior life were centered in the "heart," understood in its biblical sense as the moral and spiritual core of the human being. And throughout his writings Augustine portrayed the heart as a place of "writing," "erasure," "reading," "interpretation," and other textual operations.

Augustine's most sustained meditation on the textual self appears in his best-known work, the *Confessions*, which foregrounds the heart's role in the activities of reading and writing, as well as the heart's configuration as a "text" of memory, understanding, and affective response.[8] In particular, Augustine portrays his own heart (*cor meum*) as a record of personal experience that he transcribes outwardly in narrating his own life for others, a process of "writing from the heart" that transforms an interior record into an outward "book of the heart." The textual heart that dominates the *Confessions* is powerfully correlated with the codex, the new book format favored by Christians and in general ascendancy during the fourth century. Augustine's use of the codex as a symbol for the heart, and for interiority in general, anticipates the distinctive shape and content that the book of the heart would assume during the Middle Ages.

## "Cor Meum"

The *Confessions* has been described as essentially "the story of Augustine's 'heart,' or of his 'feelings'—his *affectus.*"[9] The heart (*cor*) is mentioned nearly two hundred times in the work and in more than seventy instances refers to Augustine's own heart (*cor meum*) in particular. Additional heart-based terms for memory and recollection such as *recordatio* and *recordari* enhance the heart's centrality to the narrative. The heart marks many of the work's formal divisions and key episodes as well, most notably Augustine's readerly conversion in the garden.[10]

As the most common term in the *Confessions* for the innermost self
and the scene of interior life, "heart" (*cor*) is by far the most prominent
of several anatomical terms used in a psychological sense, including
*pectus* (chest, breast), *viscera* (bowels), and *venter* (stomach).[11] Augustine
exploits the heart's bodily connotations in his imagery of interior writing, wounding, and circumcision, terms that often suggest a fleshly organ. But he evokes the heart mainly in its biblical sense as the center
of moral and intellectual life, including conscience, understanding, the
affections, volition, and memory. For Augustine, the heart signifies the
inner self and inward life in general—"the indivisible, authentic centre
of human life" and "the place of interiority and religious experience,
which defines individuality. . . ."[12] "My heart," as he puts it, is "where
I am whatever I am."[13]

The heart is also the distinctly *verbal* center of the self, associated
from infancy onward with Augustine's struggle to express his desires
through language to the outer world: "By making all sorts of cries and
noises, all sorts of movements of my limbs, I desired to express my
inner feelings [*sensa cordis mei*], so that people would do what I wanted
. . ." (1.8). The heart remains the center of language at every stage of
Augustine's personal history, from "speaking boy" (1.8) and adolescent
student to mature rhetoric master and converted Christian writer.

As the center of the self in an autobiographical story, the heart is
a stage for Augustine's double role as both author and protagonist, a
rhetorical division that involves constant temporal shifting between
past and present selves. For example, Augustine writes of his boyhood,
"Such was my heart, God, such was my heart which you had pity on
when it was at the very bottom of the abyss. And now let my heart tell
you what it was looking for there . . ." (2.4), where *cor* signifies both the
experiencing self of the narrated past ("such was my heart") and the
reporting self of the narrative present ("let my heart tell you"). Rather
than a unitary self, then, the heart designates a multiple and shifting
subjectivity—a double, divided consciousness required by the conversion story, with its distinction between past and present selves ("before" and "after"), and by the first-person narrative, which separates
the converted author from the unconverted persona "until they are
fused at the narrative's culminating moment."[14]

As the center of Augustine's split narrative self, the heart has a special link with the written word. Essentially, Augustine equates the tex-

tualized heart with three different psychological functions: conscience, where God inscribes his law in humans; understanding, the center of readerly intellect and affect; and memory, an internal record of personal experience, which in turn provides the basis for his published narrative. Augustine's pattern of personal and spiritual growth in the *Confessions* begins with his recognition of the divine law written on the heart, continues with his heart-centered reading of Scripture, and culminates in his new role as an author writing from his own heart to edify a literary public.

## The Inscribed Heart

Paul's metaphors of the inscribed and circumcised heart powerfully influenced the poetics of the *Confessions,* shaping for Augustine what Eugene Vance calls "a spiritual itinerary that involves the passage from the outward Law of the Letter incised in stone, the Law commanding circumcision of the flesh, to another inner Law, a universal Law 'written' in the circumcised heart." For Augustine, as Vance puts it, "the material world is that of temporal things, of carnal language and of the dead letter. The soul's world is one in which divine truth is imprinted in the living heart or the memory." [15]

Although Augustine regards the inner word, "the word in the heart" (*verbum in corde*), as a mental and even nonverbal entity, his metaphors of interior writing often have a bodily aura. [16] In his treatise *On Christian Doctrine,* Augustine allegorizes away the heart's corporeal flavor: "He [Ezekiel] wanted the heart of flesh—whence the apostle's expression 'in the fleshy tablets of the heart'—to be distinguished from the heart of stone because of its sentient life; and by the sentient life he meant intelligent life." [17] But Augustine brings out the heart's fleshly connotations when he contrasts stone and flesh as inscriptional media: "[Paul] speaks of the 'fleshy tables of the heart,' not of the carnal mind, but of a living agent possessing sensation, in comparison with a stone, which is senseless." [18] The "living" quality of the inscribed heart is evident in a personal letter that Augustine wrote to Paulinus and his sister Therasia in 396, shortly before he began writing the *Confessions.* Augustine describes two recent visitors as, "so to speak, an additional letter from you," for in their faces "we could ... read you written on their hearts."[19]

The early books of the *Confessions*, which narrate Augustine's life under the Law and his initial conviction of sin, focus on an innate natural law (i.e., conscience) that God inscribed on the heart when he created humans in his image. For example, in his famous pear tree story, Augustine portrays himself as a "son of Adam" who steals forbidden fruit and thus breaks the inner natural law that preceded the external Law of Moses: "There is a law written in men's hearts which not iniquity itself can erase" (2.4). By recapitulating the universal Fall of humankind in the story of his own youthful escapade, Augustine equates the divine law inscribed in human hearts with an Adamic inheritance that sin can partly "erase" (*delere*) but not wholly obliterate. Not simply passive recipients of this inner law, humans are responsible for "reading" and obeying it as well.

Augustine's later treatise *On the Spirit and the Letter* outlines the universal history of the heart that informs his personal account. Figuring the heart as a wax tablet, Augustine explains that God originally inscribed his law there along with his image and that sin partly deleted this divine script, which was restored by grace: "What was impressed on their hearts when they were created in the image of God has not been wholly erased. . . . [And] just as that image of God is renewed in the mind of believers by the new testament . . . , so also the law of God, which had not been wholly erased there by unrighteousness, is certainly written thereon, renewed by grace."[20] On this textual model of human moral history, which Augustine developed from the theory outlined by Ambrose, three different human epochs (creation, sin, and grace) correspond to three distinct textual operations on the heart—writing, erasure, and rewriting. And the stages of this universal history apply to every individual (ontogeny recapitulating phylogeny) as each person's heart becomes a surface for the successive actions of divine writing, human erasure, and divine *re*writing.

The *Confessions* associates the inscribed heart with not only an innate divine law but also memory—that is, the faculty of memory in general as well as the individual's specific recollections. Augustine often treats memory or recollection as synonymous with the heart by employing the term *recordatio* (and its cognate verb, *recordari*), sometimes using wordplay to emphasize the link between memory and the heart, as when he declares to God, "My heart and my memory are open before you" (*coram te cor meum et recordatio mea*).[21] Employing a key metaphor from the classical art of memory, Augustine treats memory as internal writing, pictured as letters or signs impressed by a stylus on the surface of a wax writing tablet. Thus he says that words, feelings, and sensory experience in general leave their traces as internal "images" or "impressions," without which humans would not be able to recall anything at all.[22] A heart-centered process of recollection informs Augustine's entire authorial project, as he emphasizes in the opening line of book 2, "I want to recall [*recordari*] my past impurities," and again at the beginning of book 8: "Let me remember [*recorder*] with thanks and let me confess to you your mercies." In short, the heart is central to Augustine's notion of "autobiographical memory," where memory has "a critical role in sustaining the individual's personal continuity and in creating self-knowledge. . . ."[23]

In the *Confessions,* writing on the heart belongs to a cluster of fleshly metaphors that includes the "circumcised" heart. As with the inscribed heart, Augustine applies this biblical metaphor to himself, proclaiming, for example, that "many are the temptations which I have cut off and thrust away from my heart."[24] As images of carving or cutting, inscription and circumcision convey the radically transforming power of God's word upon the inner self and even the violence of that word as it operates on the human heart. In his treatise *On the Spirit and the Letter,* Augustine equates the circumcised heart with inward and spiritual writing, with "the will that is pure from all unlawful desire, which comes not from the *letter,* inculcating and threatening, but from the *Spirit,* assisting and healing."[25] Augustine also contrasts the circumcised heart, as an emblem of spiritual renewal, with the carnal circumcision that Paul equates "with the *textuality* of the Law itself and with the *letter* of that text of stone . . . in which the Law was incised."[26] Despite its transcendental thrust, however, Augustine's inscribed and circumcised heart often figures as a surrogate body that contests Paul's uneasy distinction between spirit and flesh.

The inscribed heart takes on fleshly qualities especially by association with the wounded heart, a quasi-inscriptional trope having both biblical and classical precedent.[27] A recurring image in the *Confessions,* the wounded heart is frequently erotic. When his concubine is "torn from [his] side," Augustine says that his heart, "which clung to her, was broken and wounded and dripping blood" (6.15). Again, after the loss of another woman—his mother, Monica—his "wounded" heart heals only slowly (9.13). But the converted Augustine deprecates such earthly passions by comparison with the spiritual love figured by his wounded heart in book 9, just after his conversion: "You had shot through our hearts with your charity, and we carried about with us your words like arrows fixed deep in our flesh. . . ."[28] The "words like arrows" refer to Scripture, the study of which preoccupies the converted Augustine as its words become "fixed" in his heart—that is, his memory. Although Augustine here converts the wounded heart from an image of classical *amor* to one of Christian *caritas,* he retains its erotic undertones; indeed, the quoted passage places Augustine in a "feminine" (or "passive") role with its hint of penetration by the phallic arrows of God's word. The trope's erotic history in classical poets such as Ovid adds further sexual connotations. And so does the wounded heart's connection here with the "flesh"—literally, the bowels (*viscera*), a term sometimes having sexual meaning.[29] Augustine's erotic imagery of the inscribed and wounded heart anticipates the stories of medieval lovers and saints alike, as well as scholastic accounts of God the Father engendering Christ the Word by "writing" with the "pen" of the Holy Spirit in Mary's womb (*visceribus*).[30]

## Heart and Codex

Reading characterizes every stage of Augustine's life and is typically centered on the heart, especially in the middle books of the *Confessions,* where the divine law inscribed in the heart leads to a growing awareness of the inward effects of grace. Essentially, Augustine's heart-centered psychology of reading signifies the capacity of God's word, as externally embodied in Scripture, to convert or transform the reader's innermost self. Augustine highlights the readerly conversion of the heart by contrasting the external, bodily aspects of reading (eye movement, voicing) with its internal, spiritual effects (recollection, understanding, spiritual arousal).

Heart-centered reading is typified by Augustine's well-known account of the busy Bishop Ambrose trying to snatch a few quiet minutes with his books—"when he was reading, his eyes went over the pages and his heart looked into the sense, but voice and tongue were resting" (6.3)—where the heart (*cor*) seeking textual "sense" signifies both the understanding, which grasps this sense, as well as memory, which retains it. Often cited as an exception to the supposed rule of vocal reading in late antiquity, Ambrose's silent reading was not actually so unusual, although its practical significance in this passage should not overshadow its symbolic importance.[31] Mainly it prefigures the silent reading of Augustine's own conversion, again suggesting a transition from the external word embodied in outward texts to the word of God inscribed in the heart.[32] In the very next chapter (6.4), Augustine credits Ambrose for having taught him how to understand scriptural allegory by applying Paul's rule of letter and spirit.

The most crucial and memorable scene of silent heart-centered reading in the *Confessions* takes place during Augustine's famous conversion in the garden: "I snatched up the book, opened it, and read in silence the passage upon which my eyes first fell. . . . [And when] I had reached the end of this sentence it was as though my heart was filled with a light of confidence and all the shadows of my doubt were swept away" (8.12). As with Ambrose, the bodily movement of Augustine's eyes over the page is a counterpoint to the inward effects of reading with the heart. Again silent reading marks an inward movement from letter to spirit, from the external Law and Scripture to the word inscribed within. This heart-centered reading remains a major theme in Augustine's post-conversion narrative, both as a sign of his new life and as an ideal in his spiritual community.[33]

It is no accident that Augustine's conversion, a pivotal scene of reading with the heart, features a book in the form of a codex. In late antiquity, a book could still take the form of a parchment or papyrus scroll, as it always does in biblical usage. But from the second to the fourth centuries, the scroll steadily disappeared from Christian circles and was replaced by the codex, ancestor of the book as we know it and "undoubtedly the most important revolution in the book in the Common Era."[34] By the early fourth century, the eventual dominance of the codex was assured with the accession of Christianity to political power in the Roman Empire. The manuscript codex (usually made of parchment, although some early examples are papyrus) remained the principal book format in the West for the next one thousand years, until the codex itself was revolutionized by Gutenberg.

Why the codex first became established among Christians is still a much debated question.[35] One theory holds that Christians favored it for mainly symbolic reasons, such as the fact that it distinguished their sacred writings from the scroll of the Jewish Law or of pagan literature. Other theories argue practical reasons such as its efficiency in holding text, its convenience or portability, or the relative ease of finding passages, which may have aided Christian methods of study and exegesis. The pattern of book metaphors in the *Confessions* itself has even been taken to suggest that "the codex is better suited to interpretive discussion than the roll."[36]

In any case, by the late fourth century, the codex had become the standard format for the Christian Scriptures and other religious writings. Among other things, the codex format probably encouraged a shift to private (and even silent) reading, as suggested by the large number of miniature biblical codices that survive from the third century on.[37] The adoption of the codex by Christians for their sacred writings also endowed this form of the book with special symbolic significance. As early as the third century, the codex appears in religious art as a symbol of divine authority or revealed knowledge, and by the end of the next century, it becomes a symbol of personal religious experience and the inner spiritual life.[38] This is exemplified by Augustine's conversion scene in particular, where a codex is closely associated with the reader's heart, and by the symbolism of the codex in the *Confessions* at large.

Codices are mentioned only a few times in the *Confessions*, where the usual writing formats are the tablet and the scroll. The tablet appears not only as a memory metaphor, but also as actual writing equipment, as in Augustine's story of how he was cured of a toothache by inscribing a prayer on a tablet (9.4). The scroll appears even more often as both object and metaphor.[39] Some of the books figuring in Augustine's spiritual education take this form, including the Platonic books (*volumina*) that teach him to search for invisible truths, as well as the books that Ambrose reads.[40] And, as Karl Morrison has shown, Augustine often uses the scroll figuratively, from the "glue of love" referring to pasted sheets of papyrus and the slowly "unrolled" days at Cassiacum, to the "rolled" and "unrolled" firmament of the heavens.[41] Even humans are likened to scrolls when Christ looks "through the lattice of our flesh" to see us as we are (13.15), where "lattice" (*retia*) refers to "the network of laminations that comprised the papyrus sheets," so that the body is to the soul as the material letter of a text is to its invisible sense.[42]

The codex as object and symbol stands out against this background of tablets and scrolls. It first appears in the series of readerly conversions leading up to Augustine's own conversion in the Milanese garden. One day Ponticianus sees a codex of Paul's epistles lying on a table, prompting him to tell Augustine of another man who likewise found a (second) codex containing a life of Saint Anthony and who, while reading it, was changed within (*mutabatur intus*) as "the waves in his heart rose and fell" (8.6). The third codex to appear in short order is the one that Augustine himself seizes in the garden and that he mentions no fewer than three times—before, during, and after his pivotal act of reading.[43] Augustine could not have picked a more dramatic place to associate the codex with the heart. Structurally and thematically, this is the climax of his narrative, the "culminating moment" that divides his past and present selves even as it "converts" the protagonist into the author.[44]

The codex in the garden may have been suggested in part by practical considerations, since this particular book format facilitates the *sortes biblicae*, or reading from the first passage to which a book opens, supposedly under divine direction.[45] But Augustine's codex is more than a practical convenience; it is a psychological symbol as well. Other images of interiority appear throughout the conversion story (e.g., house, room, garden) and even begin to overlap with each other as the crisis approaches: "And now inside my house great indeed was the quarrel which I had started with my soul in that bedroom of my heart which we shared together" (8.8). The codex is the culminating symbol of the series. As a container having an interior and an exterior and as an enclosure that can be opened and closed, the codex even embodies patristic notions of the heart's "visible" and "invisible" parts, its "interior" and "exterior."[46] Augustine's sudden opening of the codex—a gesture more precise and binary than the slow unrolling of a scroll—results in an inward flood of light that suggests a heart finally opened to God's word.[47]

Besides being a kind of container, the codex also has the form of a diptych, a term originally applied to a folding pair of writing tablets but extended by patristic authors (especially Augustine) to include the twin tablets of the Mosaic Law.[48] Augustine's codex contains Paul's letters and thus embodies a Christian gloss on the Jewish Law. As such, it anticipates the medieval symbolism of the codex, whose diptychal form was used to contrast the Jewish Law with its "fulfillment" in the Gospel.[49] But Augustine's codex also embodies the *external* word of God that is internalized by the process of his silent, heart-centered reading. Augustine's act of reading, which begins with the codex but ends with the heart, involves a movement from the outer to the inner word, a transition from Law to Gospel, letter to spirit, even stone to flesh. Augustine hardly could have foreseen that medieval artists would combine the diptychal codex with the diptychal shape of the stylized human heart to make an integral "book of the heart." But the pictorial trope would grow out of an essentially Augustinian theology, and one of its sources is the symbolism of heart and codex that vividly marks Augustine's most famous moment.

After the conversion scene, the codex appears only one more time in the *Confessions*, again in a crucial passage that emphasizes this particular choice of book imagery. In a well-known chapter near the end of the work, Augustine describes how the angels read the heavenly "book" of God's face: "They read, they choose, they love; their reading is perpetual and what they read never passes away, for by choosing and by loving they read the very unchangeableness of your counsel. Their book [*codex*] is never closed, nor is their scroll [*liber*] folded up, for you yourself are their book and you are forever" (13.15).

As already noted, scroll metaphors are common in the *Confessions*, and several of them appear in this particular chapter, which opens with the "unrolled" heavens and closes with "the lattice of our flesh." But Augustine updates and revises the older imagery of the scroll by adding the metaphor of the comparatively new codex—here used to represent the divine Self, the Creator of all human selves. Augustine's equivocation between the two different metaphors, scroll and codex, reflects the fact that he is writing during a period of transition when the one was giving way to the other as the preferred literary format.[50] But it also reflects an ongoing shift in book *metaphors*, as the codex begins to replace the scroll in the Christian imagination as a symbol for the self, human or divine. Writing metaphors often lag behind writing technology, and scroll metaphors (along with those of the tablet, used throughout the

Middle Ages) would flourish long after the birth of the codex. Indeed, the fully developed metaphor of the heart as a codex would not appear until the Middle Ages, when writing technology and human psychology merged in the scriptorium of the heart. But clearly by the turn of the fifth century, the new form of the book was already beginning to reshape the textual metaphorics of the self. And Augustine's influential example helped to make the codex into the sign of unique subjectivity and personal presence that it became during the Middle Ages and for modernity as well.

## Heart and Pen

Augustine suggests that his readerly epiphany in the garden, with its inward mediation from Scripture to his heart, in turn made possible an outward mediation from heart to text in his own written works. Indeed, Augustine's post-conversion narrative is preoccupied with his own writerly role and his reading public's response, his awareness of which the "serial publication" of his *Confessions* would have enhanced.[51] Already a double figure by virtue of being both author and protagonist, Augustine enhances his dual role by continually alternating between his narrated past and his authorial present, offering a kind of running commentary, a metanarrative, on the work in progress, on his audience, and on his own role as author. A prominent feature in this part of the *Confessions* is the relation between Augustine's book and his heart.

Besides the figurative wound in his heart made by the "arrows" of God's word, the newly converted Augustine suffers several bodily afflictions as well, including a chest complaint (*dolor pectoris*) that forces him to stop teaching rhetoric (9.2) and a toothache that similarly deprives him of speech (9.4). These symptoms figure (and, in practical terms, further) a retreat from external language to interior language, to the "word in the heart." The rhetor's eloquence traditionally originated in the chest or breast (*pectus*), which Augustine consistently links to spoken language throughout the *Confessions* and elsewhere.[52] It is hardly a coincidence, then, that in his early career as a converted writer, Augustine's loss of speech, centered on the lungs, is accompanied by an intense literary production from the heart, a separate organ in the pectoral area and one associated specifically with the *written* word.

In the process of writing his *Confessions,* Augustine transcribes his inner "record" of experience outwardly for an audience, a literary public consisting largely of "Catholics of ascetic experience similar to Augustine's own."[53] Augustine's running commentary on his work in progress refers repeatedly to this audience. Early on, he asks readers not to laugh at him for succumbing to certain sins (2.7). Later, on a more positive note, Augustine claims that "when the confessions of these past sins are read and heard, they rouse up the heart and prevent it from sinking into the sleep of despair" (10.3). Years afterward, reviewing his collected works in the *Retractions,* Augustine echoes this verdict when he writes that the *Confessions* "lift up the understanding and affection of men to Him. At least, as far as I am concerned, they had this effect on me while I was writing them, and they continue to have it when I am reading them."[54] Of course, such effects stem not only from the narrated events of Augustine's life, but also from the literary shape into which he puts them, the affective stylistics of genre, scheme, trope, allusion, and allegory. Augustine "knows that the life is not a revision of events; it is a revision of his interpretation of them."[55]

In reflecting on the work in progress that he has been publishing in installments, Augustine even suggests that his book provides readers with access to his inner self, his heart:

> As to what I now am, at the very moment of writing these confessions, there are many people who want to know about this— both those who know me personally and those who do not, but have heard something about me or from me; but their ear is not laid against my heart [*cor meum*], where I am whatever I am. And so they want, as I make my confession, to hear what I am inside myself, beyond the possible reach of their eyes and ears and minds. (10.3)

Here reading is an auscultation of the heart, where the written text serves as a bodily surrogate for the author himself. Augustine's self-conscious reflection on his own literary persona, on how his writings can project a personal presence, even anticipates a modern phenomenology of reading.[56]

Yet Augustine wonders whether his audience can really know his heart through his book, since people are "very inquisitive about other people's lives, very lazy in improving their own," and, "in wanting to hear, they are ready to believe; but will they know?" (10.3). Skepticism about language as a medium of knowledge, both doctrinal and personal, is a frequent theme in Augustine.[57] In his letter to Paulinus and Therasia about two recent visitors, Augustine emphasizes the superiority of "living letters" with an unusual scribal metaphor: "We transcribed in our own hearts what was written in theirs, by most eager questioning as to everything concerning you."[58] Clearly the inscribed heart, not the written page, is the true transcript of the self. It has even been suggested that in the *Confessions* Augustine finally abandons the autobiographical narrative of books 1–9 for the scriptural exegesis of books 10–13 because "such narrative is ultimately the mediator of false presences."[59] But as an exegete of his own (still unfinished) book, Augustine tempers his doubts with an appeal to a bond of charity that assures mediation between readers and author: "That charity, by which they are good, tells them that I am not lying about myself in my confessions, and it is the charity in them that believes me" (10.3).

The heart is not only an object of Augustine's narrative, but also the source of his writerly activity. Rejoicing in his new vocation as an author, he confesses to God that he writes from a converted heart: "You rescued my tongue as you had rescued my heart. . . . My writing was now done in your service" (9.4). Likewise, he claims to serve God "with heart and voice and writing" (9.13). And, in what is perhaps Augustine's most explicit self-portrait as an author, he describes his written confessions for a literary public as an extension of his private confessions before God: "This is what I want to do in my heart, in front of you, in my confession, and with my pen before many witnesses" (10.1). "Heart" and "pen" symbolize, respectively, the inner sanctum of the self and the public sphere of letters, and their correlation suggests that Augustine thinks of himself as "writing from the heart."

There is evidence that Augustine was taken at his word, that the *Confessions* was actually recognized and reproduced as a "book of the heart" in the Middle Ages. For example, a fifteenth-century codex of the *Confessions* now at the British Library (MS Harley 3087) opens with a colored miniature that shows the saint seated at a writing desk before an open book and holding a heart in one hand and a pen in the other (figure 1). Accompanying the portrait is the passage in the *Retractions*

1. *Augustine with Heart, Book, and Pen.* Augustine at a desk with an opened codex, holding his "heart" and a pen. Miniature from a fifteenth-century manuscript copy of Augustine's *Confessions.* MS Harley 3087, fol. 1 verso. By permission of the British Library.

where Augustine admits that he is moved by rereading his own recollections. The portrait, probably intended to show Augustine in the act of writing his *Confessions,* seems to be a visual allegory for "writing from the heart." Moreover, its most likely source is Augustine's own pronouncement about heart and pen, where the grammatical balance of heart (*cor*) and pen (*stilus*) has a direct parallel in the formal symmetry of the illustration. As a pictorial gloss on this passage—and on Augustine's book as a whole, at the head of which it stands—the portrait underscores the metaphor of the textual heart in the *Confessions,* presenting this work as a veritable book of the heart and providing clues about its medieval reception.

## "The Book of the Life of Each Man"

If Augustine presents his own life as a text whose meaning is gradually revealed over time to its protagonist and reader alike, he also highlights the textuality of human lives in general. In one of the later books of the *Confessions,* he likens the human awareness of time to the recitation of a psalm, whose syllables pass from "expectation" (the future) to "memory" (the past) as they are pronounced; and the same is true "of the whole of a man's life, of which all of his actions are parts. And it is true of the whole history of humanity, of which the lives of all men are parts."[60]

Augustine's sense of life as a narrative, and of the human heart as a secret record of this life, in turn implies the need for an audience, a community of readers. According to Brian Stock, "It is this intersubjective quality that makes Augustine's *Confessions* unique in the ancient literature of the soul rather than the doctrine that the inner self is veiled, mysterious, or inaccessible. . . ." Augustine "establishes the view that knowledge about the self is revealed when the moral habits and internal patterns of a life proceed from the private to the public realm."[61]

The notion of the individual life as a secret narrative destined eventually to be revealed also informs Augustine's account of the Last Judgment in the great work of his later years, *The City of God.* Glossing the "opened books" of judgment mentioned in Revelation 20.12 and quoting from an Old Latin version of the Bible, Augustine refers not to a "book of life" per se, but to what he calls "the book of the life of each man" (*liber vitae uniuscuiusque*).[62] Augustine's phrasing suggests a book containing very individualized records, as he emphasizes by stating that this book shows "what commandments each man has done or omitted to do." Augustine even raises the possibility that there will be "a separate book for every life," although he rejects this interpretation on practical grounds: "If this book be materially considered, who can reckon its size or length, or the time it would take to read a book in which the whole life of every man is recorded? Shall there be present as many angels as men, and shall each man hear his life recited by the angel assigned to him?"

Instead, Augustine answers his own question with a psychological allegory, saying that "the book of the life of each man" signifies "a certain divine power, by which it shall be brought about that every one shall recall to memory all his own works, whether good or evil, and shall mentally survey them with a marvellous rapidity, so that this knowledge will either accuse or excuse conscience, and thus all and each shall be simultaneously judged. And this divine power is called a book, because in it we shall as it were read all that it causes us to remember."

Augustine does not mention the heart here, but he associates this very individualized record with conscience (*conscientia*), memory (*memoria*), and the mind (*mens*), interior faculties that reinforce his psychological interpretation of the opened "book." Moreover, Augustine rejects the idea that an angel will read aloud (*recitare*) from each person's recorded life, as other patristic authors had stated, specifying instead a silent perusal of the inward book whereby each person shall "mentally survey" his works "with a marvellous rapidity"—terms suggesting a primarily visual rather than an oral (or aural) conception of text. The visual text and the more private and individual mode of reading that it implies would characterize many medieval books of the heart.

Augustine's picture of the individual recalling his own life through memory as though reading a book indicates not only that the full meaning of a life is deferred until the end, but that its meaning can only be grasped retrospectively—"must be understood backwards," in the words of one of Augustine's modern spiritual heirs, Søren Kierkegaard.[63] The same principle informs the *Confessions*, which is not the record of a complete life but still embodies the idea of retrospective self-understanding. Augustine's use of texts to discover the self and his use of text as a metaphor to represent the self assume that the true self will not be fully revealed until the end of time—"that full meaning shall remain hidden until revelation of an ending which is not of our own device."[64] These ideas would powerfully shape the medieval book of the heart, which incorporated many other Augustinian notions as well. Among these were the notion of the individual's life as a legible (and interpretable) text, the portrayal of the heart as a record of the individual's life, and the psychological symbolism of the codex. In fashioning the medieval book of the heart, authors (and artists) would elaborate these Augustinian themes with varying emphases. Some would focus on the book's content, others on its legibility, and others yet on its precise authorship or its formal qualities as a book created in the image of the material codex. But in one way or another, nearly every medieval book of the heart would reflect Augustine's legacy.

## Chapter Three

# *The* SCRIPTORIUM *of the* HEART

‍⟐⟐⟐⟐⟐⟐⟐⟐⟐⟐⟐⟐⟐⟐⟐⟐⟐⟐⟐⟐⟐⟐⟐⟐⟐⟐⟐⟐⟐⟐⟐⟐⟐⟐⟐⟐⟐⟐⟐‍

The book of the heart that was created by patristic culture came into its own among the medieval monks and scholars who turned the manuscript codex into a supreme symbol of the self. In the early Middle Ages, books were already synonymous with the manuscript codices preserved mainly in monasteries, although the metaphorical book of the heart could still take the form of a wax tablet or a scroll. But by about the year 1100, the interior book was portrayed almost exclusively as a parchment codex. The codex of the heart was perfected by learned authors associated mainly with the schools of Paris and with newly founded monastic orders such as the Cistercians. Deeply immersed in a textual culture and inspired by Augustine's textual model of the universe, these authors created the most detailed model of the self as a book that had ever appeared up to this time.

To create this book of the heart, every aspect of the manuscript codex was thoroughly and ingeniously allegorized: its materials, production, structure, contents, and use. The inner book as a whole was variously identified with reason, conscience, memory, will, or emotion, and its content varied accordingly from a record of divine laws or a moral account of an individual's deeds, to a transcript of personal feelings and experience. The physical materials of the codex were allegorized in moral and spiritual terms, from its polished vellum (piety) to its securing clasp (secrecy). Even its diptychal structure was interpreted in terms of moral psychology, as when the two facing pages of the opened book were used to represent a divided self. The activities of the inner scribe and inner reader were allegorized as well, from scraping the parchment of the heart (penitence) and checking the text for error against an exemplar (accuracy of memory), to daily reading in the book (obedience to God's law) and consulting it as a commentary or gloss on Scripture (heartfelt devotion).

In scholastic and monastic writings, the book of the heart was increasingly identified with the hidden or private self. This tendency reflected the status of the material book as a locus of secrecy and mystery, as well as crucial developments in medieval book culture, such as the growth of private book ownership and the emergence of silent reading.[1] As Paul Saenger has shown, silent reading, or reading with the eyes alone, "developed only with the evolution of a more rigorous intellectual life in the twelfth and early thirteenth centuries in the *studia* of Cistercian abbeys and at the cathedral schools of the eleventh and twelfth centuries from which universities would emerge."[2] The cathedral schools and eventually the universities also fostered private book ownership and, most important, a new class of clerics living outside the monastery and accustomed to private reading. The solitary reader who studied texts in silence in turn favored the smaller, more portable volumes that became available after about 1300 and that further associated books with personal, private space.[3] Accordingly, the manuscript book came to be regarded increasingly as a visual "text," an object meant primarily for silent and individual study, by contrast with the monastic "page" of communal oral recitation.[4] In following the physical book from the choir to the study, the book of the heart, as modeled on the manuscript codex, was likewise imagined as a primarily visual text for the most private and silent reading of all.

Besides the private self, the book of the heart was also increasingly identified with the unique—even idiosyncratic—individual. In general, this may reflect the "discovery of the individual" that scholars have traditionally placed in or around the twelfth century.[5] In particular, it may reflect the rise of new literary genres such as Latin autobiography (e.g., Guibert de Nogent, Abelard) and the vernacular romance, which treated the individual life, especially inward emotional experience, as worthy of written record and which shaped it into a linear sequence of literary units.[6] It also paralleled the emergence of the book as a symbol of the self in visual art. In the twelfth century, for the first time, portrayals of the Last Judgment depict resurrected human souls holding separate books that represent their own lives. Such images illustrate what theologians and exegetes had widely come to regard as an individualized book of the heart.

## "My Book"

During the early Middle Ages, the heart was central to the monastic disciplines of reading, copying, and reciting texts. The Rule of St. Benedict (c. 535), the chief guide to medieval monastic life, constantly mentions the heart, from its opening reference to "the ear of thy heart," to its recommendations about which texts should be "recited by heart." The heart also figured in the regular chanting or singing of the divine office, which was said to resonate both outwardly and inwardly (*in corde*). But early medieval monks practiced not only the spoken *lectio*, but also the silent (or murmured) *meditatio*, and the Rule directed that books be distributed for individual reading.[7] Monks also continued the early Christian ascetic practice of introspection, a visual metaphor that implies a spatial conception of interiority and that often shades into specifically textual tropes.

Early medieval book metaphors often reflect the commonplace idea that texts in general, and Scripture in particular, resemble humans in having both a bodily and a spiritual aspect.[8] Pope Gregory I (590–604), an influential interpreter of Augustine, compared the hidden meanings of Scripture specifically to the hearts (*corda*) of men, whose faces are unfamiliar at first, but whose "very thoughts" we can trace once we get to know them; likewise we at first know only the "face" of Scripture, but upon further reading "we penetrate its meaning, as if by the effect of a familiar intercourse." In an important visual metaphor, Gregory also described how saints scan (*circumspiciunt*) themselves both outwardly and inwardly so as to "make themselves complete within their interior self" (*in sua interna*). And, in an overtly textual metaphor, Gregory's gloss on Revelation 20.12 evokes the lives of good men, where sinners will "read as in an open book the good which they refused to do themselves."[9]

Alcuin of York (c. 732–804), a leading Carolingian scholar, furthered the idea of the inner self as textual space. Alcuin had a bent for language theory and a fondness for textual tropes that rivaled Augustine's. A prolific letter writer, he often remarked on how writing made it possible to mediate oneself and one's innermost secrets to distant others. In one letter, for example, Alcuin says that written signs reveal things "hidden in the breast" and, in another, that parted friends can "speak" through letters and share matters of "the heart."[10] For Alcuin, the heart is not only an object of textual mediation, but also a "text" in its own right. In a polemical treatise that warns an erring churchman to abjure heretical doctrines, he writes, "Erase, erase quickly, holy father, that opinion from the secret chamber of your heart, lest your Lord . . . find it written in the tablets of your heart."[11] These tablets of the heart echo the biblical trope but also allude to the wax tablets still used for notes and drafts during the Middle Ages. Wax tablets were easily erased, and Alcuin is encouraging the recipient to replace the heresy "written" in his heart with the text of true doctrine. The "secret chamber of your heart" (*tui cordis cubili*) suggests a cell where the cleric might read or write, reinforcing the metaphor of interior textuality.

Some early medieval authors likened the inner self specifically to a book (*liber*), as for example an anonymous gloss on Daniel 7.10 written sometime after the middle of the fifth century and possibly as late as the eighth:

The books that until then were folded up shall be opened. We shall have to give an account of all that we do, say, and think, even of our idle words. It is written in the books of God. Some think these books recording our sins are in heaven. But I think they are our consciences, which shall then be opened, and each

one of us shall see what he has done. Nothing is hidden that shall
not be revealed. . . . Certainly I do not dare confess much of what
is written in my book to my brother or my friend.[12]

In being "folded up" (*complicati*), these books still seem to be imagined
as scrolls, although in the later Middle Ages the same terminology was
extended to the codex.[13] In any case, the author emphatically equates
these books with the individual conscience, as distinct from heavenly
books of record. Most remarkable is the self-conscious reference to
what is written "in my book" (*in libro meo*) as a private realm set off from
the scrutiny of others, whether friend or fellow monk. The designation
of interior space as "my book" would have had special force in monastic culture, where books were not held as private possessions but as
communal property.

It was not unusual for the book of the self to be imagined as a scroll
even in Carolingian times.[14] The library at Fulda, a principal Frankish
monastery, contained some volumes of Origen. And Origen's gloss on
Romans 2.14, which evokes the heart as a book to be opened at the Last
Judgment, found its way into the exegesis of Hraban Maur (c. 780–
856), abbot of Fulda, and later archbishop of Mainz. Hraban, often
regarded as an unoriginal encyclopedist, was the Carolingian master of
the condensed book, excerpting and organizing knowledge for clerical
schools. His commentary on Romans reproduces Origen's metaphor
almost verbatim, even preserving its original scroll format, although
Hraban lived in what was unquestionably the age of the codex: "These
books are now rolled up [*involuti*] and hidden in our heart, containing
written records of our deeds and marked, so to speak, with the reproofs
of conscience, and still known to no one but God. But these books of
our soul or tablets of our heart shall be opened before the throne. . . ."[15]
As a textbook of Carolingian culture, Hraban's writings illustrate that
by the ninth century the book of the heart had become a learned commonplace. At the same time, Hraban's virtually unaltered gloss from
Origen suggests how the inertial force of an outdated metaphor could
be augmented by the prestige of ancient authority. As late as about 990,
an illuminated Gospel codex that is dedicated to Emperor Otto III in
the following words, "With this book, Otto Augustus, may God invest
thy heart," portrays the emperor holding an unfurled scroll rather than

an opened codex.[16] But later authors would powerfully recreate the book of the heart in the shape of the newer book format.

## The Inner Parchment

The book of the heart assumed its definitive medieval form with the thinkers, teachers, and writers of the cathedral schools in and around twelfth-century Paris. Scholastic writers, immersed in a culture of books, and tending (like their chief intellectual forebear, Augustine) to view God, the world, and humans through metaphors of the book, produced the most elaborate and copious variety of book metaphors in the Middle Ages.[17] In describing the book of the heart, they assigned psychological significance to not only its content but also its distinctive *form*, modeled on the manuscript codex, as well as the lengthy process whereby the inner book was prepared, inscribed, collated, corrected, read, and interpreted.

A good example of how the book of the heart was recreated in the image of the manuscript codex appears in the writings of Richard of St. Victor (d. 1173), one of Augustine's most influential twelfth-century interpreters. In a treatise on the Last Judgment where he discusses the opened books of Revelation 20.12, Richard specifies a codex of the heart containing a record of the individual's deeds:

> Each person carries in his heart a written record, as it were, whereby his conscience accuses or defends him. . . . What are the consciences of those to be judged except the writing of their deeds . . . ? For those awaiting judgment, opening the books of their deeds before the judges is nothing other than not to be able to hide their consciences from them. And for the judges to read in books [*codicibus*] of this kind is nothing other than to penetrate with clear vision the things hidden in consciences. . . .[18]

The same passage refers to contemplative readers of Scripture as "transcribing" what they understand of God's truth into "the books of their hearts" (*in cordium voluminibus transcribunt*), where *volumen* (pl. *volumina*), once denoting a scroll, now is clearly synonymous with the codex.

Elsewhere Richard describes the codex of the heart in more detail. A sermon for the feast day of Saint Augustine that explicates one of Augustine's favorite passages—"My heart overflows with a goodly theme. . . . My tongue is like the pen of a ready scribe . . ." (Ps. 45.1, Vulg. 44.2)—describes the heart as a book authored by the Holy Spirit through the teaching and preaching of God's word: "The scribe is the Holy Spirit, the pen is the teacher's tongue, the ink is grace, the inkhorn is Christ, the parchment is the hearts of men, the writing is truth, and the scriptorium is earthly means."[19] Richard details how the parchment of the heart is prepared for this writing: "Truly our hearts, which we say are figured by parchment, and in which this writing of the spirit is spiritually inscribed, are prepared by bitter penitence in the same way as a material skin. They are stretched by regular abstinence, they are scraped by removing all carnality, and they are formed into quires by unflagging constancy." In Richard's extended metaphor, even the rectilinear quires (*quaterniones*), or gatherings of folded leaves, have symbolic significance, for "just as all round things are unstable, so all square things are stable and firm," a comparison that may allude disparagingly to the circular scrolls of "unstable" Jewish (or pagan) tradition.

A biblical commentary authored by either Richard or his great Victorine counterpart, Hugh (1096?–1141), uses the details of codex construction to render the parts and workings of the inner self in even greater detail: "the soul's arrangement is like the quires; its functions, like the leaves; the feelings, like the pages [i.e., recto and verso]; the movements of the heart, like the prayers written on each page; the love of God and neighbor, like the coloring of the letters. . . ." Even the flaws in the book are allegorized, as its errors and erasures are said to represent "worldly ambition and fleshly desires."[20] Unlike the scroll, with its continuous writing surface, the codex was eminently divisible into separate parts, a quality that obviously appealed to the scholastic mind seeking analogies for a complex and multipartite self. The minutely divided pages of the glossed Bibles that began appearing in the twelfth century clearly reinforced this tendency.[21]

A notable variation on the codex of the heart comes from another Parisian authority, Peter of Blois (c. 1135–c. 1212), who describes a single book of conscience whose individual sections correspond to the hearts of separate persons at the Last Judgment: "The book of conscience is now closed, for 'Deep and unsearchable is the heart of man, and who can know it?' ... That book shall be opened at that time when the hidden things of our hearts shall be revealed. Then man shall appear naked and carrying the *fasciculum* of his works. . . ."[22] The term *fasciculum*, meaning a unit consisting of one or more quires, clearly indicates the codex as Peter's model for the inner book.[23] By equating each individual's heart with only a single fascicle of the book in which they are all comprised, Peter offers a neat answer to Augustine's question of how a single "book of life" containing an account of many individual lives could be interpreted "materially."[24] Since the fascicle is a unit of scribal labor (books were often taken apart and rented out by the section to university students for copying), Peter's terminology tends to stress the link between the individual and a certain length of text.[25]

Some authorities even offered "practical" instructions for making a book of the heart modeled on the products of the scriptorium. An elaborate example appears in a twelfth-century sermon from Durham Cathedral stating that "everyone, from the time when he begins to use his reason until the end of his life, writes the book of his own conscience, in accordance with which he shall be judged in the end." There follows a detailed allegory from the scriptorium about becoming "scribes of the Lord":

The parchment on which we write for him is a pure conscience, where all our good works are everlastingly recorded to make us acceptable to God. The knife with which it is scraped is the fear of God, which removes from our conscience by penitence all the roughness of sin and the unevenness of vices. The pumice with which it is made smooth is the discipline of heavenly desire, which breaks down the smallest carelessness arising from idle thoughts, lest anything obstruct the heavenly writing on it. The chalk with whose fine particles it is whitened signifies an unbroken meditation of holy thoughts, which makes our conscience resplendent. The ruler, by which the line is guided that we may write straight, is the will of God, to which we apply the efforts of our hearts so that they may be graced with the rectitude of justice. . . . The pen, which is divided in two to prepare it for writing, is the love of God and of our neighbour, which causes all that is good in us. The ink with which we write is humility itself. . . .[26]

The sermon goes on to gloss the book's colored illuminations (divine grace), the writing desk (tranquillity of heart), and the exemplar from which the scribe should copy his own good works (the life of Christ). Although less pointed in its psychology than the Victorine allegory of quire, folio, and page, this northern English example displays a technical virtuosity almost without equal, at the same time suggesting that by the twelfth century such elaborate metaphors were ranging well beyond the center of scholasticism in Paris.[27]

A sermon by Peter Comestor (d. 1179/89), another Parisian master, displays a similar relish for technical detail but also goes on to specify the use of the inner book once it has been completed. Peter urges each "*frater*" in his audience to make his heart into a book containing God's commandments, just as a scribe prepares parchment to copy a text from an exemplar:

> You know the scribe's work. First, with the knife he begins to clean the parchment of fat and to remove all gross filth. Next with the pumice stone he smoothes away all hair and sinews, without which the script will not be legible or durable. Then he applies the ruler to serve as a guide for writing. All of which you also must do if you want to have the book I have described. This parchment book shall be your heart.[28]

In this allegory of the scriptorium and its tools, the knife signifies penance; the pumice, prayer and alms; and the ruler, the guiding example of the Fathers.

After the parchment of the heart has been prepared, according to Peter, it is ready to be inscribed. In this case, the text to be "copied" consists of the Ten Commandments: "In the first folio and on the first line, you shall write: 'The Lord your God is one God'—that is, believe in the omnipotent Father, and love him. On the second line of the same page, you shall write: 'Thou shalt not take the name of thy Lord God in vain'—that is, believe the Son to be no less than the Father in divinity but equal to the Father, and love him. . . ." All the commandments are enumerated and glossed in this way, each one serving as a memory cue for more discursive teachings. As Peter puts it, writing God's laws in the book of the heart enables the reader "to recall them to mind." The book of the heart is thus synonymous with a book of memory, as the heart assumes the formal layout, the *mise-en-page*, of the manuscript codex.

Peter's sermon concludes with advice about the care and use of the completed book of the heart. The scribe must carefully keep his book from damage and error, "not allowing any enemy to look within it, or any inserted filth to erase anything, or anything contrary to these precepts to be added between the lines." The chief "enemy" is the Devil, pictured here as a devious scribe who "might erase these laws and write instead their opposites, that is, the deadly sins" (which the sermon also enumerates). To further safeguard his book of the heart, the owner should add a clasp (*serrarium*) signifying "the grace of God against the wiles of the enemy." Thus kept from harm and error, the book of the heart can be taken anywhere and even read "with eyes closed."

Although Peter's book of the heart has a generic content (unlike the individualized moral record in the Durham sermon), its clasp and other formal features emphasize its personal, private nature. By comparison with other books, the book of the heart is portable and convenient— "a book that you will always be able to carry with you without any trouble, and you will know its teachings as soon as you have it in your possession." It is even a kind of private property with an intrinsic value assessed in monetary terms, as Peter pronounces it "more valuable than gold," though it can be had "without either coin or money." The scribe who might seek payment or reward (*praemium*) for his work, something "whereby those who write in the heart shall be remunerated," is told to look for it in heaven. In this, Peter may be modeling his book of the heart on the smaller codices that were becoming available in his time, or he may simply be distinguishing it from the large folio volumes that still dominated the scene. Whatever its specific model in the culture of the manuscript codex, his book of the heart implies the private reading and study that were increasingly common during the later Middle Ages.

## The Inner Scribe

In portraying the book of the heart as a manuscript codex, many learned authors assigned psychological significance to the specific tasks of inscribing, collating, correcting, and studying books, as some of the above examples have already suggested. In particular, medieval authors continued the patristic tendency to allegorize the examination and correction of manuscripts in ethical terms, applying the quality-control methods of the scriptorium to the inner moral self, now represented almost exclusively as a codex.[29] These scribal allegories tend to treat the book of the heart as an object of the private, silent reading that was transforming the actual manuscript codex into an increasingly visual text.

One of the many monastic works entitled *The Cloister of the Soul* describes how a book of the heart containing God's laws and originally dispensed to Adam in Paradise was "corrected" over time from later books. There were four books in all: "The first was written by God in the heart of man, the second by Moses in tablets of stone, the third by Christ in the earth, the fourth in divine foreknowledge." Respectively, these are the books of reason, correction, grace, and divine wisdom. Using the language of the scriptorium, the treatise indicates the errors and corrections to which each book is subject. The book of reason, for example, "was corrupted but not corrected," whereas "the book written by Moses in the desert was corrupted many times and many times corrected." The scribal tasks of reading and emendation signify motions of the will and the understanding: "Whenever anyone wonders what he should do, and decides the matter rationally, it is as if he reads in the book of reason. And when he sins and immediately repents, he as it were reads and studies the book of correction."[30]

Similar scribal tropes were used to interpret the opened books of the Last Judgment (Rev. 20.12) as the inner moral record of a person's life. The anonymous Cistercian treatise *De interiori domo* depicts an inner scribe who writes down every deed in such a book: "Wherever I go, my conscience does not leave me but is always present and writes down [*scribit*] whatever I do. . . . When the Lord shall come to judge, the conscience of each person shall be brought to witness, and the book of conscience shall be opened, and each sin brought to light"—literally, "placed before the eyes" (*ante oculos*).[31] As an object of visual (rather than vocal) reading, the self is here identified with the silent, spatialized text.

The same Cistercian treatise describes the inner book as a copy that may contain errors and must first be checked against a divine exemplar. Again, the copy is unique to the individual: "To each one [*unicuique*] belongs the book of his conscience. . . ." It is also portable: "When the soul leaves the body, it cannot take with it anything but the book of conscience, and from that book it knows where it should go and what it shall receive." But because the private book of conscience is destined for a very public reading and correction at the Last Judgment ("all others will be present at the discussion and correction of this book"), the inner scribe must carefully check it for errors. And if he discovers that his book is not written "according to the exemplar that is the book of life," he must correct it at once. Manuscript culture and moral psychology combine perfectly in the concluding allegory: "Let us then compare our books with the book of life, so that if they read differently they may be corrected, and not found wanting in the final collation and thus rejected."[32]

A twelfth-century treatise attributed to Hugh of St. Victor likewise mentions a Final Collation (*ultima collatio*) at which each individual's book of the heart will be checked against an exemplar kept by God. Here the opened books of Revelation 20.12 are expressly glossed as "the hearts of men" to be opened "when the secrets of the heart are revealed." Each person will be judged by his own book, so that, like a careful scribe, he must undertake a comparison (*collatio*) and emendation (*correctio*) in order to ensure that his book agrees with the divine exemplar: "Our books must be written according to the exemplar of the book of life. . . . And if they are not written thus, they must be corrected at once. Let us then compare our books with this one book, so that if they read differently they may be corrected. . . ."[33] Again, comparison and correction represent the individual's moral self-assessment according to the "exemplar" of God's word.

These scribal allegories show that the inward book was increasingly imagined in visual rather than vocal terms, as a book to be silently perused and understood rather than recited aloud, and hence as the ultimate private text. Modeled on the quality-control methods of actual scriptoria, these allegories also capitalize on the moral and spiritual discipline of the scribe's sanctified manual labor and the related idea that copying, checking, and correcting books was good for the soul—or heart. As metaphors of the inner scribe, they also exhort the cleric to maintain an accurate memory of his own moral history, thus continuing the patristic ideal of the "corrected heart." But what originated as clerical disciplines of the heart would eventually take more popular forms. The Church's growing emphasis on inward spirituality, as expressed by the decree of the Fourth Lateran Council (in 1215) that all Christians must confess their sins annually, helped to make the book of the heart a more common possession, one that already in the twelfth century Peter Comestor said was legible "to cleric and layman alike," and even "to those of us who have not learned to read or write."[34]

## The Diptychal Heart

As we have seen, the book of the heart in later medieval writings assumes not only the general form of the manuscript codex, but also its structure and layout, from quire to folio to the individual line. Authors occasionally specify alternate writing formats, as when Bernard of Clairvaux (1090/91–1153) eloquently hearkens back to the scroll in a gloss on the Last Judgment: "The book of conscience is opened, the whole length of the misery of life is unrolled, a certain sad story is unfolded, reason is brought to light, and memory is rolled open as if set before its own eyes."[35] Bernard's choice of metaphor is dictated by his theme, for the unrolled scroll and sequential story or narrative (*historia*) that he mentions both suggest a continuous, undivided self. But authors discussing topics such as sin, repentance, and salvation frequently wanted to portray a divided, disjunctive self that was more aptly pictured by the codex, with its bifoliated or diptychal structure. The medieval book is most famous as a symbol of unity or totality, but it was sometimes used to represent psychic division or moral ambivalence as well.

The symbolism of the diptychal codex can be seen in the sermon by Peter Comestor that was quoted earlier. Peter divides the Ten Commandments into their two traditional groups, each of which fills one of two facing pages in the book of the heart: "In this first folio are written those commands that pertain to the love of God himself, and in which the Trinity is expounded. In the second folio you are to write those commands that pertain to the love of your neighbor." This bifoliated book of the heart mirrors the traditional *form* of the Law, the twin tablets that had become a standard symbol by the twelfth century.[36]

The two parts of the Law are complementary, of course, not conflicting. But the diptychal codex was also used to portray a self sharply divided by sin or grace, as in an anonymous twelfth-century miscellany:

> Man speaks to his own heart, reading attentively about his own deeds in the book of his heart. This book has two leaves [*folia*]. Sinners read in one, and penitents in the other. This is what the sinner reads: "These things I have done, I remember them, and I love them." In the other leaf the penitent reads: "I have done these things, I remember them, and I am sorry for them." Let us read in the leaf of penitence lest we be exiled from the new land. . . .[37]

Here the bifoliated book of personal secrets embodies not a formal division in God's law, but a moral division in the human psyche. It suggests a complex self with a retrospective self-awareness that, like Augustine's in the *Confessions*, is divided between past and present, sin and repentance, temptation and redemption. Moreover, this book of the heart occasions a choice of how to "read" (*legere*) one's own past—specifically in terms of the feelings or affections that accompany this reading. To read the book of the heart is to recall one's past sins; each reader, sinner or penitent, says, "I remember" (*recordor*). But the differing responses of each—the sinner's love for what he reads (*delector*) and the penitent's sorrow (*doleo*)—put the personal past to very different uses. While in both cases it is the "same" past, it is a markedly different self that reads each, or that is read *by* each.

This passage implies that the ideal reader of the book of the heart is one who has already changed from reading his own life as a sinner to reading it as a penitent, a redeemed individual. He has already left off reading from one page (*in uno*) to read exclusively from the other (*in alio*), from what the sermon emphatically calls the opposite leaf (*contrario folio*). The movement from one page to the other, from left to right, hints not only at an ideal of "correct reading," but also at an Augustinian notion of reading as a process of converting ("turning") the heart. If the job of the inner scribe is to keep the book of the heart free of textual error, that of the inner reader is to keep himself free from erroneous interpretation.

## "Your Own Book"

A much longer discussion of how to read the book of the heart appears
in the Pseudo-Bernardine treatise *De doctrina cordis.* This work, widely
read and translated during the Middle Ages, has been recently reattributed to Hugh of St. Cher (d. 1263), yet another Parisian scholar.[38] It
includes a chapter on "opening" the book of the heart, which again is
imagined as a manuscript codex, followed by another chapter on the
various "impediments" to interior reading. For the most part, Hugh
leaves aside the materials and production of this book (which he treats
in detail elsewhere), emphasizing instead how the individual is to use it
for penitence and devotion in his own private "reading" and "study."[39]

What Hugh calls "the book of the heart or conscience" (*liber cordis
sive conscientie*) is again a record of the individual's life as modeled mainly
on biblical precedents, including Daniel 7.10 but especially the opened
books of Revelation 20.12. In this case, however, there is no divine original or exemplar but simply the individual's own self-authored work:
"See what sort of writing you bring for judgment in the book of your
conscience, which is to say what sort of testimony you carry in your
conscience, whether to eternal life or death." In considering what he
"writes" inwardly, the individual is asked to reflect on his own life as a
moral narrative, as a kind of autobiography. Although the inner book
authored by each person will be opened for all to read at the end of
time, its main purpose is his own edification and self-understanding
"during the earthly life." To understand oneself, says Hugh, is "to read
within" (*intus legere*).[40]

Like Peter Comestor, who advised each scribe to furnish his book
of the heart with a clasp, Hugh urges that each person stick to his own
book and not pry into others: "Read in your own book. Do not be like
those who, neglecting their own book, always want to read in another
person's, and who, neglecting their own conscience, always wish to examine and judge the conscience of others" (185). Proper reading means
not only attending to the right text, but also having the right moral and
emotional response to it: "You must often read with tears of sorrow
and penitence that come from considering your sins, and the perils and
miseries of this world, as well as the song of gladness and mirth which
comes from contemplating heavenly joys or the eternal damnation of
the reprobate" (184). Reading the book of the heart while weeping over

one's sins as recorded there will even help "erase" the miseries of the world, adds Hugh, using wordplay on *delere* (erase) and *dolere* (weep). Hugh's ethic of reading, as applied to the inner book, emphasizes both moral and affective response, constituting the individual as a self-aware reader of the text that he has authored himself.

In urging a highly personal, emotional response to reading the book of the heart, Hugh seems to model the inner book on a privately owned text intended for individual, silent reading. Hugh does allude to oral reading when he says that preoccupation with worldly things "makes such a great noise in the heart of man that what is read in the conscience cannot be heard [*audiri*]" (189). But he evokes the inner book as a visual text for silent reading as well. He urges the reader to "see" (*videre*) what is written in his heart, describing the psychology of reading in expressly visual terms: "Here we have spoken of the heart as a kind of book, where first the eye sees, then the mind understands, and finally the affections take delight" (185). Moreover, Hugh figures the book of the heart that each reader/scribe will present to Christ at the Last Judgment as a manuscript codex that has been visually examined and corrected: "Why would you wish to emend a book such as a missal or antiphonary but hand over the book of your conscience, by whose contents you shall be judged, in an uncorrected state?" (190). The human individual, not God, is clearly the author and scribe of this book. And as a record of deeds for which the individual takes ultimate responsibility, Hugh's book of the heart represents the self as a unique moral being having a specific personal history.

An individualized book of the heart like the one described by Hugh appears in not only theology and exegesis, but also the visual art of the manuscript book. By the twelfth century, the illustrated Apocalypse often included pictorial images of the "opened books" in Revelation 20.12 next to glosses specifying their increasingly personal significance. Most of these images adorned lavish volumes that never left the monastic library and were accessible only to clerics.[41] By the thirteenth century, however, such images began appearing in vernacular works meant for a wider audience that probably included lay readers and patrons. For example, the Paris Apocalypse (c. 1250–1255) includes a miniature that pictures the resurrected souls with opened books as they await Christ's verdict (figure 2). According to the accompanying French gloss on Revelation 20.12, these books "signify that all consciences shall be

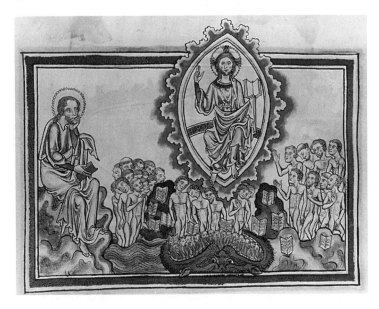

2. *Opened Hearts at the Last Judgment.* Resurrected souls present their "opened books" (Rev. 20.12). Apocalypse Commentary, thirteenth century, miniature. MS fr. 403, fol. 40v. Cliché Bibliothèque nationale de France, Paris. Reproduced by permission.

opened to see how they have kept God's commands."[42] While the gloss emphasizes the interior, metaphorical significance of the books ("conscience" being virtually synonymous here with "heart"), the pictorial image stresses their individuality by showing multiple volumes (if not quite one book for each person!).[43] As discussed in a later chapter, similar images of the heart as a book would eventually spread from the comparatively privileged space of the manuscript page to very public and accessible places such as the church wall and the popular stage.

## The Book of Experience

Besides an inner book of personal moral history, a record of good and evil deeds to be opened at the Last Judgment, learned authors cited a book of experience (*liber experientiae*) that represented the more subjective, emotional side of a person's life.[44] Usually identified with the heart, the book of experience includes the interior life of feelings, imagination, and even the senses. As such, it epitomized the growing medieval sense of the uniquely constituted self and can be seen as a correlative to the personal narratives that increasingly appear from the twelfth century on, especially the emerging genre of autobiography. Some authors invoked the internal book of experience mainly to confirm external written authority; others, especially devotional writers, used it to represent the deep feelings that they saw as essential to the religious life. In its emotional and sometimes even sensual aspect, the book of experience had affinities with the eroticized book of the heart in vernacular romances and other popular literature.

Medieval preaching manuals cite the book of experience as a supplement to Scripture and other authorities, particularly as a source of the self-understanding necessary to assimilating God's word. Guibert de Nogent (1053–c. 1125) invokes such a book when he says that the preacher can count on each listener to understand certain topics from his own personal experience: "This type of subject matter will be absolutely clear to everyone, especially since each can study within himself, as if written in a book, whatever the preacher's tongue expounds concerning various temptations."[45] Guibert's best-known work is a narrative of his own life (*De vita sua*), which was modeled on Augustine's *Confessions* and has been called the first medieval autobiography. His earlier preaching manual likewise reflects the value Guibert assigned to personal experience, maintaining that the preacher must first learn "the lessons his experience of interior struggles has taught him," since "the events of his life, both good and bad, are indelibly imprinted on his memory."[46]

A preaching manual written by Alan of Lille (d. 1202) about a century after Guibert's includes a sample sermon that cites the book of experience as essential to self-understanding, along with the books of knowledge (Scripture) and conscience. Alan associates this book of experience with the heart, which he compares (and contrasts) with a codex book: "You may read about yourself in the book of experience. You may discover yourself in the book of conscience. The book of knowledge, written in a volume [*in codice*], may reprehend you, as well as the book of experience written in the heart [*in corde*]." Alan's book of conscience is less a record of individual sins than a reminder of eventual judgment, while his book of experience, as for Guibert, represents a direct knowledge of temptations: "In the book of experience you will read that the flesh battles against the spirit, in the book of conscience that 'The day of judgement circles on remorseless wings.'"[47]

Alan taught theology at Paris, and his book of experience has a strongly scholastic flavor. But he wrote his preaching manual late in life after entering the Cistercian order, and he may have borrowed this particular book metaphor from his monastic brethren, who gave the book of experience a more independent role. Experience was a key term for spiritual life in the Cistercian order, founded around 1100, and the book of experience was part of the "new vocabulary" that they adopted.[48] In Cistercian spirituality, the book of experience signifies a special kind of private devotion, very personal and often highly emotional, that goes beyond normal communal observances.

Bernard of Clairvaux, the great Cistercian leader, invoked not only a book of the heart containing personal secrets to be opened at the Last Judgment (as cited earlier), but also a book of experience representing private and deeply felt piety. Thus Bernard opens one of his sermons on the Song of Songs by selecting the daily reading from this inner book: "Today the text we are to study is the book of our own experience. You must therefore turn your attention inwards; each one must take note of his own particular awareness of the things I am about to discuss. I am attempting to discover if any of you has been privileged to say from his heart: 'Let him kiss me with the kiss of his mouth.'" Here the book of experience almost rivals Scripture as an object of study. Unlike Scripture, however, the inner book is not a common text shared by all believers but a unique, personal record that must be studied or examined by each person (*unusquisque*) for himself.[49] In addition, it has a "sensual" content that is placed in the service of spiritual devotion.

Other Cistercian writers made similar appeals to a book of personal experience. For example, Isaac of Stella (c. 1100–c. 1169), abbot of the monastery at Étoile, declared in a sermon that believers recognize Christ's various qualities—his humanity and divinity, his weakness and strength—from the similar variety within themselves, which it is impossible not to feel (*sentire*) because "we learn [*sentimus*] of it in the book of experience with more certainty than we are taught it by the preacher's voice." The book of experience, here an object of understanding but also of *feeling*, again takes precedence over external texts. But lest the inner book assume undue authority, Isaac also cautions that everyone must scrutinize it to determine "the source of all that rises within us, the origins of thoughts and feelings, the roots of desires and urges as well as of suggestions and pleasures."[50]

Some mystical and devotional authors describe the book of experience even more elaborately, as with Guigo the Carthusian (d. 1188), who maintains that no one can understand written accounts of the soul's love for God without assistance from the "commentary" of personal experience in his own heart:

> Why do we try to express in everyday language affections that no language can describe? Those who have not known such things do not understand them, for they could learn more clearly of them only from the book of experience where God's grace itself is the teacher. Otherwise it is of no use for the reader to search in earthly books: there is little sweetness in the study of the literal sense, unless there be a commentary [*glossa*], which is found in the heart, to reveal the inward sense.

Guigo's vocabulary of text and gloss, *littera* and *sensus*, has a scholastic flavor, but his interior book represents not God's law or a record of sins, but rather the soul's joyous love for Christ, here described (as by Bernard) in very sensual terms: "Embrace Him whom you long for, make yourself drunk with this torrent of delight, and suck the honey and milk of consolation from the breast. . . ."[51] Clearly this book of experience contains something very different from the one cited by Alan of Lille. What it represents is not primarily the self as dependent creature, or as moral agent, but as aspiring lover.

The book of experience evoked by ascetic lovers of Christ actually has a good deal in common with the secular lover's book of the heart in the vernacular romances of the same period. There is even some evidence that the sensual book of the heart had its beginnings in the cloister, as we shall see in the next chapter. Both books contain mainly the lover's feelings or affections, which in both cases are similarly ineffable—"affections that no language can describe," as Guigo puts it, in words that apply equally well to erotic love. Both books also tend to stress the unique quality of these ineffable feelings, as directed toward a unique love object, and the idea that true knowledge of a thing does not come from book learning or external instruction but from one's own direct experience, whether of spiritual or fleshly things.

## Chapter Four

# *LOVERS*

෴෴෴෴෴෴෴෴෴෴෴෴෴෴෴෴෴෴෴෴෴෴෴෴෴෴෴෴෴෴

With the rise of vernacular love literature in the twelfth century, the book of the heart made its way out of the cloister and school into a more popular sphere. This new literature recreated the book of the heart in its own image, transforming it from a largely religious text into a frankly secular one. The new book of the heart was filled not with divine commands or moral records, but amorous memories and erotic feelings. The inner scribe who produced it was identified not with the biblical God, reason, or conscience, but instead with the pagan god of love (Cupid), the human lover, or even his lady. And its introspective reader now studied the commandments of love, the charms of the beloved, or his own turbulent emotional history.

The earliest vernacular love poems of the Middle Ages, the lyrics of the troubadours, tended to portray the lover's feelings or memories as pictures, engravings, or simply wounds in his heart. Later poetry, however, increasingly described the lover's emotional or sensual impressions in expressly textual terms. In part, this change reflects the fact that later medieval vernacular poetry began to assume the weight and dignity of a book culture that hitherto had existed only in the Latin-based world of the monasteries and schools. As romantic love was codified into a set of literary conventions, it also tended to become "codified" in the other, original sense of the term, meaning to be put into the form of a book (codex), or at least in the form of writing. The codification of romantic literature appears on various levels, from its physical format to its plots and metaphors. Already by the late twelfth century, Andreas Capellanus had authored a self-proclaimed Latin "textbook" of love that purported to offer a systematic treatment of the subject. Books and documents increasingly appeared as props in the stories of literary lovers, as in Dante's story of Paolo and Francesca seduced into adultery by reading a romance book, and the amorous letters exchanged by lovers in many of Chaucer's tales. As might be expected, *metaphors* of writing also proliferated, as when Sir Gawain's hostess tries to seduce him by appealing to what she calls the "text" of chivalry, the recognized rules of knighthood.[1] Secular literature that was intended for a sophisticated though not necessarily learned audience naturally extended such metaphors of reading and writing to the psychology of the lover and the experience of erotic passion.

The secular book of the heart drew upon many traditions of textual metaphor, from the classical poets to the scholastic philosophers. One of its most important ancient sources was Ovid, who had used writing symbolism in sexually suggestive ways, as with the confidante carrying a love letter "concealed by a broad band on her warm bosom," or even a secret message written directly on her body.[2] Medieval poets elaborated the sexual symbolism of writing (pen as phallus, etc.), often treating the heart as a synecdoche for the body in general and the erogenous zones in particular. They also adopted from classical poets the quasi-inscriptional metaphor of the wounded heart, in some cases transforming Cupid's arrows into a writing pen.

The erotic book of the heart drew upon religious sources as well. Poets turned the biblical "tablet of the heart" to sexual use, creating an all-too-fleshly version of Paul's living "letter" written on the heart. As shown in the previous chapter, monastic writers cite a surprisingly sensual book of experience in connection with personal devotion. And scholastics sometimes treat the book of experience in sexual terms, as when Alan of Lille cites it as a practical complement to the theory of erotic love.[3] The amorous book of the heart in vernacular literature reflected both of these impulses, sometimes treating romantic passion as an alternative religion, with its own commandments, rituals, and objects of devotion, and sometimes as an alternative course of study, with its own subjects, questions, and textbooks. In its move from religion to romance, however, the amorous book of the heart reversed the polarities of logos and eros in Christian culture. Instead of an interior writing that signified spiritual values and the transcending of carnal impulses, medieval love poets openly celebrated a writing on the "fleshly" heart that embodied sexual desires, memories, and fantasies. Even so, the idealizing tendency of medieval love literature often left the book of the heart hovering somewhere between the realm of the spirit and the realm of the flesh.

## The Cloistered Heart

In France, around the year 1100, the outlines of a very sensual book of the heart appeared in a verse epistle written by an educated woman to a male friend:

> I put [your] letter under my left breast—
>     they say that's nearest the heart. . . .
> At last, weary, I tried to get to sleep,
>     but love that has been wakened knows no night. . . .
> I lay asleep—no, sleepless—because the page you wrote,
>     though lying on my breast, had set my womb on fire.[4]

This sounds for all the world like a romance heroine lamenting her absent lover and pressing to her body his latest love letter as a kind of erotic fetish. But these verses were actually written—in *Latin*—by a young nun, Constance of Angers, to an older monk, Baudri of Bourgueil (1046–1130), who later became archbishop of Dol. Hence we are faced with the surprising possibility that the book of the heart, as a record of amorous feeling, may have had its origins in the cloister. Moreover, Constance is clearly an agent and not just an object of desire, a female author of sensual verse who invites comparison with the roughly contemporary female troubadours. It remains unclear whether these love letters from the cloister were simply an "intellectual game" or "something more materially erotic," since they maintain a "tense balance" between sensual and spiritual language.[5] For all the apparent eroticism of her verses, Constance voices a desire to transcend bodily urges: "Oh if only I could live as bride of God!"[6]

The moral tension or ambiguity in these texts is heightened by the fact that amorous language is fairly common in monastic letters of this time. For example, Bernard of Clairvaux, a near contemporary of Constance, writes almost as a lover to Ermengarde, a former countess who has become a nun: "If you could but read in my heart how great an affection for you the finger of God has written there, then you would surely see how no tongue could express and no pen describe what the spirit of God has been able to inscribe there." Sounding even more like a lover pining for his distant lady, Bernard adds that since he is absent in body but present in spirit, he and Ermengarde can at least share their hearts: "Search your heart and you will find mine there too . . ." (*Intra ergo cor tuum et inspice meum . . .*).[7]

Bernard also applied sexual metaphors of reading and writing to theological matters. For example, one of his sermons describes the Virgin Mary praising God for having "written" in her womb with the "pen" of the Holy Spirit in order to engender Christ—"Not [a word] scratched by dumb signs on dead skins, but one in human form truly graven, lively, within my chaste womb, not by the tracings of a dead pen, but by the workings of the Holy Spirit."[8] The letter by Constance to Baudri, where she is speaking for herself, and on a less clearly theological topic, evokes a similar sexual writing on the female heart or genitals—the "two-leaved book" of later popular reference.[9]

Medieval culture, in the words of Carolyn Dinshaw, tended to associate "acts of writing and related acts of signifying . . . with the masculine," and "the surfaces on which these acts are performed . . . with the feminine."[10] Since these gendered terms applied to both actual and metaphorical writing, the heart or mind was often an implicitly "feminine" surface for "masculine" inscription. And when memories or feelings were of a sexual nature, interior writing became overtly erotic, as in a letter by Heloise to Abelard recalling their affair: "Everything we did and also the times and places are stamped [*infixa*] in my mind along with your image, so that I live through it all again with you."[11] In later vernacular versions of Heloise's letters, these sensual memories are located expressly in her heart. For example, in Jean de Meun's French translation (c. 1270), Heloise says, "The things we did . . . are so fixed with you in my heart [*couraige*] that in them I do again all these things with you, so that not even in sleep do I have any rest, and often the thoughts of my heart are betrayed in a movement of my body or they surprise me in an unexpected word." [12] In Heloise's metaphor, past erotic deeds have left such sharp impressions on her inner being, and particularly her heart, that they could potentially elicit a repetition of those deeds. Her metaphor of erotic impressions is especially apt to the lingering memories of a love affair that began, according to Abelard's own testimony, with glances stolen between lessons from books: "My hands strayed oftener to her bosom than to the pages; love drew our eyes to look on each other more than reading kept them on our texts." [13]

## Making an Impression

The troubadours, the first vernacular poets to treat the heart as a personal erotic record, tended to equate sensual memories or passionate emotions with visual images rather than words per se. Even more so than the inscribed word, an image carved or impressed on the heart suggests the violence of the lover's feelings. Thus Sordello (c. 1200– c. 1270) begins one of his lyrics with the ancient image of the lover's pierced heart: "I have an arrow in my heart / Crafted by Desire and tempered by Death, / Which makes me sing...." But by the last stanza, love's arrow has become a kind of chisel:

> Love engraved
> Your features in an image
> Cut deeply into my heart,
> And so I've handed myself over,
> To do whatever pleases you,
> Finely and firmly through all my life. [14]

The lover's memory-picture of his lady resembles the mnemonic images of rhetorical tradition. But Sordello also adapts the interrelated biblical themes of writing, graven images, and idolatry to the alternative religion of sensual love. The lover exchanges the divine law written on the heart (*al cor*) for the commands of romantic love, which he is to obey for all the days of his life (*a totz mos ans*). And he exchanges the image of God for the image of his lady, worshiping this "graven" image within himself instead.

The lover's heart marked by his lady's image was something of a commonplace and also appears in a poem by Folquet de Marseille (c. 1160–1231) in which the poet claims to sing in order to forget, but the more he sings the more he remembers:

> For it is true and it seems a good thing, lady,
> That I carry your image deep in my heart,
> And it urges me never to change my feelings.[15]

The lady's "image" (*faisso*) suggests her face in particular, and this is precisely how an artist illustrated Folquet's poem in a thirteenth-century anthology where it was collected.[16] The illustration, which shows the lady's face emblazoned on the poet's chest (figure 3), is one of the earliest attempts to give visible form to the idea of the heart as a record of personal memory. According to Stephen Nichols, the poet's recorded song and pictorial image collaborate on the manuscript page to leave a vivid impression of individual identity: "Singing mediates memory and oblivion and shows how love inscribes them on the heart or psyche of the poet in the form of the image of the woman."[17] The anthology even uses special reference marks in red ink to link words in the poems to the images in the margins. One such reference mark appears directly under the word "heart" (*cor*) in the quoted passage and again next to the lover's chest in the illustration, emphasizing that "the poet's metaphor is directly transformed by the artist into a symbolic image."[18]

Troubadour poetry was born in a world of oral performance that had close ties with music and where the separate roles of composer and performer, poet and jongleur, emphasized this basic orality (and aurality). So it is not surprising to find the heart imagined there in pictorial terms as a secular altar devoted to the memory of an earthly Madonna and decorated with her image. But a volume of lyrics accompanied by illustrations and cross-references suggests a more bookish production and reception of the poetry. Indeed, the manuscript containing Folquet's illustrated poem also pictures the poet as the solitary writer. One image shows him sitting pensively at his desk with a quill pen and roll of parchment, suggesting that by this point "poetic creation . . . was considered to be *written* work."[19]

Long after the troubadours, the lover's heart could contain visual images representing feelings or memories, images that were variously

3. *The Lady's Image on the Lover's Heart.* Illustration of a poem by Folquet de Marseille in a thirteenth-century anthology of troubadour poetry. The Pierpont Morgan Library, New York. MS M.819, fol. 59r. Reproduced by permission.

likened to the products of sculpting, engraving, or painting. Petrarch continues the tradition in his worshipful account of Laura's "lovely smiling face, which I carry painted in my breast" (. . . *che depinto / porto nel petto*), where devotion to the lady's idolized image appears to be at the expense of religious icons devoted to another Lady.[20] Partly as a result of Petrarch's influence, similar pictorial metaphors continued to appear in love lyrics throughout the Renaissance. From the early thirteenth century, however, lyric and romance began to portray the lover's heart also in expressly textual terms, perhaps partly to appeal to a more literate laity increasingly familiar with written texts. Instead of containing simply a wound or an image, the heart now spelled out the name of the beloved or carried a written transcript of the lover's thoughts, feelings, or amorous memories, an interior text that is sometimes likened to a book.

## The Scholastic Lover

Although learned Latin authors generally gave the book of the heart a moral or spiritual application, they occasionally cited it in connection with bodily or even sexual matters, as in Alan of Lille's reference to a book of experience that teaches the arts of love. The scholastic tendency to portray all realms of human knowledge or endeavor in bookish terms filtered into the work of many learned vernacular poets treating the subject of love. And some of these writers evoked an amorous book of the heart that retains a very scholastic flavor. Such a book makes one of its earliest appearances in the *Roman de la Rose*, an allegorical dream-vision begun around 1230–35 by Guillaume de Lorris and completed some forty years later by Jean de Meun. Jean's part of the poem draws heavily on scholastic ideas and metaphors, and the book of the heart that it cites several times is clearly adapted from an academic model—often with deliberately comic effect.

In the first part of the poem, written by Guillaume, a young Lover crashes a garden party attended by the God of Love, Beauty, Wealth, Generosity, Courtesy, and other personified abstractions of aristocratic love. Promptly shot in the heart by the God of Love, the Lover is smitten with love (or lust) for a certain Rose. In Jean de Meun's continuation, the Lover begins a sentimental education under the tutorship of various authorities who lecture, pro and con, on the subject of love. In the first instance, Lady Reason makes a long speech about the perils of love, and the Lover replies that he has taken many mental notes on her lesson (*leçon*, "reading, lecture") but is unable to apply it to his own situation: "I can repeat it well by heart, for my heart never forgot any of it; indeed, I can make a public lecture of the whole thing, but to me alone it means nothing."[21] The scholastic book of the heart is here reduced from a *summa* of God's truth to a student's meaningless scrawl. As though attending a university lecture, the Lover transcribes Reason's speech to his heart and then attempts to "read" it, but like many students he finds that he cannot understand his own notes. And in failing to understand the notebook of his own heart, the Lover also fails to know himself.

But eventually the book of the heart turns from a set of misunderstood lecture notes into a digest of cynical worldly wisdom that the

Lover learns only too well. Long after the precepts of Reason have faded from memory, the Lover turns to a very different female personification of expertise, the Old Woman (La Vieille), who lectures him with double-edged Ovidian maxims that can be taken as either advice to women or warnings to men (e.g., "All men betray and deceive women; all are sensualists, taking their pleasure anywhere. Therefore we should deceive them in return, not fix our hearts on one").[22]

Midway through her lecture, the Old Woman comments approvingly to the Lover on the fact that he is writing down everything she says in the book of his heart (*livre du queur*), making a permanent record of her teachings so that "when you depart from me, you will study more, if it please God, and will become a master like me." Continuing her academic satire on love, she appoints the Lover a veritable Professor of Desire: "I confer on you the license to teach, in spite of all chancellors, in chambers or in cellars, in meadow, garden, or thicket, under a tent or behind the tapestries, and to inform the students in wardrobes, attics, pantries, and stables...."[23] By now the notebook of the heart has become a goliardic parody of its scholastic original and lacks only erotic doodles in the margins.

The book of the heart takes a further comic turn toward carnality with the sermon of Genius, who preaches sensuality with all the pomp and ceremony of the bishop whose ring, crosier, and miter he assumes on the dais. Praising the "natural" love between man and woman, Genius (drawing on scholastic theory) compares sexual intercourse to writing and denounces "those who do not write with their styluses, by which mortals live forever, on the beautiful precious tablets that Nature did not prepare for them to leave idle, but instead loaned to them in order that everyone might be a writer and that we all, men and women, might live...."[24] While Genius preaches, this sexual writing is "copied" or "reproduced" (which amounts to the same thing) by his audience, for "everyone who liked the sermon noted it word for word in his heart...."[25] Thus the book of the heart not only records the sermon's substance about Nature's sexual writing, but also assumes the *form* of Nature's masculine "stylus" and feminine "tablet," suggesting the implicit sexuality of all writing on the heart. Here, again, the individual is the scribe of his own heart, but what he writes there is a carnal—even carnivalesque—parody of the scholastic metaphor.

## Glossing the Heart

The book of the heart survived scholastic parody to become the ruling metaphor in one of the classic works of medieval love literature, Dante's *Vita nuova,* the poet's account of his youthful passion for Beatrice. In the famous opening chapter of this work, Dante introduces himself as a scribe who has created the work in hand by copying it from an internal book of memory: "In the book of my memory, after the first pages, which are almost blank, there is a section headed *Incipit vita nova.* Beneath this heading I find the words which it is my intention to copy into this smaller book, or if not all, at least their meaning." [26]

Dante's metaphor of the inner book, his scribal persona, and his technical vocabulary ("pages," "section," "heading," "copy") recall the elaborate metaphors of the manuscript codex in the scholastic authors with whom he was well acquainted. [27] As Charles Singleton points out in his classic essay on the *Vita nuova,* Dante presents himself not as the author of the memory book, but as a scribe and glossator who selects, transcribes, and comments on what he finds already written there. The published work is thus excerpted from an even more personal and private text, for "no one other than this scribe can ever have access to the original of this book." [28] The scribe's selective editing of his inner book reinforces the sense of undisclosed secrets. As Dante says in his second chapter, "I will move on and, omitting many things which might be copied from the master-text [*l'esemplo*] from which the foregoing is derived, I come now to words inscribed in my memory under more important headings." [29]

Dante's memory book is virtually synonymous with the heart, which is mentioned nearly seventy times in the work as a whole, not counting the heart-based terms for recollection (e.g., *ricordare*) that dominate the narrative. [30] The heart is especially prominent as a symbol or metaphor. Chapter 2 recounts how Dante's first sight of Beatrice caused a trembling of "the vital spirit, which dwells in the inmost depths of the heart," an allusion to the Aristotelian doctrine that the heart was "the locus of spiritual refinement of the vital spirits, as well as the place where the imagination makes its impressions available to the intellectual faculty." [31] Chapter 3 narrates a dream in which the God of Love brandishes the poet's heart. Finally, a sonnet in one of the work's concluding chapters explicitly pictures the poet's heart as a text inscribed with his lady's name:

> These thoughts of mine and sighs which forth I send
> Within my heart to sharper anguish grow,
> Where Love in mortal pallor lies in pain;
> For in the deep recesses of their woe
> The sweet name of my Lady they have penned
> And many words to tell her death again.[32]

Heart and memory fuse here under the metaphor of interior writing, and again the poet emphasizes, by refusing to name his lady, that the outward and public book only selectively reproduces the inner one, that the book of his heart keeps many of its secrets.

Dante's refusal to transcribe even the name of his beloved stands in sharp contrast to the exuberant carnality of naming the rose in Jean de Meun's *Roman*. Yet, in his own idealizing style, Dante, too, rewrites the scholastic book of the heart as an even more personal story of amorous passion and erotic fixation. The tension between bodily attraction and spiritual aspiration is epitomized by the work's traditional title, *La vita nuova*. Although added by later editors, it renders a Latin phrase that appears in the first chapter (as quoted above) and that, as part of a conventional tag to mark the beginning of texts ("*Incipit* . . ."), underscores Dante's manuscript metaphor. The title closely echoes the passage in Augustine's *Confessions* where Ponticianus reads from a codex (like Augustine himself soon afterward) and is born into a "new life" (*nova vita*).[33] Unlike Augustine's new life, however, Dante's begins with a conversion *toward*, rather than away from, a female object of desire. Dante also repeats Augustine's self-conscious project of transcribing a record of personal experience from the heart to the page, using even more explicit scribal and manuscript metaphors to relate the published literary work to a private book of memory. But the resulting work praises an erotic object rather than a spiritual one, a kind of earthly goddess rather than a heavenly God.

In its structure and content, Dante's inner book superbly exploits certain scholastic refinements to metaphors of the manuscript book. The most important of these is that, in technical terms, Dante's book takes the form of the gloss, and its scribe the specialized function of the glossator. As Singleton points out, the formal divisions of verse and prose in the *Vita nuova* actually correspond to different layers of memory or experience in Dante's inner book: the words of the poems are words that Dante wrote himself, whereas "those 'words' in prose which the poet, having resolved to become the scribe of the Book of his Memory, finds surrounding his poems . . . are not his." That is, the "prose" in the book of memory represents experience that Dante did not author or create but that he "found" there, already inscribed by experience on his heart (again, the "book of experience"). And it is "because the words of this 'prose' are words which he did not himself write that the scribe is now justified in turning back over them and discovering a hidden meaning in them."[34]

The hidden meanings of his earlier life that most fascinate Dante concern the death of his beloved Beatrice. Dante says that he will leave this subject "to be discussed by someone else"—literally, another glossator (*chiosatore*).[35] Yet Dante himself goes on to interpret the number nine, which marked Beatrice's death as it did so many other key moments, abandoning the role of mere scribe as he assumes that of commentator: "Why this number was so closely connected with her might be explained as follows. . . ."[36] What is new here is not that Dante annotates the memory-record of his life, something that Augustine had done long before him, but that he imagines himself as a medieval glossator adding marginal or interlinear comments to a text. Dante represents the process of self-understanding not in terms of writing per se or even reading, but specifically in terms of glossing, of opening up the hidden meanings of a text. This metaphor was firmly based on scholastic precedent and was previously applied to theological understanding and even the strong emotions of devotional reading. But here it is adapted, apparently for the first time, to a lover's amorous passion and specific emotional history.

In searching for hidden meanings in the narrative of his own life, especially in the traumatic memory of Beatrice's death, Dante anticipates psychoanalysis and its use of textual metaphor to represent obscure complexes of memory and emotion. But Dante's self-glossing resorts to expressly medieval theories of symbolism, allegory, and dream interpretation. He views the manifest events of his life and their latent significance in terms of text and gloss, *littera* and *sensus*. Essentially, his model of self-understanding is based on a scriptural hermeneutic that had turned the glossing of texts into a great intellectual industry of the High Middle Ages. As such, it hearkens back to the self-exegesis of the patristic authors who invented a "scriptural" model of the self equating the heart or soul with a book of personal secrets that would ultimately be revealed. In principle, glossing was infinitely extendable, and medieval scriptural commentaries in turn often engendered their own commentaries. But Dante's gloss on the book of memory in the *Vita nuova* is haunted less by the abyss of infinite exegesis than by its potential to turn endlessly back upon the self. Dante recognized that the narrative of his life, like Scripture, was polysemous, capable of multiple meanings. He also recognized the subjective element in choosing among possible meanings, as he admits in concluding his numerological gloss on Beatrice's death date: "Perhaps a more subtle mind could find a still more subtle reason for it; but this is the one which I perceive and which pleases me the most" (*che più mi piace*).[37] With the book of the heart, as could hardly be the case with Scripture, the lover's own pleasure is the final arbiter of meaning.

## The Scribes of Love

Whereas Dante portrays himself as a scribe who copies and interprets excerpts from a book of memory that is already written in his heart by experience, the *Roman de la Rose* depicts the Lover as a scribe who produces the book of the heart himself by taking notes on the theory and practice of love. Elsewhere poets depict an amorous book of the heart authored instead by the lover's lady, or by the God of Love. With such variations on the scribe's gender or station, the content and meaning of what is written in the heart often changes as well.

In Boccaccio's *Amorosa visione* (1342–43), an autobiographical poem heavily influenced by the *Roman de la Rose* and Dante, the lover recounts a dream in which his lady, Fiammetta, herself assumes the role of scribe and writes her name on his heart:

As I stood there it seems to me that
the gentle lady seemed to be coming towards me
to open my breast and write within,

there in my heart, placed so as to suffer,
her beautiful name in letters of gold,
so that it might never escape.[38]

The unusual details here include the opening of the chest like a tablet or a book in order to write on the heart, and of course the golden letters. But the most unusual thing of all is the gender of the scribe. Actual female writers such as Constance and Heloise were rare in the Middle Ages; even rarer were portraits, either historical or fictional, of female authors and scribes.[39] A writing woman challenged many norms.

By wielding the pen or stylus, Fiammetta claims a privilege usually reserved to men in the Middle Ages, and with it the power it symbolized. An obvious dimension of this power is sexual. By opening the "book" of the man's body to penetrate his flesh with the stylus, Fiammetta reverses the usual sexual symbolism of writing, the pattern of "male" pen and "female" page that is exemplified by Constance and Baudri. But as a female scribe, she also exerts social power. In courtly tradition, the male lover typically offers his heart to his lady as a gift, but here the lady actively claims it as her own property by writing her name on it.[40] Dante's heart was also inscribed with his lady's name, but his own feelings performed the scribal function, not the lady. In writing her own name, Fiammetta leaves a personal signature, a use of writing that increasingly marked legal and financial transactions in the later Middle Ages, especially at banking centers like Boccaccio's Florence, and a use that gradually spread among women.[41] The golden letters (*littere d'oro*) in which Fiammetta writes her name add further connotations of monetary value. Golden letters on the heart are common in medieval hagiography, as discussed in the next chapter. But in a secular context, they mark the man's heart as the lady's valuable personal property.

Another scribe who writes in the book of the heart is the God of Love. Sordello showed the God of Love exchanging his arrows for a chisel to carve the lady's image on the lover's heart. Love's arrows had even closer affinities with the quill pen: the Latin word *calamus* means "arrow" as well as "pen," and manuscript illustrations in the *Roman de la Rose* actually show the one feathered tool transformed into the other.[42] In the *Canzoniere*, his cycle of poems praising Laura, Petrarch depicts the God of Love (*Amor*) as both dictating the story of the lover's passion and writing it down in the lover's heart:

> He who speaks with me about my ills
> leaves me in doubt, so confusedly he dictates.
>     But still, however much of the story of my suffering
> I find written by his very own hand,
> in the midst of my heart where I so often return,
> I shall speak out. . . .[43]

Just as Cupid replaces the biblical God often imagined as dictator or scribe, so the writing on the heart changes from religious or moral truths to the lover's emotional history. So, too, with the internal transcript of the lover's sufferings (*miei martiri*) that is a martyr's testament, a secularized saint's life celebrating the sensual passion idealized by the alternate religion of love. Like Boccaccio with his golden letters, Petrarch may have had in mind here the many stories of medieval saints who received special marks of divine favor in their hearts.

But the most telling detail here is not the elevation of the lover's passion to secular sanctity, but its elongation into a personal narrative that Petrarch calls the history (*la storia*) of his suffering. The lover's story is presumably his passion for Laura as narrated by the *Canzoniere* as a whole. Yet the separate poems tell this story in fragments, what John Freccero calls "a composite of lyric instants" in which the persona constructed by these fragments is equally "illusory." Still, "the resultant portrait of an eternally weeping lover remains Petrarch's most distinctive poetic achievement." And although in a strict sense "the portrait has no temporality," it creates the illusion of passing time (and of fluctuating passions) as surely as the cycle's 366 poems suggest the course of a very full year.[44] Moreover, even if the *Canzoniere* seems like a *Vita nuova* shorn of the intervening prose commentary that highlights the passage of time, Petrarch clearly presents it as an outward version of the narrative—"*la storia*"—written on his heart.

Petrarch even refers to such a book of the heart in his *Secretum*, a penitential dialogue in Latin between Saint Augustine and himself ("Francesco"), and a work whose title points to the hidden heart that figures throughout it. In the third dialogue, the saint concludes a long summary of the "miseries of love" by saying that only people with a personal knowledge of these will understand what he is talking about, and Francesco in turn confesses that "all you have said is taken from the middle of the book of experience"—literally, it is "excerpted" (*excerpsisse*) from this inner book.[45] Petrarch thus repeats Dante's conceit that what is actually said about love between confidants, or published about it in a book, is merely selected from a much longer, more detailed, and essentially private record in the heart. In the *Canzoniere*, Petrarch likewise underscores Dante's affirmation that this inner story is something the lover finds already written in his heart—in his own case, as dictated and recorded there by the God of Love. Petrarch's book of experience is not necessarily confined to matters of love, since he cites it in the course of a penitential dialogue, an Augustinian confession, that ranges far beyond the only quasi-religious emotions of his erotic poems. But as such it suggests an even more comprehensive and unique book of the heart than had been imagined by the scholastic and monastic authors who first evoked the inner book of experience.


## The Embodied Book

In the fifteenth century, when the book of the lover's heart had assumed a high degree of individuality, it also took a more material turn, as poets likened its content to specific genres of secular literature or its form to deluxe illustrated manuscripts of the sort prized by wealthy patrons. The literary metaphor assumed an even more physical presence when it was transformed into a pictorial image and, eventually, into an actual manuscript codex—a logical and perhaps inevitable development that also, however, seemed to mark the limits of the metaphor.

The book of the lover's heart often has specific formal and generic attributes in the poetry of Charles d'Orléans (1394–1465), a French nobleman who spent much of his life as an English captive during the Hundred Years' War and who found his chief solace in books.[46] For example, one of Charles's lyrics portrays the lover's inner book expressly as a romance:

> When I am laid in my bed,
> I cannot rest in peace;

For all night long my heart reads
In the romance of Pleasant Thought,
And asks me to listen. . . .[47]

As a romance (*rommant*), the inner book is a vernacular work, one written in the poet's native tongue rather than Latin, and hence less a time-
less and universal text like sacred Scripture than a local, temporal, individual one. As a romance, it is also a narrative, though in this case not
the story of the lover himself, since "This book is all written / Of the
deeds of my peerless Lady." Again, like a romance, this book is for
enjoyment or pleasure ("Often my heart laughs for joy / When he
reads . . ."). Indeed, the romance of the heart is an avowedly secular text
that elevates reading for pleasure to an end in itself, a book where the
lover finds his chief delight (*souverain plaisir*).

Besides a certain generic content, Charles gives the book of the heart
a specific material form when he describes it elsewhere as a lavish illustrated manuscript:

Within my Book of Thought I found
My heart transcribing what it hears
Of my sad story, richly bound,
Illuminated with my tears.

It was erasing all the while
A much-loved image from the leaf;
Within my Book of Thought, the style
Has changed from bright-hued joy to grief.[48]

A kind of companion piece to the first poem, this lyric depicts the heart
not as reader but as scribe. In Petrarchan fashion, the inner scribe records the true story of the lover's sorrow (*la vraye histoire de douleur*), but
in this case the narrative consists of both word and image, like one of
the costly illuminated (*enluminee*) manuscripts of the time. The older
troubadour trope of an "image" in the lover's heart has now been incorporated into a specifically manuscript metaphor. Moreover, the inner
scribe is replacing a picture of happy former times with one of present
sorrow, a process of artistic "revision" that enhances the "materiality"
of the inner book at the same time it suggests a changeable record of

the lover's life. By picturing the book of the heart in terms of the manuscript art of the day, Charles seems to presage the metaphor's eventual
transformation into an actual book.

The heart had already assumed a concretely textual form around the
year 1400 in the famous Chantilly Codex, with its patterned musical
scores. One of these scores is a love song whose words and music are
put into the form of a heart (figure 4). The familiar stylized form of the
human heart seen here became increasingly common during the later
Middle Ages, when its uses ranged from family coats-of-arms to tapestries and playing cards, but this is the earliest known example of a written text in the form of a heart.[49] Heart-shaped songs or poems gained
in popularity during the Renaissance, culminating in the seventeenth-
century craze for emblems and emblem poetry.[50]

The lyrics of the Chantilly piece show that its unusual form is thematic and not merely decorative. Clearly addressing a woman, the lover
begins with a series of compliments and goes on to offer his heart to
his lady:

Beautiful, good, wise, pleasing, and elegant lady,
On this very day when the year begins anew,
I make you the gift of a new song in my heart
Which presents itself to you.[51]

Wordplay indicates that the song is figuratively held within (*dedans*) the
lover's heart, just as its words and notes are physically contained within
the heart-shaped score on the page. The parallel between heart and
page, inward and outward text, is emphasized by the substitution of a
small heart symbol (in red ink) for the word "heart" (*cuer*) in the text
(see figure 4), a rebus that also occurs in other contemporary texts.[52]
The lover's proffered heart is a common motif in literary romance and
visual art, but the Chantilly Codex transforms this gesture or image
into a musical performance. That is, the lover makes his heart into a
gift by the very act of singing the song "inscribed" there—which involves not only "reading" the inward song, but vocalizing it in words
that also issue from the "heart" (i.e., chest). More than just a reified
metaphor, the heart-shaped song is a performance script that is fully
realized only by its bodily enactment. As such, it seems to answer a
lyrical complaint by Clara d'Anduza, a thirteenth-century *trobairitz*, or

4. *A Song in the Heart*. Heart-shaped musical score with lyrics, attributed to Baude Cordier, c. 1400, beginning "*Belle, bonne, sage. . . .*" Chantilly, Musée Condé, MS 564 (formerly 1047), fol. 11 verso. Giraudon/Art Resource, NY. Reproduced by permission.

female troubadour: "I can't make music / with the strophes [*coblas*] that my heart is willing to supply."[53]

Given its increasingly specific attributes of form and content during the later Middle Ages, it is hardly surprising that the book of the lover's heart was eventually reified as an actual manuscript codex. At least four heart-shaped manuscript books survive today. One of these is a Latin prayer book embodying religious themes, which is discussed in chapter

7, while the other three contain poems or songs on amorous themes and suggest the book of the lover's heart. Of these three, two contain texts of a fairly late date, probably from the second half of the sixteenth century. But the third, a collection of French and Italian poems set to music and illustrated by colored miniatures, dates from no later than about 1475 and so is the earliest surviving incarnation of the amorous book of the heart.

This heart-shaped songbook—the Chansonnier Cordiforme, also known as the Chansonnier de Jean de Montchenu, after the fifteenth-century canon (later appointed bishop) who apparently commissioned this unusual volume—consists of seventy-two parchment folios, in a heart-shaped leather binding that opens to a double-heart shape (figure 5). Since the late nineteenth century, when it was acquired by the Baron Henri de Rothschild, this rarity has been famous among musicologists and historians of the book, though it has received little attention from literary scholars, particularly in relation to the history of the heart-book metaphor. As might be expected, heart symbolism features prominently in many of its songs, and writing metaphors are frequent. One song, for example, evokes the familiar image of the God of Love armed with a bow and shooting the lover in the heart, a motif also illustrated by a miniature in the manuscript.[54] In another song, Love declares that he will have none but the lover as his spokesman or scribe (*advocat ne secrétaire*).[55] And in the final song the lover asks the help of all who can write the praises of his lady (*Tout ce qui s'en pourra escrire*), since his heart (*cuer*) desires nothing but her.[56] The heart thus appears in the final line of the final song of this heart-shaped book. Although Jean de Montchenu held the office of apostolic protonotary, a recording secretary for the papal curia, this churchman seems to have been equally comfortable in the role of love's scribe.[57] Indeed, his book often mixes religious with secular imagery, as in the concluding song, where the lover speaks in Petrarchan fashion of his martyrdom (*mon martire*).[58]

Less well-known and less prepossessing than the bishop's lavish songbook are two heart-shaped manuscripts preserved in Pesaro, Italy. One of these, however, deserves mention here because of its unusual evolution from a collection of music into a more individual and idiosyncratic volume.[59] Pesaro Manuscript 1144 was originally created around the year 1500 as a collection of musical scores for the lute. Beginning in the 1570s, a subsequent owner, a poet named Tempesta Blondi,

5. *Heart-Shaped Songbook.* Burgundian, c. 1475. "The Chansonnier of Jean de Montchenu." Roths-child MS 2973, fols. 20v–21r. Cliché Bibliothèque nationale de France, Paris. Reproduced by permission.

inscribed love poems and even erotic verses in the volume, thus enhancing the amorous significance of its unusual shape. Yet Blondi annotated his heart-shaped book in yet another way that further altered its original significance. He personalized it by adding a record of key dates in his own life, including his marriage (in 1574) and his father's death (in 1592).[60] Moreover, an analysis of the handwriting in the volume suggests that Blondi did not add the poems and personal records all at once but over a period of years, so that the volume served as a kind of commonplace book and a personal diary.[61] As such, this heart-shaped volume embodies several of the functions traditionally associated with the book of the heart.

In a certain sense, the book of the heart found its ultimate expression in these heart-shaped manuscript codices of the late Middle Ages and Renaissance. But the reified metaphor simply compounded a paradox that had haunted the book of the heart from its origins. As noted in chapter 1, the metaphor of interior writing began in antiquity by asserting itself as the "real" or "true" writing, and by reducing literal (external) writing from reality to metaphor, to a mere copy of the writing on the mind or soul. But the book of the heart as embodied in actual

manuscript codices simply brought the process full circle by making
interior writing into *external* writing once again. Not that this further
turn of the trope canceled the metaphor, for the reified book of the
heart was the last possible step in the series; it marked the trope's logical
(and ontological) limit. Indeed, its newfound materiality only compounded its traditional symbolism, turning it into a metaphor of a metaphor, a trope of a trope. Besides a material book, there was only one
other possible form in which the metaphor could be so fully embodied—namely, literal inscription on the fleshly human heart. This possibility was not only imagined but actually realized in the medieval cult
of the saints.

## Chapter Five

# SAINTS

*L*ike the lovers celebrated by medieval romance, many of the saints celebrated in Christendom were famous for the inscriptions on their hearts. Wounds, signs, and letters on the heart were reported of saints from the early days of the Church, and by the late Middle Ages the legends of the saints, one of the most popular literary genres of the time, were filled with stories of hearts miraculously inscribed with divine testimonies and opened to be read like books. As a bodily scripture, the saint's inscribed heart transformed the metaphor of the inner book into one of its most vivid and apparently literal incarnations.[1]

The heart was a central symbol in both religion and romance, and the saint's life shared the inscribed heart with secular poetry as a metaphor of certain psychological functions, including memory, feeling, and (in different senses of the word) passion. For lover and saint alike, the inscribed heart signified remembrance, devotion, and self-sacrifice. There were important differences, of course. The lover worshiped another human being, while the saint was devoted to God. The lover's heart was usually a text for private reading, while the saint's heart was typically opened to a much larger public. And the lover's heart recorded a carnal love, while the saint's heart gave witness to a spiritual passion. Yet the line between carnal and spiritual love was not always so clear. Again and again, in saints' legends and other religious texts (and in visual art), inscription on the body carries a powerful erotic charge. This may be in part a function of genre; the saint's legend highlights the suffering, mutilated, and frequently dismembered human body. But writing on the heart carries its own subliminal suggestion of sexual penetration, not to mention the erotic import of the cries, tears, swooning, and other ecstasies that often accompany the touch of the divine finger to human flesh. Simply the insistence of many legends that it was the physical heart itself that was inscribed, opened, removed, or read keeps the body at the center of attention. Indeed, the saint's heart (like the lover's) often functions as a synecdoche for the body, a body in miniature form, as some Latin legends emphasize by wordplay on the terms *cor* and *corpus*.

On the one hand, the saint's inscribed heart, opened and revealed to multitudes, seems to be a perfect embodiment of Paul's influential metaphor, "a letter from Christ ... written ... on tablets of human hearts," a letter "to be known and read by all men." By actually incarnating this ideal, however, the saint's legend pushes the paradox of the inscribed heart further than it goes in any other medieval literary genre. For here a type of "writing" that is avowedly interior, invisible, and spiritual assumes an external, visible, and very fleshly form. With the saint's inscribed heart, the usual categories seem to break down. But as Caroline Bynum reminds us, "Medieval writers were often uninterested in certain distinctions that in the early modern and modern periods have fascinated canon lawyers, theologians, and psychiatrists—distinctions, for example, between miraculous and self-induced or between visible and invisible."[2] And, according to Karma Lochrie, the "bodily *insignia*" of medieval hagiography and mysticism challenge even the distinctions between body and soul, male and female, since "the body's capacity for amazing transformations marks and measures the soul's capacity for imitating Christ's Passion."[3] These are useful cautions to keep in mind as we turn to the inscriptions on the heart that appear in the legends of certain saints and would-be saints.

## Bodily Scriptures

Writing on the heart may be seen as a specific form of the writing on the body that appears in the legends of the martyrs as early as the fourth century. The *Crowns of Martyrdom*, by the Spanish-Latin poet Prudentius (348–410?), is famous for its metaphors of writing, as catalogued by Ernst Robert Curtius: "St. Eulalia likens the wounds which the torturers inflict on her to purple writing in praise of Christ.... An angel who measures each individual wound writes down the passion of the martyr Romanus while it is in progress.... The martyr himself is an 'inscripta Christo pagina.' ..."[4]

Prudentius's most elaborate example of bodily scripture appears in his account of Saint Cassian, a rhetoric teacher who refused to worship at the pagan altars, causing the authorities to condemn him to death at the hands of his own students, who hated him for his reputedly harsh and stern ways. In an ironic application of their learning, they stab Cassian to death with their styli:

> Countless boys round about (a pitiful sight!) were stabbing and piercing his body with the little styles with which they used to run over their wax tablets, writing down the droning lesson in school.... The one end enters the soft flesh, the other splits the skin. Two hundred hands together have pierced him all over his body, and from all these wounds at once the blood is dripping.[5]

As the blows pierce deep into Cassian's flesh and strike his vital organs (*viscera, vitalia*), the blood drains from his heart (*praecordia*) through the many puncture wounds in his body, and his soul is released. But not before the boys have shouted many cruel taunts about their perverse writing on his body. Theirs is a sarcasm in the original sense, from the Greek word *sarx*, a literal tearing of the flesh:

> "Why do you complain?" calls one; "you yourself as our teacher gave us this iron and put the weapon in our hands. You see we are giving you back all the thousands of characters which as we stood in tears we took down from your teaching.... You may examine and correct our lines in long array, in case an erring hand has made any mistake. Use your authority; you have power to punish a fault, if any of your pupils has written carelessly on you."[6]

Cassian's martyrdom clearly has sexual—and specifically, homo-erotic—overtones. In addition, it reifies the "violence of the letter" that some postmodern critics have taken to be characteristic of West-ern writing in general.[7] The saint's inscribed body, as a site of state-sanctioned violence, even brings to mind its modern mechanical counterpart in Kafka's "Penal Colony."[8]

At the same time, however, violent inscription on the saint's body evokes the Christian apologist's concern with what might be called the body of evidence for martyrdom. Prudentius is prompted to immortal-ize Cassian in writing by a visit to the martyr's tomb, where he contem-plates a picture (*imago*) of the saint's passion. Unlike the ultimate record of the martyrs that is "written in heaven," earthly records are some-times lost or stolen, and, as the poet stresses in an account of two other martyrs, "we are denied the facts about these matters."[9] In composing his poetic supplement to a fragmented hagiographic tradition about Cassian, Prudentius dwells almost obsessively on the prior "text" of martyrdom—the saint's body itself, which is the original (if not the ultimate) record of the saint's passion. By treating the saint's body as a kind of scripture, the poet borrows authority from this fleshly record, this sacred corpus, of which his own written memorials can only claim to be a somewhat removed "copy."

As the essentially passive victims of torturers and executioners, the saints do not "author" these bodily scriptures, but they sometimes serve as the primary interpreters or exegetes. Thus Saint Eulalia counts the strokes of the torturer's claws or pincers and "reads" the marks left by these instruments on her body: "'See, Lord,' she says, 'Thy name is being written on me. How I love to read [*legere*] these letters, for they record thy victories, O Christ, and the very scarlet of the blood that is drawn speaks the holy name.'"[10] Here, too, Prudentius grounds his own literary text on the prior authority of the saint's body. Although, aside from any surviving relics, this prior bodily text is largely consti-tuted by the later literary one, Prudentius, in a master stroke of poetic license, reverses the relation by having the saint herself "establish" and interpret the bodily scripture.

## Golden Legends

As a special kind of bodily scripture, the inscribed heart is a popular motif in hagiography from the thirteenth century on, either as an addi-

tion to the legends of earlier saints or as an original feature in the recorded lives of contemporary ones. Its widespread occurrence in romance and love lyrics probably aided this popularity, for saints' legends
borrow many features from secular literature. Another factor was the
growing cult of devotion to the heart of Christ, which eventually became the official Cult of the Sacred Heart.[11] Already in the twelfth century, Bernard and other authorities evoked the wounded heart of the
crucified Christ as an object of worship, and an English mystical text
of the same century describes Christ's heart as an opened "love letter"
that is to be read by the devotee, clearly a romance trope adapted to
mystical use.[12] Since the core of the typical saint's legend is an imitation
of Christ and the *passio sancti* is patterned on the *passio Christi*, the saint's
inscribed heart finds its ultimate model in the wounded heart of
Christ.[13] The imitation of Christ's wounded heart is central to the most
famous legend of saintly stigmata, that of Saint Francis (1182–1226),
which recounts how a vision left "a most intense ardor and flame of
divine love in [his] heart" and "a marvelous image and imprint of the
Passion of Christ in his flesh."[14] After Francis, the legends of other
saints began to report similar stigmata, including signs and writing on
the heart.

One of the most famous instances of bodily writing is the legend of
Ignatius of Antioch (d. c. 110 C.E.), whose heart is said to have been
inscribed with the name of Christ. Apparently this motif did not become part of the saint's legend until the later Middle Ages, when it
appears in accounts like the one in *The Golden Legend* (c. 1260), the most
popular medieval collection of saints' lives.[15] According to this account, Ignatius refused to worship the pagan gods and was condemned
by the Emperor Trajan to torture and death in the arena:

> In the midst of all sorts of tortures blessed Ignatius never ceased
> calling upon the name of Jesus Christ. When the executioners
> asked him why he repeated this name so often, he replied: "I have
> this name written on my heart and therefore cannot stop invok-
> ing it!" After his death those who had heard him say this were
> driven by curiosity to find out if it was true, so they took the
> heart out of his body, split it down the middle, and found there
> the name *Jesus Christ* inscribed in gold letters. This brought many
> of them to accept the faith.[16]

Here the heart is unambiguously corporeal, as emphasized by the Latin phrasing of the legend: "they took the heart out of his body" (... *cor ejus ab ejus corpore*).

Thus removed from the saint, the heart is not only a relic to his memory but also a text, a bodily scripture, that is opened like a book to be read by the others in attendance, resulting in their conversion. The moment at which the saint's heart is opened for examination by a reading public is depicted in Botticelli's painting *The Extraction of the Heart of St. Ignatius* (figure 6), created about two centuries after the story of Ignatius was popularized in *The Golden Legend*. Originally part of a church altarpiece, the painting shows two witnesses cutting open the saint's heart to read its inscription, suggesting the reception of this bodily scripture by a community of readers. Both the legend and the painting play out the familiar topos of conversion-by-reading, as exemplified in Augustine's *Confessions*, except that here the audience reads the message directly from the saint's heart, rather than from a more conventional text. In fact, the painting was once incorrectly identified as a scene from the life of Augustine, no doubt because the inscribed and legible heart is a central Augustinian theme.[17]

The recorded life of Ignatius in turn extends the same opportunity of reading and conversion to later "witnesses," who are not able to examine the heart itself but are at least able to read about it, and to read its inscription at secondhand, in his legend (or in visual art). Indeed, the name of Christ inscribed on the saint's heart in the arena is the original of the "copy" in the published legend, a copy that exists at many removes from the bodily original by virtue of a scribal culture. In theory, the inscription recorded in a conventional manuscript book has the same power to convert and edify as the original writing on the saint's heart; it even reaches through time to a later and potentially much larger audience. On the other hand, as with Prudentius, the copy can never fully represent the original. As implied by the script in "gold letters" (*litteris aureis*) on the saint's heart, conventional writing can never capture the aura of miraculous writing. The golden legend that is literally embodied in the saint's inscribed heart supplies "that which is to be read," or "reading material" (the literal sense of *legenda*), to a later audience. But hagiographic tradition, as a kind of literary reliquary, can only point back to the original book of the saint's heart.

Another version of the Ignatius legend recorded by Vincent of

6. *Opening the Saint's Heart.* Sandro Botticelli, c. 1485. "The Extraction of the Heart of St. Ignatius." Predella panel of the San Barnaba Altarpiece. Florence, Galleria degli Uffizi, no. 8393. Alinari/ Art Resource, NY. Reproduced by permission.

Beauvais (d. 1264) in his *Speculum historiale* states that the saint's heart was not simply cut open to be read, but also divided up to provide individually legible relics. According to Vincent, when the saint's heart "had been divided into small pieces, the name of the Lord Jesus Christ was found written in golden letters, so that it might be read, on each part."[18] The division of the inscribed heart suggests the fragmentation of the consecrated Host in the Mass. It also resembles the scribal reproduction of a text, although here the process of textual multiplication is a divine miracle, a kind of automatic writing that attends the communal effort to multiply, share, and incorporate the bodily scripture of the saint's heart.

## Logos and Eros

Many medieval legends of the inscribed heart feature female saints, whose inward markings invite comparison with the erotic writing on the heart in secular literature.[19] Some of these holy women are saints of the early church whose stories, like that of Ignatius, acquired this motif only in much later hagiography. For example, the "standard" version of *The Golden Legend* depicts Catherine of Alexandria without inward markings, but in John Capgrave's later English legend (c. 1450) she has a divine token "impressed . . . / upon her heart." Besides this sign on her heart, Catherine retains the memory of her marriage to Christ "imprinted on her vitals [*entrayle*]"—that is, written in her womb.[20] This is not so much an imitation of Christ as an imitation of Mary, in whose womb God "wrote" with the "pen" of the Holy Spirit in order to engender Christ, according to authorities such as Bernard of Clairvaux.[21] Sacred literature, like secular, often exhibits a gendered notion of writing that treats the heart as a "female" page for the "male" pen.[22] Although this pattern shapes the stories of both male and female saints, as we have already seen with Cassian's legend, it has a special prominence in the latter.

The inscribed heart of the female saint is sometimes a text for private devotion, as in the case of Gertrude (the Great) of Helfta (d. 1301/02), who recorded the following Latin prayer: "Most merciful Lord, write your wounds in my heart with your precious blood, that I may read [*legam*] in them your suffering and your love alike. Then may the mindfulness of your wounds remain with me unceasingly in the recesses of my heart, that sorrow for your suffering may be aroused in me and the ardor of your love may be kindled in me."[23] Among female saints, as among males, the inscribed heart could also assume a very public role, as with Clare of Montefalco, whose "spiritual sisters came to believe so intensely that Christ had planted his cross in her heart that at her death in 1308 they threw themselves upon her body, tore out her heart, and found incised upon it the insignia of the Passion."[24] Clare's widely reported legend, concurrent with that of Ignatius, turns the stigmatized heart into a kind of erotic fetish.[25] Similarly, Saint Catherine of Siena (d. 1380) is said to have exchanged hearts with Christ and afterward to have borne a scar on her breast.[26]

One of the most remarkable inscriptions on the female heart appears in the early-modern legend of Maria Maddalena de' Pazzi (1566–1607), a Carmelite nun who was canonized in 1669.[27] While still a novice in her late teens, Maria began to experience miraculous ecstasies. Since she was often unable to recall the revelations, her superiors ordered other nuns to record her utterances during the ecstasies themselves, and afterward she would read and correct the transcripts. As one official account puts it, "The spirit of God dictated to her such exalted things, that her superiors assigned two sisters as her secretaries to record them, and a large volume of these was printed. . . ."[28]

Less than a year after these ecstasies began, Maria's own body provided the medium for another, less conventional, kind of writing that also achieved a "publication" of sorts. At the age of eighteen, on the eve of the Feast of the Annunciation in 1585, while meditating on the Gospel of John, she is said to have received on her heart an inscription from the hand of Saint Augustine. According to her confessor, Vincenzio Puccini, who authored a *Vita* that was reprinted in an English translation of 1687, "St. Augustine at two different times engraved upon her heart these four words, *Verbum caro factum est,* 'The Word was made flesh': the first time in letters of blood, to communicate to her a perfect knowledge of the supereminent love of Jesus Christ for mankind, when he died upon the cross; the second time in letters of gold. . . ."[29]

One of these inscriptional moments is depicted in a late baroque painting (c. 1702) by Giovanni Camillo Sagrestani that decorates a Florentine chapel dedicated to this saint (figure 7). Maria's posture and expression in the painting clearly recall the swooning Saint Teresa in Bernini's famous sculpture.[30] But here the angel's fiery dart turns into Saint Augustine's quill pen, and the momentary piercing of the heart becomes a permanent inscription. Unlike Botticelli's *Extraction,* which shows the saint's inscribed heart as a finished text on the point of reaching its literary public, Sagrestani represents the act of miraculous inscription itself. He comes as close as possible to showing the heart in the process of becoming a legible text.

The text of the inscription on Maria's heart, a familiar scriptural passage ( John 1.14), suggests the old patristic and scholastic theme of copying God's word into the heart. As such, it extends the familiar theme of Christ's incarnation (Maria's namesake is of course the Magdalene, but her name also recalls the Mary in whom the Word became incarnate) to the more unusual incarnation of the divine word as an inscription in Maria's flesh. Indeed, to the viewer familiar with Maria's history, the painting emphasizes the *scribal* import of the quoted words, the transformation of written word into flesh, or, conversely, flesh into written word.

Late medieval artists commonly portrayed Augustine as an author or scribe, but here Augustine writes on human flesh rather than the

7. *Inscribing the Saint's Heart.* Giovanni Camillo Sagrestani, c. 1702. *Saint Augustine Writing on the Heart of Saint Mary Magdalene of Pazzi.* Florence, San Frediano in Cestello. Scala/Art Resource, NY. Reproduced by permission.

more conventional media of parchment or paper. This very corporeal writing is also a gendered writing, since the male hand writes on the female "heart" with a pen having phallic significance, as suggested by other details in the scene, such as the cupids transformed into angelic *putti.* The feathery quill wielded here by Augustine even recalls his own heart "wounded" by the divine logos—"your words like arrows fixed deep in our flesh."[31]

If writing on the body, and specifically on the heart, often carries an erotic charge, this charge clearly can assume different sexual orientations. The legend of Cassian, with its male-on-male inscriptions, suggests a homoerotic subtext. Maria's legend, with its male-on-female inscription, enacts the notion of writing as a masculine privilege and a sexual poetics that treats the female body and heart as a receptive page for the male pen (a pattern implicitly reinforced here through the painting's own production by a male hand applying paint to the "female" canvas). In the Pauline grammatology that informs this painting, the spirit conquers and converts the flesh much as the fully conscious man wields the authority of the stylus and all that it signifies over the swooning woman. As with other representations of the inscribed heart, Sagrestani's painting tends to blur the distinction between spirit and flesh, literal and figurative, and even interior and exterior. But it clearly insists upon the male/female difference, as embodied here in the Church Father's active authority (in all of its senses) over his receptive spiritual daughter.

## The Strange Case of Henry Suso

Medieval legends about saints whose bodies had received special marks of divine favor moved some religious devotees to seek similar signs on their own bodies. The legend of Ignatius in particular seems to have inspired the fourteenth-century Dominican friar Henry Suso (or Seuse, c. 1295–1366), one of the most unusual of all medieval aspirants to sainthood.[32] Suso prayed repeatedly that God would inscribe a sign of love on his heart, until one day, in a fit of pious fervor, he took a stylus to his own flesh.

Like his teacher Meister Eckhart, Henry Suso was one of the best-known mystics of his time. The son of a German knight who was instead drawn to the church, he entertained visions of spiritual knighthood and took to great extremes the courtly style of religious devotion to Mary and Christ that was then in vogue. It was typical of this style for the devotee to alternate between gender roles, and in his writings Suso is sometimes the (male) "servitor" of a feminine Eternal Wisdom and sometimes the (female) "spouse" of Christ. Still, Suso seems to have identified especially with women; at a young age he took his mother's surname (an unusual step at the time), and he spent most of his career as a spiritual director of nuns, for whom much of his writing was originally intended.

Suso's admiration for Ignatius is spelled out in a letter describing his devotion to the name of Christ. First he cites Paul, who "lovingly inscribed the sweet name of Jesus in the deepest depths of his heart"; this is almost certainly an allusion to the Pauline "tablets of the heart," which appear again in connection with Suso's act of self-inscription. Then Suso offers Ignatius as an even more graphic example of the "lover" who carries Christ's name in his heart: "During his excruciating martyrdom, St. Ignatius repeated the name of Jesus with intense fervor. When he was asked the reason for this, he replied that the name of Jesus was engraved in his heart. After his death, the astonished executioners opened his heart and found written there in golden letters: 'Jesus, Jesus, Jesus.'"[33] Suso tellingly treats the saint's opened heart not as a public text that leads to multiple conversions, but as a private love token of the individual's relation to God, a pattern repeated in his own case.

Suso's attempt to write on his own "heart" was apparently an early episode in a long series of unusual devotional practices that have attracted more attention from modern critics than any other feature of his life or work. Besides practicing more typical self-deprivations of diet and sleep, Suso wore undergarments and gloves fitted with nails and carried for eight years a heavy nail-studded cross on his naked back. He also flagellated himself with a special brass-tipped scourge. These and many other self-mortifications are reported in his vernacular *Life,* a work that often has been ascribed to one of Suso's followers but that he probably compiled himself.[34] Suso's attempts to achieve a martyr's spiritual ecstasy through self-inflicted bodily suffering make for painful reading but include occasional comic moments. For example, after sixteen years of self-flagellation, Suso received a whispered reprieve from God, and "he lost no time throwing his flagella into the Rhine."[35]

According to the biography, Suso went to his cell one day to be alone, his soul burning with divine love and desiring to have some bodily sign of this love from God:

> He cried out, "Oh, sweet Lord! If only I could devise some love token which would be an everlasting badge of love between thee and me, an authentic document that I am all thine and that thou art the only beloved of my heart, written in letters which my fickleness can never erase." In his burst of fervor, he pushed back his scapular, bared his bosom, took a sharp stylus, and called on God to help him, saying: "Almighty God, give me strength this day to carry out my desire, for thou must be chiseled into the core of my heart." Then stabbing the stylus backwards and forwards, in and out of the flesh, he engraved the name of Jesus (IHS) over his heart. Blood gushed out of the jagged wounds and saturated his clothing. The bliss he experienced in having a visible pledge of oneness with his truelove made the very pain seem like a sweet delight.[36]

Suso's do-it-yourself approach sets him apart from the saints he admired and sought to emulate. By taking the divine right of bodily inscription into his own very human hands, he could not authorize his sanctity, let alone his actual sainthood (although he was finally beatified in 1831 by Pope Gregory XVI).[37] But like the traditional saint's stigmata, Suso's self-inflicted scars remained legible for the rest of his life: "When the wounds that he had made were healed, the sacred name still remained above his heart in letters the width of a cornstalk and the length of the joint of his little finger."[38]

Suso's further description of the resulting scar is also very revealing. In the first place, he portrays his fleshly inscription in romantic and even erotic terms, calling it a "love token" (*minnezeichen*) from his divine "truelove," a source of ecstatic "bliss" and "sweet delight." These terms illustrate a nearly complete intermingling of religious and amorous devotion, medieval traditions that shared the central symbolism of the heart as a place of inscription, among other things. Suso, who has been called a "minnesinger in the spiritual order," borrows from both the

poetic-erotic and biblical-theological traditions and blends them almost completely with each other.[39]

Besides genres, Suso also combines genders. As Karma Lochrie
notes, the corporeal imitations of Christ's suffering practiced by medieval saints and mystics involved "as much rapture as mortification,"
and Suso's reported experience clearly points to both pain and ecstasy.
Bodily insignia challenged not only the distinctions between body and
soul, literal and figurative, interior and exterior, but also "female/male
binarism."[40] Suso's passion, in both the religious and the romantic
senses of the term, similarly tends to blur the boundaries of sex or gender by "feminizing" his heart under the imagery of wounding, inscription, and penetration. Suso's feminized heart reflects his frequent identification with the feminine, as well as his mystical or contemplative
persona as Christ's (female) "spouse," qualities that would have appealed to his local audience of nuns.

Besides using romantic and erotic terms, Suso also borrows from a
scribal or legal vocabulary in characterizing his fleshly inscription as a
document, deed, or contract (*urkúnde*). During the later Middle Ages,
written records were proliferating to attest agreements between individuals and corporations. Suso's language points directly to a reciprocal
interpersonal bond between himself and God (*enzwischan mir und dir*),
here evidently modeled on a marriage or betrothal contract, as signified
by an inscription on the heart instead of a more typical external record.
But instead of documents written on individual sheets, the term *urkúnde*
can also refer to a wax tablet—that is, a diptychal format that has a
special resemblance to the heart.[41] Indeed, Suso writes on his flesh specifically with a metal stylus (*grifel*), a tool normally used for writing on
wax-covered tablets.[42] By applying this tool to his own flesh instead
of to wax, Suso implicitly makes his heart into a "tablet" of memory
and devotion.

Another account of Suso's self-inscription explicitly cites the Pauline "tablets of the heart" as a precedent. The *Horologium sapientiae*, a
Latin compendium of Suso's teachings that enjoyed a large medieval
readership (nearly 250 manuscripts survive), uses language that is at
once both violent and technical:

Taking a sharp iron stylus, he stabbed the bare flesh above his
heart where he could see the vital pulse throbbing most strongly,

piercing himself so forcefully that every stab was followed by a flow of blood that ran from his chest and dripped down drop by drop. And he stabbed himself so often and so mercilessly here and there that finally in this way he had cut the famous name of his spouse, which is "IHC," in great capital letters. . . . [He] bore his love's name, "not in tablets of stone" or on embroidered garments, or written in red ink or black, "but in the fleshly tables of the heart" and in letters of blood, forming a chaplet of blooming scarlet flowers; and he rejoiced to wear upon his heart what could not be effaced.[43]

Like the vernacular *Life*, the Latin text reports that Suso's self-inflicted wounds eventually healed into a permanent religious tattoo, "and his flesh perfectly preserved that name, letter by letter, in that place." As a self-styled divine lover (*divinus amator*), Suso regards these lasting signs of love etched into his own flesh as superior to the "worthless name" embroidered onto the clothing of the conventional earthly lover. However, as an overt emulation of Paul's "tablets of the heart," Suso's fleshly inscription is as paradoxical as the heart-shaped books that attempt to externalize an inherently interior kind of writing. More than paradoxical, it is ironic. For, by stabbing himself with a stylus while attempting to give fleshly form to a biblical trope, Suso not only reverses the priority of the spirit over the letter, but also seems to ignore Paul's appended warning that the letter—here, literally—can kill.

Although originally the sign of a private contract between God and himself, Suso's fleshly inscription was reproduced or published in various ways for the spiritual benefit of others. Manuscripts of the *Life* and the *Horologium* often reproduce the inscription in enlarged (or colored) letters, thus transcribing the original writing on his body to a more conventional medium (i.e., animal rather than human skin).[44] In addition, manuscript illustrations of Suso show him with a bared chest on which the inscription is clearly visible, an image for contemplation by others.[45] Suso's fleshly inscription was also reproduced in cloth to be worn by fellow devotees to Christ's name. When one of Suso's female followers learned of the inscription, she, "fired with a like fervor, embroidered the name of Jesus (IHS) with red silk on a small piece of cloth and wore it as a love token. She also made many more of these love tokens and asked the Servitor to touch them to his heart and distribute them among his spiritual children." [46] These copies of the original inscription made public and external what was originally written in secret "on the heart," offering Suso's inscribed "heart" in simulacrum to others as a model of devotion, not unlike the divided pieces of Ignatius's heart.

Indeed, the fetish embroidered with the initials that Suso had carved into his chest, then touched to his body in a mimetic gesture, and finally distributed among others sounds more like a saint's relic, or even a consecrated fragment of the most sacred body of all. Although Suso cites Paul and Ignatius as models, his fleshly inscription ultimately imitates Christ and marks his devotion to Christ's Passion. The "deed" or "contract" (urkúnde) written on his flesh even resembles the "Charter of Christ," a popular late medieval devotional topos that likens the suffering Savior's body to a written document—his skin to parchment, his wounds to words, his blood to ink, and so on. [47] It also recalls Suso's own evocation of Christ promising that wisdom may be "read from the opened, wounded book of my crucified body." [48]

Other late medieval mystics also aspired to inscriptions on their hearts, although not necessarily in so fleshly a fashion as Henry Suso attempted. For example, Suso's approximate contemporary, the English mystic Richard Rolle of Hampole (c. 1300–1349), appears in several fifteenth-century manuscript illustrations with a similar inscription on his chest. [49] But saints and would-be saints were not the only medieval people to have taken seriously the idea that their hearts should be marked with the name of Christ or remembrances of Christ's Passion. A substantial body of vernacular religious writings shows that the metaphor of the heart as a text, and often as a veritable book, eventually became a widespread devotional ideal among the laity.

## Chapter Six

# *EVERYMAN*

᠄᠄᠄᠄᠄᠄᠄᠄᠄᠄᠄᠄᠄᠄᠄᠄᠄᠄᠄᠄᠄᠄᠄᠄᠄᠄᠄᠄᠄᠄᠄᠄᠄᠄᠄᠄᠄᠄᠄᠄

We have seen that after the twelfth century the book of the heart took a sharply individual turn, whether in scholastic glosses on the personal book of knowledge or memory, vernacular poems about the lover's heart as a record of erotic passion, or the legends of saints whose hearts received special signs of divine favor. This individual turn also characterizes the book of the heart in popular religious literature and art, the vernacular texts and images designed to teach doctrine and devotion to the laity. In some cases, the popularized book of the heart was meant for not just a literate but a theologically sophisticated audience. But the mystery and morality plays performed in public festivals, and the sermons and visual art of the churches, presented the book of the heart to a much larger and more varied public, helping to make it familiar to almost everyone and encouraging the literate and the non-literate alike to apply this metaphor to their own lives.

The book of the heart in medieval popular piety was associated chiefly with the individual commemoration of Christ's Passion and preparation for the Last Judgment, two episodes in sacred history on which the clergy especially wished to focus the laity's attention, and both of which readily lent themselves to the notion of writing on the heart. In the first case, the heart was pictured as a record of events centering on the Crucifixion and thus serving as a devotional "text" for religious exercises often involving strong emotions, the so-called "affective piety" of the late Middle Ages. In connection with the Last Judgment, the heart was pictured instead as a comprehensive record of a person's life—every thought, word, and deed—that would be revealed at the end of time in order to determine his or her ultimate fate. In both cases, the book of the heart represented the moral or spiritual core of the individual.

The popularized book of the heart reflected various social and religious changes during the later Middle Ages that encouraged laypeople to look to their own hearts as a center of spiritual life and as a kind of textual space. With the decree of the Fourth Lateran Council (1215) that each person was to make confession at least once every year, penance evolved from a mainly external rite to one that "required an emotional state of interior contrition," thus encouraging spiritual introspection among the laity.[1] The individual's emotions were also central to the sharpening focus of public and private worship on the commemoration of Christ's Passion. Affective piety encouraged participation in—even "imitation" of—Christ's bodily suffering through intense feelings centered on "the heart of the believer," as well as through new devotional practices such as "prayer of the heart."[2] At the same time, late medieval piety emphasized the individual's preparation for death and the afterlife through a process of inward self-examination. Especially after the Great Plague of 1348 and its repeated outbreaks, religious art abounded with images of the sudden, unexpected appearance of Death and his summons to an individual moral "reckoning."

During the later Middle Ages, book metaphors also seem to have grown in popularity as actual books proliferated among the laity and as reading and writing became more widely familiar practices, in turn encouraging new mental habits and reshaping notions of selfhood. Even the scholastic authors who loved to describe the book of the heart in the specialized terms of the scriptorium or classroom had recognized the potential appeal of this metaphor to the laity and the world outside of academe. Thus Peter Comestor wrote that the inner book was unique because it could be examined by cleric and layman alike ("... tam a clerico quam a laico").[3] From about 1100 to 1300, lay literacy seems to have been limited mainly to the "pragmatic reader," who used texts in the course of commercial or legal business, but the period from about 1300 to 1500 saw the gradual emergence of the "general reader," who increasingly read "for recreation and profit."[4] The expansion of lay literacy was marked by a rise in vernacular documents such as letters and wills, and "the growth of a more organized book trade," including books on moral and religious subjects intended to instruct the laity.[5] These changes in the material culture of the book complemented the inward, individual thrust of late medieval piety, and the lay readers and book owners who formed a growing public for religious books began embracing textual metaphors for their own lives and inward experience. As a result, people from a wider social sphere began to imagine and understand themselves in expressly textual terms—to read, inscribe, or interpret their own hearts as a kind of book.

## "The Book of Man's Soul"

The inner book's prominent role in lay piety reflects the tendency of late medieval theology to stress that believers should not simply hear and obey God's word, but also interiorize it by "writing" that word in their hearts. Ever since Augustine, theologians had emphasized the Pauline distinction between the death-dealing Law and the life-giving Gospel, and the need for Christians to carry God's word within themselves as a "letter . . . written on [their] hearts." Toward the close of the fourteenth century, the threat of nominalist philosophy prompted some theologians to identify Scripture more closely than ever with the heart.

A case in point is the position taken by the English theologian John Wyclif in a series of Oxford lectures delivered around 1378. Wyclif defined Scripture in terms of a five-level hierarchy ranging from the Trinity down to the physical text. The fourth, or next-to-last, level is "the truth as it is believed, as it is inscribed in the book [*libro*] of the natural man, which is his soul"—as distinct from the fifth level of Scripture, the material codex consisting of mere parchment and ink.[6] Although Wyclif essentially restates the classic Augustinian view of the relative importance of spirit to letter, he emphasizes that Scripture inheres less in the outward text itself than in the reader's inward reception of it, an interior process of faith and understanding that is ultimately a kind of *imitatio*, that hallmark of late medieval piety.[7]

Wyclif's Latin lectures were confined to university circles, but a later (c. 1449) vernacular treatise by Reginald Pecock, bishop of Chichester, made a similar appeal to an inner book as the ultimate arbiter of scriptural truth. One of the first churchmen of his time to put his theology into English, the language of the laity, Pecock argued that the natural law cited in Scripture and elsewhere "is more truly inscribed in the book of man's soul than in the outward book of parchment or vellum. . . ."[8] Pecock was attacking the "heretical" views of scriptural sufficiency held by the Lollards, among whom he numbered Wyclif himself.[9] Yet Pecock's theology of Scripture is very similar to his opponent's, including his emphasis on the book of the heart: "If there be any apparent conflict between the words written in the outward book of Holy Scripture and the verdict of reason written in man's soul and heart, the external words ought to be expounded and interpreted and brought into accord with the judgment of reason." Like earlier authorities, Pecock not only pictures the heart (or soul) as a book, but even treats it as a "gloss" on Scripture rather than vice versa ("the judgment of reason ought not to be expounded, glossed, interpreted, and made to accord with the aforesaid outward writing in Holy Scripture"). Again, Pecock reflects the traditional priority of spirit over letter, but with a notable emphasis on the "sufficiency" of the internal book that later (Protestant) theologians would identify with individual conscience, and that led to Pecock's own trial and censure on charges of heresy.[10]

The letter/spirit distinction also defines the book of the heart in late medieval ascetic works that eventually became popular among the laity. The most influential of these was the *Imitation of Christ*, by Thomas à Kempis, originally composed in Latin around 1425. The *Imitation* embodied the ideals of the Modern Devotion, the collective name given to the semi-official fraternal orders that flourished in northern Europe from the late fourteenth century on. These ideals included withdrawal from the world as well as retreat within oneself for the private cultivation of an interior, heart-centered spirituality.[11]

In the dialogues between "Jesus" and the "Disciple" that comprise much of the *Imitation*, Scripture is the main "exemplar" that the devotee is to copy into the book of his heart for the purpose of study and devotion: "Write my words on your heart and earnestly reflect upon them. . . . What you do not understand through your reading and studying, you will know when I come to you."[12] This inner book is essential, since external books are useless without inward understanding: "Some people carry their devotion with them only in books, others in holy pictures, and others in outward signs and symbols. Some have me on their lips, but little in their hearts."[13] True understanding comes only from the divine author, teacher, and reader of hearts: "A book teaches one lesson, but it does not teach everyone equally, for deep within you, I am the Teacher of truth, the Searcher of the heart, the Reader of thoughts...."[14] The *Imitation* was translated into many European vernaculars during the fifteenth century, including Middle English, and printing eventually extended its influence far beyond ascetic communities. These popular versions reflect the individual and inward turn of late medieval piety that found expression in the book of the heart inscribed with the mysteries of the Passion or the ultimate secrets of the self.[15]

Another fifteenth-century ascetic work adapted the book of the heart to women readers in particular. This was the originally Latin treatise *De doctrina cordis* (probably by Hugh of St. Cher, thirteenth century), discussed in an earlier chapter, that details the form, content, and uses of the inner book. Many vernacular translations of this work survive, some addressed specifically to women.[16] A Middle English version, entitled the *Doctrine of the Hert*, which survives in at least four manuscripts, clearly is meant for a female reader, probably a nun, since it addresses her throughout as "Sister."[17] This reader is instructed to read and study the book of her heart constantly: "Your heart or conscience is a book wherein you should read during this life, for it is the book whereby you shall be judged...."[18] Listing the contents of this inner book ("lamentations, songs, and woe"), the treatise emphasizes that "these lessons must be read often, for even if you have no other books, this one will serve you for your whole life."[19] Without necessarily implying a scarcity of actual books, this may allude to the fact that in the cloister, books were still regarded as communal property, so that a nun's only private, personal text would have been the book of the heart. Although the *Doctrine of the Hert* was probably aimed at an audience of female clerics rather than laywomen, it attests to the widening appeal of the heart-book metaphor.[20]

## "My Heart Book"

Popular religious writings mention various figurative books in connection with Christ's Passion, including the "books" of Christ's own body and heart. Examples include an early (1225–1250) English mystical treatise urging the believer to open and read the "love-letter" of Christ's heart, Richard Rolle's mystical comparison of Christ's wounded body to a decorated book ("Jesus, thy body is like a book all written with red ink"), and the popular "Charter of Christ" with its comparison of Christ's body to a legal document offering release from sin.[21] These fleshly "books" became powerful objects of devotion in both literature and art, and the heart of Christ (although not always as a "text") eventually inspired its own well-known cult.[22]

The most personal and individualized of all fleshly "books" of the Passion was the believer's own heart inscribed with the story of Christ's suffering. As a devotional "text," the book of the heart was eminently private, portable, and permanent. As a focus of affective piety, it symbolically unified the individual with Christ through a "transcription" of the sacred wounds to an inward, individual "copy" of the Passion. As such, the book of the heart embodied an *imitatio Christi* that was no longer limited to a saintly elite but that everyone could aspire to. Furthermore, popular literature about heart-centered devotion to the suffering Christ tended to elide the priesthood, putting the individual into a direct personal relation with Christ.

Popular accounts of the ordinary heart inscribed with Christ's wounds and suffering had various Latin precedents. The transfer of Christ's wounds to the believer's heart, described in terms of writing, is explicit in Gertrude of Helfta's prayer to Christ: "Write your wounds in my heart with your precious blood, that I may read in them your suffering and your love alike."[23] A similar transference informs a pseudo-Bernardine prayer that reads, in part, "Write your wounds in my heart with your most precious blood. . . ."[24] And the same idea is elaborated at great length in John of Howden's *Philomena* (thirteenth century), which urges a personified Love (*Amor*) instead of Christ to itemize and record each scene of the Passion in "the book of my heart" (*cordis mei . . . volumine*).[25]

Two popularized English versions of the *Philomena* depict Christ himself authoring the story of his Passion in the book of the believer's heart. The longer work, the *Meditations on the Life and Passion of Christ* (c. 1400), illustrates the adaptation of a popular motif from saints' legends to more ordinary lives when it urges Christ to write "your name ... within my heart-root." By implication, anyone might aspire to having a heart inscribed with Christ's name. In the poem's most explicit and personal reference to a book of the heart, Christ is asked to write scenes of his Passion "upon my heart-book," a phrase that renders the *liber cordis* (or *cordis volumen*) of learned tradition into plain English. But this popularized book of the heart remains part of a sophisticated theology of writing. For example, Jesus is said to have written on his own body with nails in order to record all humanity in the "book that never fails"; and Mary is asked at the poem's conclusion to open "this same book" in Christ's presence so that he will have mercy on the author.[26] The book of Christ's body and the book of the believer's heart are thus linked by a more conventional book of the Passion whose purpose is to mediate the one fleshly text to the other.

The *Meditations* were in turn distilled into a briefer English poem (c. 1400), a metrical prayer (*orisoun*) of about 150 lines that likewise treats the book of the heart as the ultimate devotional text on Christ's Passion. The *Orison's* opening lines strike a highly individual tone as they introduce the poem's governing image of the inscribed heart:

> Jesus, who hast me dearly bought,
> Now write with spirit in my thought,
> That I might with devotion true
> Recall thy passion all anew.
> For though my heart be hard as stone,
> Thy writing makes it all thine own;
> The nail or spear, a stylus keen,
> Shall make the letters all be seen.[27]

The rest of the poem evokes the various episodes of the Passion (arrest, trial, scourging, etc.), urging Christ to write a record of each event on the believer's heart. Early on, this interior record is expressly likened to a book of the heart, "Write upon my heart book" ("... my hert boke" [29]), a metaphor later reinforced by some apparent wordplay on bookbinding.[28]

The poem's opening contrast between the Old Law of Moses

("stone") and the New Law of Christ ("spirit") recalls Paul's well-known gloss on the letter, the spirit, and the "tablet of the heart." Yet this spiritual writing takes on a very corporeal aspect in the poem's vivid imagery of nails as styli and of Christ's blood as ink:

> Jesus, write within my heart
> How blood out of thy wounds did spurt;
> Inscribe it with your blood so often
> That my heart will finally soften. (49–52)

As shown in earlier chapters, the idea of bodily "scripture" goes back to early Christian martyrologies, and it reappears in scholastic glosses on the book of Christ's body, as well as the popular "Charter of Christ." Here the comparison of Christ's blood to the rubricator's red ink (with allusion to the curing and softening of parchment) directly links the wounds inscribed on Christ's flesh to the writing on the individual believer's heart.[29]

The fleshly inscription on the believer's heart deepens with the related image of the heart wounded by Christ's arrows of love:

> Let Love his bow begin to bend,
> Love's arrows toward my heart to send,
> That they may pierce, and I may feel,
> For only wounds like his can heal. (109–12)

A reflex of the spiritualized Amor in the *Philomena*, this passage suggests an analogy between spiritual writing on the heart and the carnal writing on the body that medieval secular poetry borrowed from classical models like Ovid. The heart wounded by the arrows of divine love also recalls Augustine's powerful image of his own converted heart wounded by divine "words like arrows fixed deep in our flesh."[30] In the *Orison*, the believer's inscribed and wounded heart "imitates" the penetration of Christ's flesh and thus undergoes an inward conversion through participation in Christ's Passion.

This conversion is figured by the scribal metaphor of a transcription of Christ's wounds to the individual heart. The word "write" recurs as an imperative verb addressed to Christ more than a dozen times throughout the poem, each time in connection with a different episode of the Passion (e.g., "Write the strokes . . ."). Christ, the author of human salvation, thereby becomes the author of the inner book as well, transcribing his wounds from the exemplar of his own body to a copy in the believer's heart and turning the sacred scenes of the Passion into devotional passages of a personal memory book.

But the *Orison* cannot fully transcend its own materiality (on the page) by effecting a spiritual writing (on the heart). Indeed, its actual devotional use heightens the tension between spirit and flesh that reflects the *Orison*'s ultimate debt to the Pauline "letter from Christ . . . written . . . on tablets of human hearts." According to one modern editor, "the *Orison* was intended for practical devotions," and its content suggests "a petitioner's desire to share more fully in the experiences he has been rehearsing." The many surviving manuscript copies suggest, moreover, that the *Orison* "must have been fairly popular in the fourteenth and fifteenth centuries," largely because of "its usability as a private prayer."[31] The most obvious clue to the *Orison*'s practical use is a rubric that accompanies it in two manuscripts: "In the saying of this orison, pause at every sign of the cross and think about what you have said. For I have never found a more devout prayer of the Passion, whosoever should say it devoutly."[32] These "instructions for use" offer a glimpse into the private devotions of the medieval laity, showing that the *Orison*'s efficacy was thought to depend on the combined effects of thought, feeling, gesture, and voice. In order to prompt Christ's act of inscription, the believer must turn the inert, silent text of the manuscript page into an actively spoken prayer. The spoken prayer mediates between Christ's body and the believer's heart in much the way spelled out by the longer *Meditations*, with the exhortations to Christ as author or scribe effecting a "transcription" of wounds from the fleshly book of Christ's body to the fleshly book of the believer's heart.

❦❦❦❦❦❦

The French moralist Philippe de Mézières (d. 1405) provides another glimpse into how the laity used the book of the heart in their practical devotions, especially the belief that active prayer accompanied by sacred signs or gestures could transcribe Christ's wounds to the individual's heart. In a vernacular treatise on marriage that shows a special concern for women readers, Philippe devotes most of one chapter to the

Latin prayer cited earlier: "O gracious Jesus, write your wounds in my heart with your most precious blood so that I may always know what is required of me and what I must do, and so that I can read, feel, and clearly understand the pain of your holy Passion and your love for us. . . ."[33] Philippe translates the prayer "for the married woman and others also who perchance do not understand Latin" and adds a detailed French gloss, which indicates that by about 1400 the book of the heart was being adapted for the laity in general as well as laywomen in particular.

Using a term typically applied to elite (monastic) reading habits, Philippe states that one should ruminate (*ruminer*) this prayer often and devotedly with mouth and heart while crossing and striking the breast three times in saying the words "read, feel, and understand."[34] Philippe then tells the story of a preaching friar who throughout his life constantly repeated Christ's name while crossing himself over the chest; after his death, his breastbone was found to be marked with a sign of the Cross, a result of his constantly recalling (*recordant*) the sacred name. Everyone should pray thus, since Christ desires "to write in our hearts his sweet name" as a reminder (*memoire*) of his Passion. Philippe's remarks indicate the popular appeal of prayers invoking divine inscription on the believer's heart and the popular belief that spiritual writing can be manifested in bodily signs. Like the English *Orison*, Philippe's gloss also points to a popular belief that not only saints but more ordinary people could aspire to having Christ's name written on their hearts.

Although both the French and English prayers are clearly meant to be read *aloud*, they have affinities with an emerging devotional practice of the late Middle Ages known as "prayer of the heart" (*prière de coeur*), a type of silent prayer. As Paul Saenger has shown, this new devotional ideal was based on the traditional view of the heart's centrality to the person and involved a "shift from the mouth to the heart as the primary organ of prayer. . . ."[35] This shift of emphasis, apparent by the late fourteenth century and well established by the end of the fifteenth, is widely attested in prayer treatises, prayer-book rubrics, and prayer texts used by the laity in England, France, and the Low Countries. Scriptural examples of heart-centered prayer, once used mainly to warn against religious ostentation, now became models of direct communication with God. By the 1460s in France, prayer of the heart was increasingly valued in private devotions and was dramatically changing the laity's experience of public worship as well.

Private, heart-centered prayer gradually became customary at public celebrations of the Mass, "especially at the elevation of the Host," the climax of the Mass as a commemoration of Christ's Passion. Thus a fifteenth-century French treatise on prayer states that the believer profits most from the Mass not by listening but by remembering "with his or her memory and heart the passion of our Lord." At first recited by memory, private prayers at public Mass were eventually collected in prayer books carried by the laity, so that "a significant portion of vernacular prayers could be read silently from small portable codices. . . ." Reflecting the new ideal of silent, private, heart-centered prayer, the rubrics in these portable prayer books typically state that the texts are to be read "*en pensé, de coeur,* or *en coeur.*"

Like the ideal of heart-centered reading celebrated by Augustine, heart-centered prayer shifted the emphasis from voice and body to inward experience, to the word in the heart. At the same time, however, it tended to heighten the corporeal, fleshly aspect of this inner word, for as a focus of personal piety in the context of the Mass, it emphasized the parallel between the wounded heart of Christ and the heart of each believer as a record of Christ's Passion. This is also the central theme of the vernacular prayers considered here, with their imagery of Christ's wounds "transcribed" to the believer's heart. These guides to popular piety treat the believer's heart as a kind of personal prayer book that commemorates the Passion better than any external book, thus making this inward book the ultimate devotional text.

## "My Book of Reckoning"

Besides personal piety centered on Christ's Passion, the book of the heart also appeared in popular portrayals as a cumulative record of the individual's life, the secret thoughts, words, and deeds to be opened at the Last Judgment. This popularized book of the heart (or conscience), which appeared in works of instruction about penance and death, ultimately derived from sources examined earlier in this study, especially patristic and scholastic glosses on the "opened books" of judgment in Daniel 7.10 and Revelation 20.12.

In general, popular portrayals of the Last Judgment in the later Middle Ages followed learned precedent in replacing a single collective book of record (the "book of life") with many individual books and exchanging external books for interior, psychological ones. The earlier, one-book model makes its most famous literary (and musical) appearance in the *Dies Irae*, which cites a single comprehensive external book of reckoning, a "written book in which all is contained."[36] By the thirteenth century, however, learned authors had already established the alternative metaphor of a separate and unique book for each person, a book often identified with the heart or conscience. Typical is a Latin treatise that long went under Saint Bernard's name stating that at the Judgment, "the conscience of each person shall be brought to witness, and the book of conscience shall be opened, and each sin brought to light."[37]

The popularized book of the heart containing a record of the individual's life reflects many features of late medieval culture. Besides the personal, inward turn of penitence after the Fourth Lateran Council decreed annual confession, it coincides with the rise of lay literacy and the spread of private record-keeping in the form of account books and ledgers, especially among an urban middle class increasingly accustomed to commercial bookkeeping and the documentation of their lives in parish and legal records. It also parallels the growing use of written evidence in litigation, where documents had largely replaced oral memory by the fourteenth century.[38] The ecclesiastical courts furthered the impact of writing on ordinary lives through the notorious device of the "archdeacon's book," where crimes were recorded and fines assessed.[39] Lay readers as well as nonliterate folk who witnessed artistic or dramatic portrayals of the Last Judgment may well have regarded the Doomsday "books" evoked on stage as ultimate versions of daily realities. And during the fifteenth century, when the preoccupation with death reached its height in Europe, popular treatises on "The Art of Dying" gave the internalized book of reckoning a further immediacy.

A book of the heart or conscience is suggested in popular English religious writings already at the end of the twelfth century. One of its earliest appearances is in an anonymous metrical homily known as the *Poema morale* that may have been composed as early as 1175 and that survives in at least nine manuscripts dating from 1225 to about 1300, indicating a popularity that lasted a century or more.[40] The poem mentions devils who have written down everyone's sins, but the greatest witness will be "a man's own heart," for "All that each man hath done since he came to manhood, / As if he saw it written in a book, so shall it seem to him then."[41] The metaphor is not fully realized here, since the book is not expressly interiorized or individualized, but this passage from "one of the most important of the early Middle English poems" illustrates a crucial phase of its popular development.[42]

The individualized book metaphor makes a similar appearance in the *Cursor Mundi* (c. 1325), a popular metrical summary of doctrine that pointedly shows how figurative books were becoming increasingly common in lay instruction. The *Cursor* warns the reader to avoid condemnation and punishment at the Last Judgment by confessing his sins with an "open heart," and to review his thoughts, words, and deeds as though reading from a written record: "Confession should be made with good preparation, / So that you consider your deeds / As if you had written them in a book."[43] The *Cursor* thus pictures the ultimate opening of the individual's book at the Judgment in terms of a more immediate and regular practice, since by this time annual confession was required of everyone. Significantly, it also pictures the individual as the scribe of his inner book, as the one who has "written" his own sins there.

By the middle of the fourteenth century, the inward book of reckoning had become explicit in popular religious writings, as shown by the *Prick of Conscience* (c. 1350), a lengthy summary of Church doctrine that has been called "the most popular English poem of the Middle Ages" because it survives in over a hundred manuscripts from all parts of England.[44] The section on the Last Judgment, based on Daniel 7.10, details how the book of each person's conscience will be opened before God's throne:

All secret things shall then be known,
As Daniel's prophecy has shown:
*Sedit iudicium et libri aperti sunt.*
"The judge shall sit with opened books,"
And read men's sins where'er he looks.
The books betoken each man's heart
Or conscience, says the gloss, in part:

*Consciencie omnibus revelabuntur.*
"The truth," it says, "of what's been done
Shall then be known to everyone."
One's every sin, both great and small,
Shall him accuse; the books tell all.

This passage clearly signals the metaphor's arrival among the literate laity. Explicit mention of the biblical gloss (*þe glose*) indicates a learned source for the popularized metaphor, while the bilingual presentation marks the metaphor's transition from a clerical to a lay audience. The vernacular text drives home the point that conscience is like a "book," warning readers (or listeners) that their itemized sins shall accuse them. And just for good measure, devils who "write down all sins" will provide additional written evidence.[45]

Toward the end of the Middle Ages, the *Imitation of Christ* further popularized the idea of an individual book of the heart that would be opened at the Last Judgment. Drawing on the usual biblical sources (e.g., Rev. 20.12), the Latin *Imitation* refers to an ultimate reading of each individual conscience: "The time will come when Christ, the Teacher of teachers, the Lord of angels, will appear to hear the readings [*lectiones*] of the gathered hosts and to examine each person's conscience."[46] This passage duly appears in the vernacular *Imitation,* including the Middle English text (c. 1450), which warns that Christ shall appear "to hear the reading [*lesson*] by all the angels, that is, to search the conscience of all men . . ."—where *lesson* (from Latin *lectio*) likewise portrays the individual heart or conscience as a written record, if not necessarily as a separate "book" for each individual.[47] The Middle English *Doctrine of the Hert,* cited earlier, provides an even more detailed gloss on the opened book of the heart or conscience, "the book whereby you shall be judged."

Compared to poems or treatises studied by individuals or read aloud in small groups, the medieval drama brought the book metaphors of the Last Judgment to an even larger popular audience. Most of the English cycle plays on the theme of the Last Judgment show devils gathering up record books ("accompts," "rentals," etc.) to bring to the divine tribunal as evidence against sinners, scenes obviously meant to impress a lay audience increasingly familiar with writing, books, and documents of various kinds.[48] But the most vivid and elaborate examples appear in the morality play *Everyman* (c. 1500) and its Flemish analogue *Elckerlijc*, where the personal account book is a stage prop mentioned some two dozen times in the text and displayed throughout the play.

When Death confronts him at the outset to demand "thy book of count," Everyman replies that his book is not ready, establishing it as the play's chief symbol of man's inner moral being:

> To think on thee, it maketh my heart sick,
> For all unready is my book of reckoning.
> But twelve years if I might have abiding,
> My counting-book I would make so clear
> That my reckoning I should not need to fear.

Although the play does not directly equate book and heart, it aligns them here in adjacent lines ("my heart . . . , / . . . my book"). Moreover, like the book of the heart inscribed with Christ's suffering, Everyman's account book is emphatically individualized as "*my* counting-book," "*my* reckoning," and (later) "*my* writing," "the books of *your* works and deeds," and so forth.[49] And since many of the play's "characters" are personified psychological qualities (i.e., Knowledge, Discretion, the Five Wits), the book can also be seen as symbolizing one of Everyman's interior aspects. Indeed, what the book as a stage prop represents— "accounting" or "reckoning"—is primarily a mental, interior function. And it is this perfect merging of moral and commercial vocabulary, the religious and the secular, the interior and the exterior, that makes Everyman's book of reckoning such a powerful metaphor for a late medieval audience who were living increasingly recorded and documented lives.

Besides the morality play, the book of the heart also appeared in the visual art located in churches to instruct the laity, literate and nonliterate alike. Whereas the illuminated scenes of Judgment in medieval Bibles or books of hours would have been seen only by monks, scholars, or relatively wealthy patrons, the sculpture, paintings, and stained-glass window scenes in churches were accessible to a large and socially diverse audience. In art, as in literature, the metaphorical books of the Last Judgment tended over time to be multiplied, individualized, and interiorized. In one of the earliest surviving Judgment scenes, a twelfth-

8. *Everyman's Book of the Heart.* Resurrected souls with individualized features carrying "opened books" (Rev. 20.12) over their "hearts." Anonymous, c. 1490. Albi, Cathedral of Sainte Cécile, west interior wall, fresco of the Last Judgment (detail). Vanni/Art Resource, NY. Reproduced by permission.

century sculptural panel at the cathedral of Autun, the archangel Michael holds an open book representing a single, comprehensive divine record—the biblical "book of life."[50] By contrast, the famous fresco of the Last Judgment in the cathedral of Sainte Cécile at Albi, in southern France, which dates from the end of the fifteenth century, shows each resurrected soul carrying an open book on his or her chest (figure 8). Although surviving examples today are rare, this sort of image was hardly unique in its time.[51]

In the Albi fresco, the books are as individualized and "realistic" as the life-size human figures holding them, a fact emphasized by colored illuminated initials and other textual details that are visible in the painting. As such, these individualized books are the visual equivalent of the personalized "counting-book" carried by Everyman, which appeared on the European stage at about the same time. Alternatively, they have been compared to the parchment roll containing the individual's itemized sins (and inscribed, "Behold thy sins") that appears in the late medieval illustrated *Art of Dying*.[52] According to Philippe Ariès, the Albi fresco represents the transformation of the "book of life" from a universal record book to "an individual account book" that each resurrected soul carries around his neck "like a passport, or rather like a bank book to be presented at the gates of eternity."[53] The fresco's imagery points to a Catholic sacramental theology in which "works are indispensable" to personal salvation.[54] Indeed, it is a pictorial gloss on the biblical inscription visible in one of bordering scrolls—"And the dead were judged by those things which were written in the books, according to their works" (Rev. 20.12, Douay)—where "works" (*opera*) are objectified as books by means of a kind of visual pun. Opened wide and worn on each person's chest—"over the heart"—these individual books of reckoning are vivid emblems of the fully revealed inner self.

As a visual image of the book of the heart, the Albi fresco embodies the metaphor's last step before its full pictorial realization. About the time that this fresco was painted, probably in the 1490s, an anonymous Flemish artist was giving the book of the heart its definitive late medieval form by combining the heart and the book into a single image.[55] Actual heart-shaped codices had already appeared by this time, as discussed in chapter 4, but these were mainly romantic embodiments of the metaphor that pointed to the heart's sensual rather than its spiritual import. In contrast, the Flemish artist who rendered the book of the heart as a fully formed pictorial image was illustrating the metaphor's moral and religious significance. Moreover, he placed this image into a rich symbolic context referring to both Christ's Passion and the Last Judgment, to affective devotion as well as moral self-examination. This brilliantly realized book of the heart is the subject of the next chapter.

## Chapter Seven

# PICTURING
## *the* METAPHOR

〜〜〜〜〜〜〜〜〜〜〜〜〜〜〜〜〜〜〜〜〜〜〜〜〜〜〜〜〜〜〜〜〜〜〜〜

We have seen that as the book of the heart acquired a more individual content and a more popular presence, it also assumed ever more concrete forms, from the saint's inscribed heart to the heart-shaped manuscript book. The urge to embody the book of the heart in a fleshly (or physical) form also helped perfect it as a visual image. Some artists had placed heart and book into close proximity, as in the portrait of Saint Augustine that adorns a fifteenth-century copy of the *Confessions* (see figure 1). Others had placed the book over the heart, as in the Albi fresco of the Last Judgment that shows resurrected souls holding opened codices on their chests (see figure 8). But not until the end of the fifteenth century were the two symbols actually combined into a single form, the heart-shaped book that appears as an accessory in some early personal portraits, as if to emphasize the subject's interior life and individuality.

The pictured metaphor appears, possibly for the first time, in two portraits painted around 1485 by an anonymous Flemish artist known as the Master of Sainte Gudule.[1] This painter, who probably managed a busy workshop in Brussels from which more than two dozen religious and devotional works survive, was once regarded as a minor imitator of Rogier van der Weyden.[2] But more recent scholarship has ranked the Master of Sainte Gudule well above his contemporaries: "Of all the painters from Brussels around the turn of the 15th century, the Master of the View of Sainte Gudule is the one whose artistic personality is the most pronounced. His extravagant style sets him off from that of his more sclerotic contemporaries, whose works are still ruled by the imitation of the great early Flemish painters."[3]

What sets this master apart is an expressiveness that at times borders on caricature—"the agitation of his figures, their frenetic and excessive gestures, their ugly faces often tending toward a grimace."[4] Praised today for "an expressivity rare among Flemish painters" and even hailed as "a distant precursor of Northern expressionism," the Master of Sainte Gudule reflects in his own distinctive style the general movement toward in-depth psychological portrayal.[5] As Norbert Schneider remarks, "The portraits painted towards the end of the fifteenth century focused increasingly on inward states, on the evocation of atmosphere and the portrayal of mental and moral attitudes."[6] The Master of Sainte Gudule could hardly have signaled more clearly his concern with inward states than he does in the two portraits considered here, where the subject holds an opened heart-shaped book containing visible—though not quite legible—handwriting.

One of these portraits presents the subject expressly as a reader, while the other, which includes some writing tools, presents him also in the role of author or scribe. Together the two paintings vividly illustrate the medieval book of the heart as created in the image of the manuscript codex, including its specific form, production, and use. At the same time, they give striking expression to sophisticated notions of the self as a book where reading and writing represent mental functions such as memory and recollection. Since both portraits have a religious theme, they point mainly to the book of the heart in its devotional or moral significance. And yet the many clues of setting and circumstance in each painting do not necessarily reveal the character of what the subject is reading, or writing, in his heart-shaped book. Unlike the book of the heart in many of its literary instances, the perfected visual metaphor, with its ultimately inscrutable writing, conceals as much as it reveals.

Reading the Heart

In the first of these remarkable paintings, now at the Metropolitan Museum of Art in New York, the subject holds an opened heart-shaped book while apparently engaged in prayer or meditation (figure 9). The setting clearly signals a religious theme; behind him there stands a church, its walls and pillars cut away to show an altar where a priest conducts a mass. Except for the unusually shaped book, the painting resembles many other late medieval portraits that show individuals engaged in devotional reading. Indeed, scholars have generally assumed that the heart-shaped book in this painting represents a prayer book.[7] The portrait was painted in the final decades of the fifteenth century when personal prayer books were increasingly common among the laity, along with devotional practices such as the heart-centered prayer discussed in chapter 6. The sitter holds one of the book's leaves between thumb and forefinger, as if turning the pages to follow a liturgical program. One study of late medieval devotional painting simply cites the heart-shaped book in this portrait (and its twin) as evidence that the subject is engaged in prayer.[8]

The celebration of the Mass portrayed in the painting's background indicates the nature and focus of his worship—namely, the remembrance of Christ's Passion. Memory was often regarded as a specific function of the heart, as embodied in terms such as *recordatio*, with recollection figured expressly as the "reading" of an inward book.[9] In this eucharistic setting, the heart-shaped book may even symbolize the popular devotional ideal of the heart inscribed with a record of Christ's Passion. Gertrude of Helfta had pictured herself as reading from a record written in her heart by Christ: "Lord, write your wounds in my heart with your precious blood, that I may read in them your suffering and your love. . . ."[10] And the English poems examined in chapter 6 likened the reader's heart expressly to a book ("my hert boke") containing the memory of Christ's Passion.[11] The painting may likewise picture the believer "reading" from a Passion book written in his heart by Christ.

At the same time, the heart-shaped book may allude to the abundant heart symbolism of the Mass itself. The liturgy of the Eucharist variously mentions the heart as a place of God's Word (*Dominus sit in corde*

9. *Reader with Heart-Shaped Book.* The Master of Sainte Gudule, Flemish, c. 1485. *Young Man Holding a Book.* The Metropolitan Museum of Art, Bequest of Mary Stillman Harkness, 1950 (50.145.27). All rights reserved, The Metropolitan Museum of Art.

*tuo*), the lifting up of hearts (*Sursum corda*), and the sacrifice of the heart (*Unde et memores*).[12] During the *Sursum corda* the celebrant raises his hands, following the biblical idea that the heart is raised with the hands (*cum manibus*), a gesture approximated in the painting, where the sitter likewise holds a "heart" in his hands.[13] The specific liturgical scene shown in the painting, however, is the Elevation of the Host. The Elevation, which directly follows the consecrating words "*Hoc est enim corpus meum,*" was introduced in the twelfth century and gradually acquired "sacramental efficacy" as a visual substitute for Communion. As the climax of the Mass, the Elevation "provided a focus for the emotions of the

medieval congregation," since it symbolized "the body of the Savior
. . . visibly suspended on the cross." The Elevation was also the part of
the Mass "especially" associated with heart-centered prayer.[14]

In formal terms, the painting identifies the heart-shaped book with
the consecrated Host, which Catholic theology interprets as the substance of Christ's sacrificed body, the Corpus Christi. Medieval devo-
tional literature further identified Christ's Body (*corpus*) with the believer's heart (*cor*), often treating the heart as central to the worship of that
Body (e.g., "The precious body of Jesus Christ / With all my heart I
worship").[15] The painting suggests a similar identification by aligning
the heart-shaped book and the elevated Host on the same vertical axis
(and by placing each object in a pair of hands), so that the viewer's eye
is drawn from the book in the foreground to the Host in the background, a visual effect that the artist clearly took pains to achieve.[16]
The painting even hints at a theological pun derived from the fact that
the word *cor* is "contained" by the word *corpus,* as emphasized by the
celebrant's practice of making the sign of the Cross (in some cases, over
his heart) while pronouncing the latter word (*Cor + pus*).[17]

The Eucharist scene also relates the cordiform book to the Incarnation and the mystery of the Word made flesh. Medieval sacramental
theology viewed the Host as "food of the heart" and likened the break-
ing of the Host to the opening of Scripture.[18] In the painting, the elevation of the Host above the heart-shaped book identifies the Savior as
both food and word, as *Corpus Christi* and *Verbum Dei,* as sustenance for
both the body and the heart. The Incarnation is also subtly suggested
by the outlined image of the Virgin holding the infant Christ that appears just over the altar behind the priest, located precisely where the
sitter's horizontal line of sight intersects with the vertical line through
the book and the Host.[19] Clearly visible in the full-sized portrait, the
image of the Christ child directly above the Host hints at "the child in
the Host," a popular idea and image in late medieval theology that
linked the Nativity to the Passion and stressed their typological relation.[20] Within this formal and symbolic pattern, the heart-shaped book
suggests the mystery of the Incarnate Word—that is, both the Word
that became flesh, and the Word inscribed in human, fleshly, hearts.

Heart symbolism relating to the Elevation of the Host also involves
the kneeling figure in the painting's background, which some critics
have identified with the sitter himself.[21] From the thirteenth century

on, kneeling at the Elevation was encouraged by Church authorities.[22] And the Second Council of Lyon (1274) had decreed that at the mention of Christ's name during the Mass, everyone was to bend "the knees of the heart" (*genua cordis*).[23] The knees of the heart are mentioned in a supplement to the Vulgate Bible that was eventually incorporated into the liturgy of the Mass: "And now I bend the knees of my heart, calling on thy goodness, O Lord."[24] In the painting, the kneeling worshiper is positioned directly above the heart-shaped book and is the nearest background detail. Kneeling figures are common in other contemporary illustrations of the Elevation, such as Rogier van der Weyden's *Altarpiece of the Seven Sacraments,* probably the model followed by the Master of Sainte Gudule.[25] By aligning the kneeling figure with the heart-shaped book, the painter identifies heart-centered prayer as both a bodily and a spiritual exercise, a matter of inward and outward devotion alike.

The heart-shaped book itself has further theological significance as a diptych, originally a hinged pair of writing tablets that could be opened and closed like a book.[26] Patristic writers (including Augustine) used the Latin word *diptychum* as a synonym for the twin tablets of the Law, and medieval artists widely represented the Law tablets with rounded tops, creating what became their standard image (round-topped wax writing tablets were also known in the Middle Ages).[27] Since the Old Testament refers to the Law written on the heart, the heart-shaped book in the portrait, as a round-topped diptych, carries a double association with the Law. But the heart-shaped book represents the Gospel as well, not only by its association with the consecrated Host, but also by being yet another kind of diptych—a codex. Medieval iconography contrasted the codex as a symbol of the Gospel with the tablets (or scrolls) of the Jewish Law.[28] Moreover, the book of the heart, imagined as a codex containing "a letter from Christ," was held to have superseded the stone tablets of the Law. Scholastic authors even described a book of the heart containing the Ten Commandments accompanied by glosses from the Gospel, suggesting a "transcription" from the original tablets to an inward book.[29]

The stylized form of the heart seen here—which became common during the fifteenth century and is now standard on playing cards, valentines, and the like—readily lent itself to the format of the codex book. Indeed, the separate diptychal forms of the heart and the codex—each consisting of two halves that are mirror images of each other—combine perfectly in the heart-shaped book of the painting. Moreover, the portrait's rounded top suggests that it (or its London twin) originally may have been part of yet another kind of diptych—a hinged painting that paired the devotee's image with a sacred scene, often a Virgin and Child.[30] Folding icons in small portable formats were popular objects of personal devotion in the fifteenth century. As part of a diptych, the image of the open heart-shaped book (itself a double diptych combining heart and codex) would have had a formal parallel in the opened panels of the painting.[31] In any case, as a symbolic diptych, the heart-shaped book folds into itself an entire Christian grammatology, summarizing the historical and personal progression of God's word from Law to Gospel, letter to spirit, stone to flesh, and exterior to interior. As such, the book of the heart ostensibly transcends all external, material texts. However, by turning into a concrete visual image, it turns paradoxical as well, an interior writing embodied in an external physical form.

Given its unusual form, the heart-shaped book depicted by the Flemish master in these two portraits might seem to be simply a visual trope, a pictorial conceit, except that some actual heart-shaped manuscript books survive from the Middle Ages, as discussed in chapter 4. Three of these cordiform books are collections of songs or poems that represent the amorous book of the heart. But one is a Latin prayer book that clearly embodies the metaphor's religious rather than its romantic side (figure 10). Preserved in Paris at the Bibliothèque nationale, this heart-shaped book is strikingly similar in form and size (and even its red leather binding) to the cordiform books in the paintings by the Master of Sainte Gudule.[32] Scholars have even cited the heart-shaped prayer book as a physical analogue to the books in the paintings.[33] Unlike the famous heart-shaped songbook also at the Bibliothèque nationale, the prayer book opens to form a single (rather than a double) heart. Consisting of 151 paper folios and measuring a little over six inches (165 mm) long and about seven inches (180 mm) wide when open, it can be comfortably held in the manner shown in the portrait (as I have personally confirmed during an on-site examination). Its layout and lettering, including the reduced characters that fill the bottom corners of the tapered pages, show that the book was conceived from the beginning as a heart-shaped volume. Possibly other such prayer

10. *Heart-Shaped Prayer Book.* Latin book of hours formed as a heart, French, fifteenth century. Latin MS 10536, fols. 24v–25r. Cliché Bibliothèque nationale de France, Paris. Reproduced by permission.

books once existed and the Master of Sainte Gudule knew of them or even used them as models. (As a volume containing the Hours of the Virgin, the heart-shaped Paris prayer book has a special relevance to the eucharistic scene in the painting, with its image of the Virgin over the altar.) But whether the artist worked from physical exemplars is finally less important than what his heart-shaped books suggest about the devotional ideals and practices of his time, and about the book of the heart as a symbol or metaphor of the inner self.

## Inscribing the Heart

The Master of Sainte Gudule's other portrait of a man holding a heart-shaped book (figure 11), now at the National Gallery in London, differs from the first in several important details. For one thing, it omits the indoor scene of the Mass and shows instead a church exterior. Even more telling, it includes with the heart-shaped book some writing

tools—namely, a pen case and an inkwell that lie on the ledge or win-
dowsill in the foreground. Since the pen was a common emblem of the
scribe, it has been proposed that the sitter is a clerk or secretary, possibly one attached to a chapter of Augustinian canons affiliated with
the building in the background, a particular church that still stands in
Brussels.[34] The turned-back cuff of the sitter's left sleeve, "which seems
to be associated with manual labour," lends support to this theory.[35] It
has even been proposed that the sitter, as the clerk or secretary to a
chapter of Augustinian canons, is holding a copy of one of Augustine's
works or that the heart-shaped book alludes to Augustinian doctrine.[36]
The prominent scribal imagery of heart and pen in the *Confessions*,
which appears in Augustine's fifteenth-century iconography, makes this
idea plausible though by no means certain.

As in the first portrait, the heart-shaped book may point to heart-
centered prayer and related devotional ideals, with the scribal tools perhaps indicating that the sitter holds a personalized prayer book of some
sort: "The numerous initials and divisions in the text suggest a devotional rather than a secular manuscript."[37] In the fifteenth century, as
Paul Saenger has shown, "silent prayer created a new intimacy between
the devotee and the book" that increased the demand for portable, personalized, and sometimes idiosyncratic prayer books among the laity:
"The choice of texts in books of hours was sufficiently wide to permit
scribes or *libraires* to assemble the kinds of prayers preferred by the purchaser of the book, and to adjust these prayers to the appropriate gender and name. These books, although mass-produced, were far more
personal than those of previous epochs." The purchaser might not only
commission a personalized prayer book, but also coauthor it by in-
serting "his or her own requests or desires" into spaces left in the book
for that purpose, a feature that enhanced the personal quality of heart-
centered prayer.[38] Even without the pen case and the inkwell, the unusual cordiform design of the book in the painting suggests a personalized possession.

But it is more likely that the second painting, like the first, depicts a
metaphorical book of the heart, and that the scribal tools point to figurative writing rather than to actual clerical functions. As we saw in
chapter 3, scholastic authors were fond of picturing the individual as a
scribe writing in a book of the heart modeled after the manuscript codex, and of allegorizing scribal tools and tasks. "You know the scribe's

11. *Scribe with Heart-Shaped Book.* The Master of Sainte Gudule, Flemish, c. 1485. *Portrait of a Young Man.* The pen case and inkwell (lower right) suggest an author or scribe. Reproduced by courtesy of the Trustees, The National Gallery, London.

work," says one twelfth-century sermon that elaborately describes the making of the "parchment book [that] shall be your heart."[39] Another sermon glosses the pen and ink in particular, as follows: "The pen, which is divided in two to prepare it for writing, is the love of God and of our neighbor.... The ink with which we write is humility...."[40] Besides preparing the parchment and inscribing the text, authors allegorized other scribal tasks, such as "collating" the book of the heart with a divine exemplar, "correcting" it of copying errors, and so forth.

What the scribe pictured by the Flemish master is writing (or reading) in the book of his heart could be any number of things specified in the metaphor's literary tradition—scriptural passages such as the Ten Commandments, a devotional memory, a moral account of his own life, or a more inclusive record of personal experience. The believer inscribing God's word in his heart appears in the very popular *Imitation of Christ*, which urges, "Write my words on your heart and earnestly reflect upon them," adding that "what you do not understand through your reading and studying, you will know when I come to you"—terms that could easily apply to the scene in the painting.[41] Another commonplace depicted the believer as a scribe recording the Ten Commandments in his heart, where the scribe again signified memory. The scribe of devotional memory was usually pictured as Christ himself, as noted in connection with the first portrait, but he (or she) could also be the devotee, as in a fourteenth-century French play where a queen vows to praise the Virgin from "a book that I will write in my heart," an especially apt precedent if the portrait was originally part of a diptych featuring the Virgin.[42]

The heart-shaped book in the portrait might also represent a moral record of the subject's life, a book of the heart modeled on scriptural references to "opened books" containing personal secrets (Dan. 7.10, Rev. 20.12). Already in the fourth century Saint Ambrose had cited a very individualized moral record, "the book of your heart" (*liber cordis tui*), warning the believer not to erase God's writing from this book "and write with the ink of your evil deeds"—themes that could well be illustrated here.[43] The later authors who minutely described the book of the heart as a manuscript codex tended to emphasize the role of the inner "scribe" who recorded the individual's every deed. "Wherever I go," wrote one twelfth-century cleric, "my conscience does not leave me but is always present and writes down whatever I do...."[44] The painting may point to a similar ideal of moral self-examination and mental record-keeping. The book as a symbol of the individual's life was familiar to the late medieval urban middle classes, especially as a moral account book modeled on the daily business ledger. Other visual art of the same time, such as the Albi fresco of the Last Judgment, shows resurrected souls holding individual books of account for a final reckoning. And morality plays that circulated in the Low Countries, among other places, featured a personal book of reckoning or account book that equally points to inward transactions.

Typically the scribe who records his own life in the book of his heart is also responsible for correcting it against an exemplar that represents the ultimate truth. As one twelfth-century authority put it, "Let us then compare our books with the book of life, so that if they read differently they may be corrected, and not found wanting in the final collation and thus rejected."[45] A similar idea found popular expression in the account-book metaphor of the morality plays, where Everyman—or his Flemish counterpart, Elckerlijc—was obliged to correct or settle ("clear") his moral accounts.[46] The scribe in the portrait appears to have just put aside his writing equipment, as if having finished correcting the book of his heart for the day.

The fact that the book in the painting lies open at its center may be a further hint that the sitter is recording (and reviewing) his own life. The phrase "middle of the heart" (*medium cordis*) appears in the Latin Bible in connection with God's law.[47] Petrarch, in a penitential context, refers specifically to truths taken from "the middle of the book of experience."[48] But if the opened book represents an individual's life, its halfway point might equally indicate the middle of that life. Modern captions and catalogs typically describe the men in these two paintings as "young," but in terms of typical medieval life spans, they are not necessarily so youthful. The background in the London portrait includes a cemetery containing several large gravestones—a reminder of death, a memento mori, that enhances the book as a symbol of a life at its midpoint.[49]

Another feature of this portrait (and its twin) also hints at the individual scribe who writes or annotates a personal moral record in the book of his heart. Despite their almost palpable form and detailed page layout, where individual lines and even letters are discernible, the books in these paintings defy all attempts (including the use of mirrors and magnification) to decipher their tantalizingly mimetic script. This indecipherability may be a deliberate feature, and not a result of accident or wear. As one art historian says about the book in the London portrait, "The initials are blue and red and the script is decorated with cadels or flourishes," yet "the writing is fictive."[50] Possibly the obscure script is meant to draw attention away from the "letter" and toward the "spirit," as befits the religious theme of writing on the heart. But equally possible is that it represents the inherently *secret* content of the inner book. The heart's inscrutability was a biblical theme that later authors adapted to the inner book of a person's life. Patristic and scholastic authorities treated the book of the heart as a most private text whose contents were known solely to the individual and God until their "public" revelation at the Last Judgment: "The book of conscience is now closed, for 'Deep and unsearchable is the heart of man, and who can know it?' [Jer. 17.8] . . . That book shall be opened at that time when the hidden things of our hearts shall be revealed. . . ."[51] Authorities such as Hugh of St. Cher even warned the individual not to pry into other books of the heart: "Read in your own book. Do not be like those who, neglecting their own book, always want to read in another person's. . . ."[52]

Theological motives for picturing an inscrutable (or "illegible") self may have been reinforced by certain stylistic features of late-fifteenth-century portraiture. As one art historian remarks, without specific reference to the Master of Sainte Gudule, "The tendency to psychologise went so far that it eventually provoked a retreat from the open expression of thoughts or feelings. The sitter no longer revealed himself *as an open book* but turned to a mysterious, inward world from which the spectator was more or less excluded."[53] In the portraits considered here, the book of the heart is evidently "opened" for the individual's own reading and correction but apparently "closed" to the eyes of others.

The emphatically private book in either portrait could also stand for a more comprehensive "book of experience" that includes not just moral awareness (conscience), but unique personal memories or emotions. One Carthusian authority defined the book of experience as the "commentary" (*glossa*) of personal emotion "in the heart" that is more essential to spirituality than any external text, an idea consistent with the affective piety suggested in both portraits.[54] But the scribal tools in the second portrait also hint at another book of experience cited by some medieval authors—namely, the inward and private "original" (or "exemplar") of their outward and public writings. Although the man in the portrait may not be holding one of Augustine's works, as a writer and reader of his own heart, he strikes a very Augustinian pose. In a passage that could have inspired the second portrait, Augustine described his own authorship as an act of writing from the heart: "This is what I want to do in my heart, in front of you, in my confession, and with my pen before many witnesses."[55] Petrarch, in a fictional conversation with Augustine, confessed to personal sins and temptations "excerpted" from a more comprehensive "book of experience."[56] And Dante, in an amorous rather than a penitential vein, posed as a scribe selecting from the private record of experience in his heart "the words which it is my intention to copy into this smaller book. . . ."[57]

Yet the portrait of the "author" as a young man, if such it is, suggests more than a private book of the heart revised and edited for public consumption. It portrays the individual as the author, in some sense, of his own life. In the second portrait, a self-conscious and even self-creating subject is intimated by the sitter's double role as author and reader, as one who apparently has just laid aside his scribal tools to read what he has written. Here reading and writing may simply represent the modes of affective piety or moral self-examination explored above, the commemoration of the Passion or the anticipation of the Judgment. But they may equally point to a more far-reaching conception of the individual as one who inwardly "writes" the story of his own life, and who grasps the meaning of that story by a process of retrospective understanding that is pictured here in terms of "reading" his own heart. If so, the portrait hearkens back in yet another way to Augustine, who helped to inaugurate the codex as a symbol of the self and to codify the genre of spiritual autobiography, the self-authored and self-interpreted moral life. Not that the Augustinian persona who writes and reads his own life is in any sense autonomous, independent of the divine Author, Reader, and Exegete. For here all writing and reading of the heart take place within the moral space represented by the church building that frames each portrait. The symbols of Ecclesia suggest that the true and essential self signified by the book of the heart remains a divinely interpreted text whose ultimate meaning will not be fully revealed until the end of time.[58]

## Heart and Identity

In the art of the early European portrait, sometimes the artist is anonymous, sometimes the subject is, and sometimes both are, as with the two paintings considered here. In this context, the book of the heart, a key medieval emblem of selfhood, presents a double cipher. Like many anonymous painters of this period, the Master of Sainte Gudule is a scholarly hypothesis based on an analysis of the various paintings now attributed to him, rather than on any external historical evidence. As such, he first arrived on the scene in 1923 and has since become a fixture in early Flemish art.[59] But as one study of the anonymous Flemish masters reminds, these artists have "only an imaginary name, in the absence of a real identity."[60] The Master of Sainte Gudule thus belongs to a familiar hermeneutical circle: he supposedly produced the paintings, but now the paintings emphatically produce *him*.[61] Attempts to distinguish the master's "hand" in the paintings attributed to him, to define his "characteristic" style or "signature" (notions of artistic identity expressed as scribal metaphor), only emphasize his provisional or tentative status.[62]

While the artist's identity rests on a theory of stylistic unity that in principle renders him and his oeuvre infinitely revisable, the subjects of his portraits may seem to stand on more solid ground. After all, these portraits mirror our own gaze with a convincing likeness of human feature and expression, not to mention an exactness of hairstyle, clothing, and architecture that invites scholars to assign precise dates and locales and even to designate the subjects' identities. The London portrait, for example, was once believed to depict King Louis XI of France (1423–1483), an identification no longer credited.[63] More recently the same portrait has been linked, on the basis of the background architecture, to a certain Philippe Cottereau, appointed as Keeper of the Charters of Brabant in 1484.[64] Scholars even debate whether the subject of the New York portrait is also seen kneeling at the altar in the rear, or whether the subject of the London painting appears again within the same panel as the smaller image of a man approaching the church.[65] Serious inquiry about whether it is "the same person" simply underscores the fact that a lifelike image seems to document a real person, endowing him (or her) with a bodily presence and an apparent existence.

The striking verisimilitude of face and feature in early Flemish portraits, due largely to perspectival techniques and the ability of oil paints to capture light and texture with lifelike fidelity, is a major reason for their continuing appeal some five hundred years later: "Almost no other genre of painting is capable of transmitting such an intimate sense of lived presence over so great a distance in time. This undoubtedly is linked to our subconscious attribution to the portrait of authenticity: we expect a faithful rendering that shows us what the sitter was really like."[66] In its capacity to show us what persons were "really like," the portrait began to rival the book as a symbol of personal presence or identity. About a century after the Master of Sainte Gudule, Montaigne introduced himself in his *Essais* (1580) as both text and image: "It is myself that I portray. . . . I am myself the substance of my book. . . ." A similar equation of selfhood with both writing and portraiture appears in Montaigne's eulogy for his friend Étienne de la Boétie: "He alone partook of my true image, and carried it off with him. That is why I so curiously decipher myself."[67]

In the Flemish portraits, the seemingly true image of the man is strangely at odds with the emblem of the hidden or undeciphered self that he holds in his hands. If Renaissance portraiture "was thought to show not just someone's appearance but the soul through the appearance," the heart-shaped books in these paintings, with their indecipherable script, suggest that the soul ultimately remains hidden from view.[68] In addition, the pictorial book of the heart embodies a paradox noted earlier: interior writing presented in exterior form. The heart-shaped books in these portraits are in fact the one exception to the rule of verisimilitude that governs the rest of each panel. Unless we insist that they represent physical objects, the cordiform books are symbols, and not even disguised symbols at that. They occupy a space where the artist's usual fidelity to outward reality and even to "inward states" gives way to an almost surreal expressionism. In both portraits the front borders of the sitter's gown are rolled back suggestively to expose a row of ribbon ties running like a suture down his tunic, as if, inspired perhaps by Ignatius of Antioch or Henry Suso, he has plucked his own heart from his chest.

This surreal symbolism appears within an otherwise naturalistic arrangement of space and physical objects according to the laws of perspective, an external and material world of bodies and buildings where the sitter's dramatic gesture toward an interior world seems almost out of place, the symptom of an expressionism where personal "character" verges on caricature. Still, as an image of interiority, the open book in the foreground visually echoes the bodily and architectural interiors behind it, manifesting "the relations between interior and exterior space" that seem to have intensely interested the Master of Sainte Gudule.[69] The different interior and exterior views of the church in the two portraits even suggest that the artist may have been experimenting with physical space as a correlative for the subjective, interior space signified by the book, and of course embodied in the sitter himself.

In picturing the heart as a book, the human subject as a text, and subjectivity as reading and writing, the Master of Sainte Gudule gave striking expression to a quintessentially medieval metaphor of the self. And he was not the only artist of his time to render the self-text metaphor in terms of a heart-shaped book. A now-lost Flemish painting depicts a similar cordiform book held open by a female saint, Catherine of Alexandria, who carried a divine inscription on her heart, according to some medieval legends.[70] Ever since patristic authors like Augustine first elevated the codex to a symbol of the inner life, the book had been historically bound to the idea of the subject, of a personal presence. For much of the Middle Ages, the interior book mainly underwrote the subjectivity of a privileged clerical elite, until the romance, the saint's life, popular piety, and visual art greatly extended its social range and psychological applications. In translating what had long been a literary metaphor into a visual vernacular, the Master of Sainte Gudule significantly extended its imaginative reach and appeal. And the perfected visual metaphor appeared at a time, in the late fifteenth century, when the manuscript book—as both a written medium and a model of the inner self—was spreading to a much larger, more inclusive reading public, a public that soon was to grow even larger with the advent of the printed book. Indeed, the Flemish master documented the popularity of the manuscript codex as an image for the self, helping to ensure its further dissemination, at the very time when that image was about to be profoundly transformed.

## Chapter Eight

# *After*
# *GUTENBERG*

∾∾∾∾∾∾∾∾∾∾∾∾∾∾∾∾∾∾∾∾∾∾∾∾∾∾∾∾∾∾∾∾∾∾∾∾∾∾∾∾∾∾∾∾∾

*I*f the codex book is historically bound to the idea of the subject, of an interior presence, it needs to be stressed that during the Middle Ages this subject was conceived in essentially scribal terms. The book of the heart that appears in earlier chapters as a verbal trope, visual image, and physical artifact is the product of a manuscript culture, and the human subject it represents is accordingly imagined as the author, scribe, or reader of a manuscript book. The pre-Gutenberg trope is epitomized by the Flemish portrait in the previous chapter (figure 11) that shows the subject with not only a heart-shaped codex, but also a pen case and an inkwell, scribal tools that indicate a handwritten book. But this portrait of the scribe with a heart-shaped manuscript book was actually created several decades *after* the birth of printing and during a period of radical change in book production and use, as the older manuscript culture was giving way to a new typographical one.

The advent of movable type, which transformed the codex from a unique handmade artifact into a mass-produced object, also recreated the textual self in the image of the printed book, as evidenced by the new typographical connotations acquired by old psychological terms such as "imprint" and "impression." Even the Benedictine abbot Johannes Trithemius, who wrote a treatise *In Praise of Scribes* (1492) to promote the spiritual benefits of hand-copying books in the age of movable type, asserted that "every word we write we imprint [*imprimimus*] more forcefully on our minds"—apparently a typographical metaphor.[1] Commentators have seen irony in the fact that within two years of authoring his treatise, Trithemius had it printed for wider circulation. But the abbot's expediency is less ironic, given his educational goals, than the fact that he borrowed a metaphor from the new technology to recommend the old one, that the monastic mind nurtured by the traditional discipline of the hand-copied book was now to be modeled (in part, at least) on the qualities of the new printed one.

As the printing revolution altered the formal properties of the inner book, various religious, philosophical, and scientific trends revised its content and significance. In the moral and theological sphere, Protestant authors continued to relate the book of the heart to a heavenly exemplar even as they reconceived it in legal or financial terms that suggested a more worldly or secular self. At the same time, medical discoveries were beginning to demystify the heart, especially with William Harvey's revolutionary work in the early 1600s. And an emerging empiricist (and often materialist) psychology encouraged a more cerebral centering of the self, with the result that the book of the heart was increasingly rivaled by a book of the mind or brain. The book of the brain, substituting sensory experience for innate ideas and abandoning its relation to a heavenly original, represented a more secular, materialist, and autonomous subject—a truly modern self.

Just how the medieval book of the heart was transformed by such factors as printing, Protestantism, and empiricist psychology is a complex story that can only be outlined and briefly illustrated in this chapter.[2] The changes that took place between about 1500 and 1800 appear in a variety of literary forms, including lyric poetry, drama, religious and philosophical writings, and the novel. The novel in particular, as a distinctly modern and very popular genre, had a key role in extending questions of textual selfhood to a larger and more diverse readership than ever before, and thus in both domesticating and demystifying the book of the heart. The early novel often retained the older language of the heart but was also psychologically innovative, and it staged more vividly than any other genre the transition from a medieval to a modern book of the self.


## The Book of Conscience

The inherited notion of the heart as a book containing God's word, a devotional memory, or a moral record of the individual's life was well suited to the Protestant culture of individual Bible study and self-examination. For Protestants in particular, new hermeneutical models articulated by scholars such as Erasmus encouraged "a dynamic imitation or reproduction of Scripture" whereby the text was to be "wholly absorbed by the reader and located in the *pectus*, that intuitive focus of the self which is presumed to guarantee profound understanding and living expression."[3] Noting the reciprocity of heart and book in early Protestantism, Stephen Greenblatt describes how spiritual writings were "precisely designed to be absorbed," so that it is not always clear "where the book stops and identity begins." (The transplanted Protestant culture of colonial America continued this merging of self and text, as in the *New England Primer*'s hortatory couplet "My *Book* and *Heart* / Shall never part," which encouraged readers to incorporate its teachings.)[4] Although print is often seen as "a form of depersonalization" that reconstituted "the word of God in the age of mechanical reproduction," it actually reinforced the Protestant immediacy of self and text. As solitary reading replaced the communal rituals of auricular confession, the printed book acquired what Greenblatt calls "an intensity, a shaping power, an element of compulsion. . . ."[5] A complement to private devotional reading was the Protestant practice of introspection, of "reading" one's own heart (or conscience, a nearly synonymous term at the time) for signs of sin or grace, as reflected in the spiritual diaries and autobiographies that began appearing from about the middle of the seventeenth century.[6] Added to all this, the printing press was spreading the practices and mental habits of literacy among a much larger and more socially diverse populace. "It was natural," comments Frederick Kiefer, "that such a culture would increasingly conceive of experience in terms of books, that people would speak about their lives in language inspired by the print shop, library, or study."[7]

The Protestant intimacy with books is reflected by the many tropes that represent the heart as a small, personal, or portable text of some sort. Thus Thomas Pecke's poem "Cordial Prayer" (1659) urges, "Make a clean Heart thy devout Prayer-book," and Christopher Harvey's very popular *Schola cordis* (School of the Heart), first published in 1647, similarly asserts, "My Heart's my Prayer-book...."[8] In a 1593 treatise, Thomas Nashe enjoins the doubtful reader, "From thy birth to this moment of thine unbelief, revolve the diarie of thy memory"— where "diarie" suggests "a daily record of matters affecting the writer personally," the word's earliest sense in English.[9] And one of John Donne's sermons emphatically describes the individual's heart as a small, portable volume—"his manual, his bosom, his pocket book, his *Vade Mecum*, the Abridgement of all Nature, and all Law, his own heart, and conscience...."[10] Since Donne also imagined this book of the heart in typographical terms, as discussed later, he may be alluding to the small-format "pocket books" carried on one's person, or "bosom books" carried near the heart, that were common at the time.[11]

As for many other Protestant authors, Donne's book of the heart contains a divine law and so is partly authored by God. But when writers treat the book of the heart as a record of the individual life, they tend to stress its human and highly individual authorship. For example, in *The Conscionable Christian* (1623), Richard Carpenter invokes a kind of inner autobiography when he compares conscience to "a noble and divine power and faculty, planted of God in the substance of man's soul, working upon itself by reflection, and taking exact notice, as a Scribe or Register, and determining God's Viceroy and deputy, Judge of all that is in the mind, will, affections, actions, and whole life of man." Carpenter's metaphor turns overtly judicial as he describes how "conscience, as a Scribe or Notary, sitting in the closet of man's heart, with pen in hand, records and keeps a Catalogue or Diary of all our doings, of the time when, place where, the manner how they were performed, and that so clear and evident, that go where we will, do what we can, the characters of them cannot be cancelled or razed."[12] The double sense of the word "character," both textual and ethical, further emphasizes that each person is responsible for "writing" his own life.[13]

A 1649 sermon by the "Puritan" divine Thomas Watson likewise treats the conscience as an individually authored book that will be opened at the ultimate Trial: "Men have their sins written in their conscience; but the book is clasped: (the searing of the conscience is the clasping of the book:) but when this book of conscience shall be unclasped at the great day, then all their hypocrisy, treason, atheism, shall appear to the view of men and angels. . . ." This book is not the sole record of an individual's life, for "God not only observes, but registers, all our actions," as if keeping a "day-book." However, a person is fully responsible for everything in his own book, since only he has had access to this preeminently private text: "Are not thy sins written in the book of conscience? Hadst thou not that book in thy own keeping? Who could interline it?" [14] The secrecy or privacy of the inner book had been a medieval commonplace, but Protestant authors especially seem to have imagined this book as a personal possession or a kind of private property.

Some authors carefully distinguished, however, between the human "pages" of the inner book and the divine writing imposed upon them. For example, Christopher Harvey's *Schola cordis* (1647), where the heart is mainly a record of divine law, depicts God telling the believer: "A self-writ heart will not / Please me, or do thee any good, I wot, / The paper must be thine, / The writing mine." [15] This distinction is reinforced by the accompanying emblem, which shows an angelic scribe writing with a quill pen on a heart held by another figure that presumably represents its human owner (figure 12). Although entitled "The table of the Heart," this section of the work repeatedly evokes the heart as a codex book. Besides the quill pen in the emblem, the prefatory epigram mentions a heart consisting of "tender leaves of flesh," where "leaves" clearly suggest a codex; and the main poem goes on to stipulate that the value of the divinely inscribed heart "lies in the lines, not in the leaves of th' book." [16] Although orthodox and didactic in the extreme, the *Schola cordis* hints at the possibility of a more secular and autonomous inner book by its very denunciation of the "self-writ heart," a phrase that evokes the more worldly tropes that began to rival the old theological metaphor.

Protestant authors portrayed the heart or conscience not only as a prayer book, a diary or journal, and a legal record, but also under the more commercial image of an account book or ledger. The metaphor of a financial accounting was readily available in Scripture's moral vocabulary of "debts," "forgiveness," and "redemption," and it had been openly staged as a book of reckoning in the medieval morality play.

12. *The School of the Heart.* God's angelic scribe writes on the "leaves" of the human heart. Christopher Harvey, *The School of the Heart,* 3rd edition (1676), p. 102. William Andrews Clark Memorial Library, University of California, Los Angeles. Reproduced by permission.

The medieval Church, of course, had notoriously exploited the financial possibilities of penance. But Protestants, in some cases perhaps reflecting the mutual attraction of Calvinism and commerce, exhibited an unprecedented fondness for an expressly fiscal book of the heart. Robert Burton (writing in 1621) pictures conscience as "a great Ledger book wherein are written all our offences...."[17] John Downame (in 1604) warned of a final settling of accounts: "We know not how soon our Lord and master will call us to a reckoning and therefore it behoveth us to have our accompts always perfect and the books of our consciences made up in readiness."[18] And Thomas Watson, in *God's Anatomy upon Man's Heart* (1649), changes the monastic "collation" of manuscripts into a Protestant audit by detailing how God will compare the individual account book with a heavenly record: "God writes down, *Item* such a sin: and if the Book be not crossed, there will be a heavy reckoning; to every believer, the debt book is crossed, the black lines of sin are crossed out in the red lines of Christ's blood. . . ."[19]

Besides a ledger, the Protestant book of the heart could also take the form of a narrative, a discursive record, whose text even required deciphering. For example, Watson's "debt book" is also a kind of diary: "We cannot write our sins in so small or strange a character, but God can read them, he hath a key for them . . . we cannot read his handwriting: but He understands our Hearts without a commentary. . . . He hath an eye in your heart, He is *kardiognostes*."[20] While the "sin . . . crossed out" seems to reflect a financial troping of the Psalmist's plea that God "blot out" or "erase" his sins, the term *kardiognostes* (heartknower), which goes back to patristic times, suggests a heart containing a linear narrative of some sort.[21] Watson also differentiates the book of the human heart, which God can understand "without a commentary" however obscure its text, from the divine "hand-writing" in Scripture or the Book of Nature, which humans can understand only with a gloss. Like Carpenter, Watson uses "character" in a double sense, textual and ethical, adding the idea that what is inscribed on the heart is a cipher to which God alone holds the "key."[22] In the seventeenth century, "character" also meant a person's distinctive style of handwriting, so that here it may suggest the moral signature of the unique individual.[23] But however unique the "character" of each person's inner book, it still presumes a heavenly original that "God writes down" and that provides a "key" to its ultimate meaning.

John Donne's "pocket book" of the heart likewise features a cryptic or illegible text, which here represents the individual's self-deception and refusal to read or understand God's inner law. But Donne innovatively pictures the heart as a *printed* book with handwritten annotations:

This book, though he shut it up and clasp it never so hard, yet it will sometimes burst open of itself; though he *interline* it with other studies and knowledges, yet the Text itself, in the book itself, the testimonies of the conscience, will shine through and

appear: Though he load it and choke it with Commentaries and
questions, that is, perplex it with Circumstances and Disputations, yet the matter itself, which is *imprinted* there, will present
itself. . . .[24]

Although "imprinting" can refer to the older imagery of wax seals or
wax writing tablets, Donne's extended metaphor pointedly contrasts
"imprinted" words with "interlined" ones, suggesting a printed book
with handwritten insertions or additions.[25]

For centuries the formal features of the manuscript codex such as
its separate pages or chapters had been used to represent functional or
moral divisions in the psyche.[26] Since patristic times, authors had also
portrayed the divided book of the heart in terms of inconsistent scribes,
scripts, or inks. The printed book, as a new model for the book of the
heart, offered a new formal distinction that could be treated in moral
or psychological terms. Donne is one of the first writers to exploit the
possibilities of typography by dividing the "text" of the inner book
into script and print. In Donne's metaphor, the typographical ("imprinted") text represents the universal laws of God uniformly marked
on human hearts, while the handwritten ("interlined") text represents
individual doubts and excuses that obscure this divine knowledge and
that "choke" or "perplex" self-knowledge as well. Donne thus aligns
the printed word with truth and perspicuity, and handwriting with obscurity and even self-delusion.

Donne's divided book of the heart may also reflect his own divided
religious sensibility. Born a Catholic, Donne had converted to Protestantism in his twenties, and in his later years as an Anglican divine he
emphasized the link between the Church of the Fathers and the re-
formed Church of England across the divide that (in another sermon)
he calls "the middle age."[27] In the autobiographical *Pseudo-Martyr*
(1610), Donne even described his own conversion in textual terms: "I
had a longer work to do than many other men; for I was first to blot
out certain impressions of the Roman religion. . . ."[28] In the sermon
quoted above, the "Commentaries" and "Disputations" may hint pejo-
ratively at medieval scholasticism, and "interlining" at the medieval
biblical gloss in particular. Donne seems to locate the book of the heart,
and hence the human subject (and even himself), on the same historical
divide, at once both theological and textual. That is, he treats handwrit-

ing as a symbol of "medieval" error and obscurity, while equating the "modern" printed word with truth and clarity, with letters that "will shine through and appear"—despite a widespread recognition that printed books were often rife with errors.

On a lighter note, the contradictory inner book is amusingly portrayed in Robert Herrick's poem "To His Conscience," which begins with a familiar judicial metaphor: "Can I not sin, but thou wilt be / My private Protonotary?"—a protonotary being the chief secretary in a court of law.[29] Most of Herrick's eighteen-line lyric consists of appeals by the sinning self for leniency from the surveilling self: "Can I not woo thee to pass by / A short and sweet iniquity?" The sinful self even wonders if a bribe will work: "And wilt not thou, with gold, be tied / To lay thy pen and ink aside?" But in the end conscience is unyielding ("It will not be"), and the sinner must relent to escape censure.

Besides the mental tribunal, Herrick's poem calls up a long literary tradition of self-alienation, from Paul's divided self ("It is no longer I that do it, but sin which dwells within me" [Rom. 7.17]) to medieval debate poems where the higher self (soul, reason, etc.) condemns the lower (body, passions, etc.). But Herrick's dramatic monologue boldly reverses the usual ethical polarities, identifying the persona ("I") with the erring and inferior part of the self, and the judging, recording, and traditionally superior part with "thou." All of this may be simply a *jeu d'esprit* from the contrarian parson who, at the height of the Puritan revolution in 1648, published a huge collection of sensual verses— "Upon Julia's Clothes," "Upon the Nipples of Julia's Breast," and the like. But the speaker's identification with cupidity rather than conscience offers a rare dissenting voice (however tongue-in-cheek or enfolded in irony) from the dominant tradition, which equated the interior record of divine laws and human failings with one's "true" self. Long before Freud's concept of the superego, Herrick coyly suggests that conscience is less an "I" than a "thou," an intrusive other in the sanctum of the self, a legalistic voyeur intent on recording all.

Whether the Protestant book of conscience was pictured in narrative, financial, or legal terms, it represented a model of personal identity that was ultimately based on a heavenly book. Even Herrick's brief concluding mention of "the Judge" hints at the traditional dependency of self upon God, whereby personal identity and the ultimate significance of an individual's life are determined by the heavenly Author, Reader, and Interpreter. George Herbert, whose poetry is replete with divine inscriptions on the heart, suggests something similar in a poem entitled "Judgement," where God demands "every man's peculiar book," presumably the familiar record or ledger of conscience, but instead the speaker thrusts into God's hand "a Testament."[30] On the one hand, this gesture suggests "the undoing of the self as an independent entity" that is a hallmark of Herbert's poetry.[31] On the other hand, even this disappearing book of the self remains firmly related to God's writing. By the late seventeenth century, however, this was changing, as the book of the heart was revised into a more secular, autonomous text.

## The Unclasped Heart

A more secular book of the heart characterizes the early modern literature of romantic love, which often appropriated theological metaphors of the book for its own amorous or erotic purposes. Like its antecedents in the medieval love lyric and romance, this inner book is usually imagined as a record of sensual feelings, fantasies, or experience that can take various inscriptional forms, including an image, a name, or a narrative. The Petrarchan poetry that swept over Renaissance Europe carried such tropes everywhere. But important differences arose as the traditional book of the lover's heart was reimagined from the Renaissance to the eighteenth century in increasingly subjective, materialist, and egalitarian terms.

The lover's heart inscribed with an image of the beloved, a trope that passed from the troubadours through the *dolce stil nuovo* to Petrarch and his imitators, is common in Renaissance poets, often with a heightened eroticism. For example, a sonnet by the Elizabethan poet Giles Fletcher (c. 1548–1611) explains to an embarrassed mistress why she appears naked in a painting when she has never posed thus for the artist: "I showed my heart, wherein you printed were, / You, naked you, as here you painted are."[32] Although medieval poets had invoked the "heart" (imagination) as a gallery of erotic images, this frank sensuality is a far cry from the troubadour with his lady's face imprinted on his heart. Not only men but women, too, carry erotic imprints in their hearts, as in this passage from a Spenserian-style romance by Francis Rous (1598):

One Knight there was whom she above all wights
Most dearly lov'd, whose image deeply lies,
Sealed below upon her softened heart,
From which his pressure never can depart.[33]

The "pressure" (impression) on the lady's "softened heart" is at once
erotic and writerly, a suggestion of pen as penis (or vice versa) that has
ample medieval precedent. The painted or imprinted heart and its
erotic overtones similarly characterize the homoerotic (or homosocial)
liaison celebrated in Shakespeare's sonnets. Sonnet 24, for example,
compares the poet's eye to a painter who "hath steel'd, / Thy beauty's
form in table of my heart," so that the "true image" of the beloved still
hangs "in my bosom's shop" and is visible through the "windows" of
the eyes.[34]

The heart assumes a more booklike form when likened to a narrative
record of amorous experience along the lines of Petrarch's "story of my
suffering" or Dante's "book of my memory." In the famous opening
sonnet of Sidney's *Astrophil and Stella*, the frustrated poet finally turns
from seeking inspiration in "others' leaves" to reading—and transcribing—his own book of experience: "'Fool,' said my Muse to me, 'look
in thy heart and write.'"[35] Spenser's sonnet cycle, the *Amoretti*, opens
with an even more elaborate version of this metaphor, offering rhymes
to the lady on "leaves" that are "written with tears in heart's close
bleeding book"—where "close" indicates the secret, private nature of
the inner book, and "bleeding" its source in the lover's spiritual and
bodily suffering.[36] The inner book is also implied by a Restoration-era
song lyric referring to "the heart's unfeigned story" and a love poem by
Aphra Behn that features "the story of my Heart.[37]

Following another medieval precedent, Renaissance poets sometimes extended the imagery of the book from the inward to the outward person. Shakespeare, the first English poet to speak of "reading"
a person's character from both external appearance and the heart, often
resorts to bodily book metaphors.[38] For example, Lady Capulet's
speech to Juliet offers an extended portrait of the lover as a book:

Read o'er the volume of young Paris' face,
And find delight writ there with beauty's pen;
Examine every married lineament,

> And see how one another lends content;
> And what obscur'd in this fair volume lies
> Find written in the margent of his eyes.
> This precious book of love, this unbound lover,
> To beautify him, only lacks a cover.[39]

Here the "book" or "volume" comprehends the whole person, body and soul alike. Moreover, the lover's inner self ("what obscur'd in this fair volume lies") is not actually inscrutable but quite legible in his face ("the margent of his eyes"). Unlike the book of conscience, then, known only to God and the individual himself, the lover's heart sometimes can be "read" by others. At the same time, the "precious book of love" is here invested with a religious aura, with a hint of the lover as a sensual *logos*, a god made flesh.

But Shakespeare also presents the lover's heart as a more secret book that is opened to others only as a special confidence, as with the "unclasped" book of the heart in *Twelfth Night*. When Duke Orsino declares his love for Olivia to Viola (who is disguised as a man), "I have unclasp'd / To thee the book even of my secret soul," he also commands her to "unfold the passion of my love" to Olivia. The next scene continues the metaphor as Olivia questions Viola (acting as a go-between) about the Duke's professed love for her:

*Olivia.* Where lies your text?
*Viola.* In Orsino's bosom.
*Olivia.* In his bosom? In what chapter of his bosom?
*Viola.* To answer by the method, in the first of his heart.
*Olivia.* O, I have read it; it is heresy. Have you no more to say?[40]

The book of the heart equipped with a "clasp" to signify its personal, private content originates as a moral or religious trope with scholastic authors and reappears in writers such as Donne and Watson, as we have seen. The book of the heart "unclasped" to a lover or a go-between is thus a romantic counterpart to the book of conscience, which only the individual himself can "unclasp" to God. Here the allusions to exegetical "method" and doctrinal "heresy" coyly contrast the amorous book of the heart with a spiritual one, emphasizing its sensual content and even the absence of a divine or heavenly original.

The book of conscience is similarly co-opted by the amorous book of the heart in the early novel. The novel inherited certain features of the medieval romance and the Renaissance epic, but sometimes these borrowings returned as parody, as when the hero of *Don Quixote* (1604) professes his gratitude to an innkeeper's wife in absurdly elegant language: "Beauteous lady . . . , I shall bear the services you have done me eternally inscribed in my memory, so that I may remain grateful to you all the days of my life."[41] On the other hand, the book of the heart had a serious and central role in a novel such as Madame de Lafayette's *La Princesse de Clèves* (1678), which depicts how the heroine's ill-fated love for the Duc de Nemours begins when his appearance and actions make "a deep impression on her heart."[42] The trope accumulates significance as the princess reads a misplaced love letter that she believes Nemours to have written to another woman, only to learn that he is not its actual author. Her initial relief is followed by other more unsettling feelings: "Although the suspicions aroused by the letter had been wiped out [*effacez*], they had given her an idea of what it might be like to be deceived, and gave her feelings [*impressions*] of suspicion and jealousy she had never had before."[43] The ambiguous letter that was the object of the heroine's intense reading, rereading, and interpretation is thus transformed into a powerful metaphor of her own ambivalent psyche. As such, it suggests a close association between ideas and feelings, intellect and affect, as these mark the record of personal memory. Even if false ideas or mistaken beliefs are mentally "erased," they leave behind associated feelings that become an indelible part of one's experience. Impressions on the heart appear throughout de Lafayette's novel, and in reference to both male and female characters, who can never wholly obliterate certain feelings once they have been inscribed within.[44] In the final scene, the dying princess cannot erase from her heart either the alluring image of her absent lover or the reproachful memory of her dead husband—a double text, a book of conscience and book of passion, that together embody doubt and a sharply divided self.[45]

As the chivalric world of the romance gave way to the bourgeois world of the novel, the book of the heart lost its aristocratic cachet and was domesticated and democratized. Much as Protestant sermons and tracts carried the religious book of the heart into homes everywhere, the novel did so for its romantic counterpart. Reading—and writing on—the heart is an amorous commonplace of the eighteenth-century novel. Thus the heroine of Henry Fielding's *Amelia* (1751) hears her husband declare, "If you could look into my Breast, and there read all the most secret Thoughts of my Heart, you would not see one faint Idea to your Dishonour."[46] Here the "secret Thoughts" written in the lover's heart mimic the writings in the book of conscience, but they refer to a purely earthly passion.

The inscribed and legible heart is thematic to the novels of Samuel Richardson, who, as both a printer and a psychological novelist, was "acutely aware of *impressions*."[47] In *Clarissa* (1747–48), the relation of self to text is heightened by the heroine's personal letter diary, which she obsessively reads and rewrites in order to understand her own "heart." Clarissa also describes her own psyche in textual terms, as when recording that Lovelace "was disappointed that he had not made a more sensible impression upon me" or recalling "a dream which has made such an impression upon me" that "still the frightful images raised by it remain upon my memory."[48] The heroine of *Pamela* (1740) likewise keeps a diary to "sink the impression still deeper," but more for self-congratulation than self-examination.[49] Impressionable hearts also abound in *Sir Charles Grandison* (1753–54), where Miss Jervois treats the eponymous hero's face and heart alike as a veritable Scripture: "I do love to study him, and to find out the meaning of his very looks as well as words. Sir Charles Grandison's heart is the book of heaven—May I *not* study it?"[50] A woman's name can be in turn a sacred scripture in a man's heart: "Mr. Greville loves you more than you can possibly imagine.... [Y]our name is written in large letters in his heart."[51] In their moral aspect, the hearts of Richardson's characters often resemble a book of conscience, just as their letter writing recalls earlier Puritan writers who combined "writing in the heart" with an epistolarity that ultimately derives from the apostle Paul's inward "letter from Christ."[52] But when a woman determines to "study" a man's heart as a "book of heaven," theology is ironized in the service of sentiment. A later exception to the ironized book of conscience, one that marks a return to a more Puritan notion of the inner book, is Nathaniel Hawthorne's *Scarlet Letter* (1850), where biblical, Augustinian, and saintly precedents for the inscribed and legible heart vividly converge in Arthur Dimmesdale's "red stigma."[53]

Literary characters whose inward experience is formed substantially of "impressions" are not confined to the sentimental novel, nor are their impressions limited to matters of the heart. Indeed, a survey of eighteenth-century English novels suggests that authors are almost as likely to locate impressions in the "mind."[54] Even Richardson's heart-centered characters sometimes place romantic passion in a more cerebral location ("Love at first sight . . . must indicate a mind prepared for impression").[55] The reasons for this equivocation between heart and head include early modern developments in medical science and philosophy, including the rise of an empiricist psychology that in turn affected imaginative literature. Beginning already with Montaigne (who speaks of "deciphering" himself) and continuing with Hobbes, Locke, and Hume, the inner self began to be imagined less as an integral soul stocked with innate ideas and sustained by divine will than as the site of successive sensations (or "impressions") where the sole basis for personal identity was precisely the recollection of these feelings—what Georges Poulet has termed "*la mémoire affective*."[56] This new experiential self continued to be pictured in textual terms, but less often with reference to the heart than to the mind or brain.

## The Book of the Brain

The publication of William Harvey's treatise on the circulation of blood, *De motu cordis* (1628), marks an important stage in the modern demystification of the heart as a symbol of the self. Harvey's treatise—of which an English translation, *The Motion of the Heart,* appeared in 1653—offered a scientific or medical counterpart to the moral and religious "anatomies" of the heart in the seventeenth century. Early modern "natural histories" of the heart often combined physiology with poetic conceits about this organ as "the seat and fountain of life," "the sun of our body," and so forth. Similar conceits appear in Harvey's writings, but there the heart, with its auricles ("little ears") and ventricles ("little bellies") and its alternately vaginal and phallic propulsion of fluids, represents a miniature self, a homunculus, that is emphatically corporeal rather than spiritual—a place of motion, not emotion.[57] As one scholar says, "It was increasingly obvious from Harvey's work onward that the heart was a muscle best understood as a pump."[58]

Ancient authorities such as Plato and Galen had located the rational soul in the head, and some medieval authorities followed the Platonic-

Galenic tradition rather than the Aristotelian-Hippocratic one, which favored the heart.[59] If Harvey helped to vindicate the Galenic physiology by redefining the heart as a pump, Descartes (1596–1650) extended Platonic anthropology by locating the soul not just in the brain but specifically in the pineal gland.[60] The empiricists Locke and Hume also identified the self or consciousness with the brain (or "mind"), clearly shunning the language of the heart. In general, heart language—and the heart-centered self—held on longer among the writers and thinkers of the Catholic Counter-Reformation than among Protestants, who more readily embraced the New Science.[61] The modern "migration of the body's perceived center from the heart up to the head" has been attributed to "Western man's growing trust in reason."[62] But another factor may have been that as the motions of the heart were being revealed by anatomists like Harvey, the motions of the brain remained still largely mysterious. As scientists and philosophers transferred more and more of the human subject from the metaphysical to the material side of the ledger, the brain became a logical last resort for the self, soul, or essential "person."

Shakespeare reflects the shift from heart to head and its implications for the self-text metaphor. As we saw earlier, Shakespeare evokes a book of the heart, but he also refers interior writing to the brain. For example, Sonnet 59 cites the "brains" of poets, the "record" of memory, and the time when "mind at first in character was done"; apart from an etymological trace in "record," the heart is absent here. Sonnet 108 is even more exclusively cerebral, beginning, "What's in the brain that ink may character / Which hath not figur'd to thee my true spirit?" Sonnet 122 begins similarly, "Thy gift, thy tables, are within my brain / Full character'd with lasting memory," although it goes on to equivocate between "brain and heart" as the site of personal memory.[63] The notion of identity as personal memory, conceived in turn as a writing in the brain, points to a secular, immanent notion of the self rather than a transcendental concept of a divinely created soul.

The book of the brain is explicitly mentioned in *Hamlet,* a play that abounds with self-text metaphors, from the sentry's opening challenge, "Stand and unfold yourself," to the frequent and explicit imagery of reading, writing, tablets, and books throughout.[64] In act I, after the ghost of his father reveals the murder and vengefully commands him

to "remember me," Hamlet answers by vowing to write down his filial
duty in the book of his memory:

> Yea, from the table of my memory
> I'll wipe away all trivial fond records,
> All saws of books, all forms, all pressures past
> That youth and observation copied there,
> And thy commandement all alone shall live
> Within the book and volume of my brain. . . .

Here memory resides emphatically in the head (what Hamlet has
just termed "this distracted globe") and is figured expressly as "the
book and volume of my brain."[65] The sole trace of the heart in this
passage is the mention of "records," at most an implicit metaphor compared to the explicit book of the brain. Hamlet's use of the book-brain
metaphor also reflects the play's essential worldliness, which subordi-
nates Christian values to those of personal and political revenge. Hamlet's promise to write "thy commandement" within himself carries an
echo of Scripture. But, in a telling shift from religious to secular matters, the heavenly God writing a divine law in his creature is replaced
here by an earthly king and father dictating the law of retribution to
his son, and for political and dynastic reasons as much as for moral or
theological ones.

Toward the middle of the seventeenth century, even an empiricist
(and anti-metaphorical) philosopher such as Hobbes still could appeal
seriously to a "Law of Nature . . . written in every man's own heart," an
idea that remained current during the following century in writers from
Johnson to Rousseau.[66] But the empiricist notion that the mind held
no ideas except for those imprinted there by the senses, as articulated
by Aristotle and Aquinas, had already been reasserted in its general
form by influential authors such as Richard Hooker (1554?–1600), who
wrote that the human soul is "at the first as a book, wherein nothing is
and yet all things may be imprinted."[67] By the end of the seventeenth
century, the traditional book of the heart inscribed with innate ideas
was being seriously challenged by a model of the mind (or brain) as a
tabula rasa bearing only the sense impressions of experience, as formulated more precisely by Locke.[68] Locke's picture of the mind as a book

of experiential "impressions" swept the philosophical field and had a shaping influence on imaginative literature throughout the next century and a half.

Early in his *Essay Concerning Human Understanding* (1690), Locke roundly rejected the Platonic theory of innate ideas marked on the soul before birth, the "received Doctrine, That Men have native *Ideas,* and original Characters stamped upon their Minds, in their very first Being." Locke pictured the mind instead as a cumulative record of sense experience from infancy on. Rather than Aristotle's tabula rasa, however, Locke likened the mind to "white Paper, void of all Characters, without any *Ideas.* . . ."[69] The "white Paper" of the mind receives the "impressions" produced both by the senses and the internal processes of thought. Locke's account of the latter illustrates how he places the mental self securely in the head: "The memory of Thoughts, is retained by the impressions that are made on the Brain, and the traces there left after such thinking. . . ."[70] As a recent commentator notes, Locke "generally avoids using 'heart' language in his exposition of the understanding," and throughout the *Essay* he "uses the term 'imprint,' first to deny that innate ideas or principles are impressed by the 'finger of God' into the mind or heart, then to indicate all the impressions made upon human sensation by the force of external objects."[71]

Locke's vocabulary of "impressions," "characters," and "stamping" often seems to owe more to the printed—than to the handwritten— word. As Charles Taylor remarks, "Locke *reifies* the mind to an extraordinary degree," and one of his favorite metaphors is "a quasi-mechanical process, a kind of imprinting on the mind through impact on the senses."[72] In this, Locke's metaphors reflect the "print logic" that had slowly spread through society after Gutenberg and that was clearly established in England by around 1700, according to one recent assessment.[73] In her study of printing and its cultural effects, Elizabeth Eisenstein suggests that the new technology of the written word may have encouraged a parallel mechanization of the human body: "The use of the same visual devices to delineate machine parts and human organs—both hidden from readers before—may have encouraged new analogies between pump and heart or between mechanical piping and plumbing and human venous or arterial systems."[74] Regarding psychology, Walter Ong similarly claims that print culture "encouraged human beings to think of their own interior conscious and unconscious resources as more and more thing-like, impersonal and reli-giously neutral."[75] Relocated from heart to head, transformed from a handwritten to a printed text, the modern book of the self tended to abandon its religious or romantic sources and turned resolutely secular, a textual self conceived as the subject of knowledge, perception, or mere sensations that had lost its basis in traditional metaphysics.

During the next century, Locke's picture of the mind as a quasi-mechanical record of impressions became the norm for educated Eu-rope and was extended further by philosophers such as Hume and Condillac. The influence of empiricist psychology on the novel's themes and narrative modes is well attested. The original title of Jane Austen's *Pride and Prejudice* (1813)—"First Impressions"—has been traced not only to the sentimental novel (the phrase occurs repeatedly in Richardson), but also to Hume's philosophical doctrine of "impres-sions."[76] The most famous novelistic debt to empiricist psychology is doubtless Laurence Sterne's *Tristram Shandy* (1760–67), which cites Locke by name several times and employs the association of ideas as an explicit plot hinge.[77] However, another very popular novel of time, Charles Johnstone's *Chrysal, or the Adventures of a Guinea* (1760–65), il-lustrates even more overtly the impact of empiricist psychology on eighteenth-century ideas about literary "character" and the nature of the human subject.

Johnstone's novel, an example of what has been called "panoramic fiction," is the history of a gold coin as told by a spirit (Chrysal) that accompanies its progress through the world, beginning with the miner who digs up the ore.[78] Chrysal first enters the miner's heart to "read the events of his life, which I doubted not but I should find deeply im-printed there"; but the miner's heart is filled with the love of gold, and so Chrysal travels to the head, "into the *censorium* of his brain," where "the spirit of consciousness, which you call SELF," is busily engaged in "running over a number of *niches*, or impressions, on the fibres of the brain."[79] This spirit, who is of female form but fundamentally andro-gynous ("Every spirit is of both sexes, but as the female is the worthier with us, we take our denomination from that" [9]), explains her actions to Chrysal as follows:

> This place, where we are, is the seat of memory; and these traces,
> which you see me running over thus, are the impressions made

on the brain by a communication of the impressions made on
the senses by external objects.—These first impressions are
called *ideas*, which are lodged in this repository of the memory, in
these marks, by running which over, I can raise the same *ideas*,
when I please, which differ from their first appearance only in
this, that, on their return, they come with the familiarity of a
former acquaintance. (10)

Exactly how alterations in the physical brain can raise ideas in the immaterial mind is coyly said to be "not quite fully settled among the
learned" (10). But without the continual touching of these impressions,
"a man would no longer continue the same person, for in this acquaintance, which is called *consciousness*, does all personal identity consist"
(10–11). The author's own footnote to this passage cites Locke.[80]

Chrysal's fantastic voyage into the human psyche takes a further
twist when the spirit refers to "this man whom, as I am *his self*, I shall
henceforth, for conciseness and perspicuity, call *my self* . . ." (11). Here
the rhetorical shifts of literary fiction turn into dizzying philosophical
perspectives, as personal identity or consciousness dissolves and re-
forms around the grammatically promiscuous "self." The shifting pronouns suggest not only the infinite regress of any homuncular psychology, but also the potential interchangeability of grammatical persons
(and genders). At the same time, the eighteenth-century orthography
sets apart the *self* as if to suggest an irreducible being that, like a scholastic essence, can be separated from the accidents of person and gender.
But the empiricist self is an autonomous secular text that does not pre-
sume a divine original. And the eternal soul inscribed with indelible
divine laws and personal records, the book of the heart or conscience,
has been exchanged for memorial impressions on the tabula rasa of the
mind or brain that are now the sole guarantee of personal identity.

## Chapter Nine

# CODEX *or* COMPUTER?

❖❖❖❖❖❖❖❖❖❖❖❖❖❖❖❖❖❖❖❖❖❖❖❖❖❖❖❖❖❖❖❖❖❖❖❖❖❖❖❖❖❖

The notion of the individual psyche as a unique and secret yet somehow legible text lingered into modernity. But even as the book of the heart was gradually displaced by the book of the mind or brain, textual tropes as a whole were increasingly rivaled by metaphors drawn from other technologies. Especially after the Industrial Revolution, the human mind came to be modeled on an engine or a machine. And the mechanical self of the nineteenth century was in turn transformed by the electronic and media revolutions of the twentieth, as new psychological metaphors from the movies, television, and the computer entered popular use. At the turn of the millennium we casually talk of mental "software," brain "circuitry," and even people who are "missing a chip." Or we treat our mental life as a movie, experiencing events in "slow motion," "replaying" our memories, and offering our "take" on things. Nor are these verbal effects of social and technological change limited to popular culture or speech ways. A conceptual revolution in the cognitive sciences has enshrined the computer as the dominant metaphor for the human psyche, completing the break with a long tradition of textual metaphor that stretches back to antiquity.

In this concluding chapter, I first examine some modern continuations of the old textual trope, especially the metaphor of the palimpsest, a manuscript containing more than one layer of writing, which nineteenth-century authors used to picture hidden memories or feelings and which psychoanalysis applied in a more technical sense to the notion of the unconscious. Second, by way of summarizing one of this book's key themes, I consider the ideology of the codex that from the early Middle Ages until quite recent times has reinforced the power and appeal of textual metaphors. Finally, turning to industrial and post-industrial culture, I discuss how machines and the modern media inspired new and very popular personal metaphors that have largely eclipsed the old idea of the self as text and that may signal the demise of a certain notion of the self altogether.

## Palimpsests

During the nineteenth century, the book of the brain became in turn a "palimpsest," as modeled on a manuscript that had been erased and reused in ancient or medieval times (when parchment was expensive), but whose original script could be recovered in the laboratory.[1] A mental palimpsest thus contained multiple "layers" of memory or experience, each superimposed on the last but all equally indelible. Although the palimpsest evoked the pre-Gutenberg manuscript book, as a metaphor it was meant to suggest the complex and cryptic "modern" mind, as well as the promise of modern science to uncover and decipher the hidden traces of an earlier age—collective or individual.

For example, in *Aurora Leigh* (1857), Elizabeth Barrett Browning describes how the innate and divine ideas in the human "soul" are overwritten by the sensations of bodily life:

> Let who says
> "The soul's a clean white paper," rather say,
> A palimpsest, a prophet's holograph
> Defiled, erased and covered by a monk's,—
> The apocalypse, by a Longus! poring on
> Which obscene text, we may discern perhaps

Some fair, fine trace of what was written once,
Some upstroke of an alpha and omega
Expressing the old scripture.[2]

On this essentially Neoplatonic view (which rejects Locke's empiricist "white Paper" of the mind), the "obscene" monastic script represents bodily experience that obscures the "fair, fine trace" of man's intimations of immortality, as well as the divine beginning and end of human life suggested by "alpha and omega."

Thomas De Quincey employs a less metaphysical but more elaborate version of the same metaphor in *Suspiria de Profundis* (1845), a sequel to his *Confessions*. In keeping with a modern cerebral psychology, De Quincey adapts the palimpsest metaphor not to the soul or heart but the brain, picturing individual memory as successive layers of experience preserved in the mind like texts inscribed on and then erased but never wholly obliterated from a parchment: "What else than a natural and mighty palimpsest is the human brain? Such a palimpsest is my brain; such a palimpsest, oh reader! is yours. Everlasting layers of ideas, images, feelings, have fallen upon your brain softly as light. Each succession has seemed to bury all that went before. And yet, in reality, not one has been extinguished."[3]

Like Browning, De Quincey concedes the ultimately divine origin of this inner human text—"our own heaven-created palimpsest, the deep memorial palimpsest of the brain. . . ." But for him the palimpsest of the brain represents not the divine ideas inscribed on the soul prior to birth, but rather the fundamental "human unity" of life's accumulated experiences that form a person from birth onward. Indeed, De Quincey lays special stress on the childhood traumas that are preserved, like ancient writing, on the palimpsest of memory: "the deep, deep tragedies of infancy, as when the child's hands were unlinked for ever from his mother's neck, or his lips for ever from his sister's kisses, these remain lurking below all, and these lurk to the last." In contrast to the chemicals used to treat manuscript palimpsests, "alchemy there is none of passion or disease that can scorch away these immortal impresses. . . ." De Quincey cites his own recurring dream of his sister's funeral to illustrate that no feeling or experience is ever fully erased from the mind.

Like Augustine, founder of the confessional autobiography, De Quincey invokes a private and interior record of experience—here, a palimpsest of memory—that provides in turn the basis for his external, published account. More important, De Quincey's evocation of "the deep, deep tragedies of infancy" that "remain lurking below all" strikingly anticipates psychoanalysis, which arrived on the scene toward the end of the century and used the same palimpsest metaphor to describe the unconscious. The key term made a quasi-technical appearance in an 1893 essay on dream interpretation by the English psychologist James Sully: "Like some palimpsest, the dream discloses beneath its worthless surface-characters traces of an old and precious communication."[4] Freud in turn footnotes Sully's comment in a passage of *The Interpretation of Dreams* (1900) where he distinguishes between a dream's "manifest" and "latent" content.[5] A textual model of the mind is explicit in Freud's discussion of dream "revision" (*Bearbeitung*), which compares dream interpretation to the deciphering of "enigmatic inscriptions" that are "intended to make the reader believe that a certain sentence—for the sake of contrast, a sentence in dialect and as scurrilous as possible—is a Latin inscription."[6] In Freud's metaphor, the apparently innocent Latin inscription represents the conscious (manifest) dream-text, and the "scurrilous" sentence its censored (latent) content, much as manuscript palimpsests were often shown to conceal "pagan" texts overwritten by Christian ones.

Freud also used a modified palimpsest metaphor to describe the unconscious in his 1925 essay "A Note upon the 'Mystic Writing-Pad.'" The device in question consists of a thin tablet of wax, covered by several transparent sheets that can be marked by a stylus and then lifted to "erase" the writing. Freud likens the faint traces of writing that remain on the tablet, like the underwriting in a palimpsest, to unconscious memories that are never wholly "erased" from the psyche: "I do not think it is too far-fetched to compare the celluloid and waxed paper cover with the system *Pcpt.-Cs.* [perception and consciousness] and its protective shield, the wax slab with the unconscious behind them, and the appearance and disappearance of the writing with the flickering-up and passing-away of consciousness in the process of perception."[7] Freud describes the mystic pad as "a return to the ancient method of writing on tablets of clay or wax," without noting that the writing tablet also served as a psychological *metaphor* in antiquity. But he regards the mystic pad as the superior writing tool because it combines the permanence of a paper record with the infinite capacity of an erasable slate, qualities that also recommend the mystic pad as a psychic metaphor. With its double-layered structure, the writing pad illustrates the conjoined yet distinct functions of the conscious and the unconscious minds. Freud's metaphor even accounts for the process of recovering unconscious memories, for the traces of writing remaining on the lower tablet are, he notes, "legible in suitable lights." Accordingly, to read the Freudian self is to discern the faint signs of the unconscious psyche that are all but obliterated in the conscious mind.

It is no coincidence that the multilayered, fragmentary, or cryptic mind also figures in the modern novel. Sometimes ambiguity or obscurity inheres less in the psyche itself than in the attempts to interpret it, as when Edith Wharton, in *The House of Mirth* (1905), presents her heroine Lily Bart as "a keen reader of her own heart," although others find that "in interpreting Miss Bart's state of mind, so many alternative readings were possible. . . ."[8] But avant-garde writers increasingly pictured the psyche as a multilayered text that remained mysterious even to its own possessor. In Virginia Woolf's novel *To the Lighthouse* (1927), nearly contemporary with Freud's essay on the "Mystic Writing-Pad," the mind is an obscure text that even takes different forms in men and women. Typical of the male characters in Woolf's novel, James Ramsay searches his book of memory, "the infinite series of impressions which time had laid down, leaf upon leaf, fold upon fold softly, incessantly upon his brain."[9] In contrast, Woolf renders the female psyche as an inscribed heart (a traditionally more "feminine" organ than the brain) that is not modeled on the codex or even the scroll, but rather a much more archaic form of writing—namely, ancient Egyptian tablets. Thus Lily Briscoe, contemplating Mrs. Ramsay, "imagined how in the chambers of the mind and heart of the woman who was, physically, touching her, were stood, like the treasures in the tombs of kings, tablets bearing sacred inscriptions, which if one could spell them out, would teach one everything, but they would never be offered openly, never made public."[10] Inscribed within a feminine interior that is both womb and tomb, these hieroglyphics of the self are remote and mysterious. As "sacred inscriptions" that may never be "spelled out," they represent a knowledge or wisdom that is older and better but also less accessible than that embodied by the "masculine" book of the brain. Yet Lily seeks something that transcends language and can never be fully represented by it: "It was not knowledge but unity that she desired, not inscriptions on tablets, nothing that could be written in any language known to men, but intimacy itself, which is knowledge. . . ."

Besides psychoanalysis, other modern schools of psychology have also posited textual models of the mind, from the theory of "imprinting" formulated by Konrad Lorenz to the "palimpsest phenomenon" cited in recent clinical studies of depression.[11] But psychoanalysis, which has claimed for itself the role of Champollion in deciphering the Rosetta stone of the mind, characteristically insists on recovering the lost text of repressed memories. One of Freud's most influential successors, Jacques Lacan, who famously declared that the unconscious is structured like a language, also portrayed the unconscious specifically as a written text: "The unconscious is that chapter of my history that is marked by a blank or occupied by a falsehood; it is the censored chapter. But the truth can be rediscovered; usually it has already been written down elsewhere."[12] These written clues include such things as inscribed "monuments" (the body) and "archival documents" (childhood memories). By such means, each person must reclaim his own history through a kind of introspective philology, first recovering the "text" by examining "the traces that are inevitably preserved by the distortions necessitated by the linking of the adulterated chapter to the chapters surrounding it," and then interpreting this text by a process in which "meaning will be re-established by my exegesis."

Lacan's picture of the mind as a unique and cryptic text recalls many features of the traditional book of the heart, especially the notion of the individual's life as a secret or obscure narrative that requires some sort of code, key, or gloss. But the inner book of Lacan's secular psychoanalytic subject has lost not only one of its "chapters," but also the metaphysical (and perhaps even the moral) function it had in an earlier theological age—not to mention the divine and transcendental Exegete whose interpretation once provided the last word on the book of the self. So now the human author of the inner book must also serve as its ultimate interpreter, and the book's final meaning, once its missing parts have been restored, will be determined solely by "my exegesis."

## The Ideology of the Book

Both psychoanalysis and the modern novel evoke a textual notion of selfhood and personal identity that was long associated with the book in its most familiar form, the codex. The ideology of the codex originated in late antiquity, when writers began to endow this new and ascendant form of the book with an aura of personal presence and unique subjectivity. The scholastic Middle Ages enshrined the manuscript codex as its preeminent psychological metaphor, and modernity continued to invest the codex book, in its printed form, with human qualities in general and with the attributes of unique selfhood in particular. A classic expression of this ideology, as it came to characterize both literary modernism and modern literary theory, appears in Stéphane Mallarmé's essay "Le Livre, Instrument Spirituel" (1895), which celebrates the printed book as a vessel of pure mind or spirit (*l'âme, l'esprit*, or *la conscience*).[13]

Mallarmé treats the book as a container and emphasizes that its foldings ( *pliage*) endow it with a kind of human presence. These foldings, he says, have "an almost religious significance" and "form a tomb in miniature for the soul," while at the same time the uncut pages possess a "virginal" quality. But whatever its bodily or even sexual qualities, the book represents mainly an incorporeal self, for it is possessed by "consciousness alone." Hence Mallarmé regards the book as a "spiritual instrument" through which the poet inscribes himself on the minds of his readers: "From time immemorial the poet has knowingly placed his verse in the sonnet which he writes upon our minds or upon pure space." Although a manifesto of modern poetics, Mallarmé's essay echoes the scholastic ideal of the book as a universal model when he declares that "all earthly existence must ultimately be contained in a book." The essay's setting, "a garden bench where a recent book is lying," even recalls the scene of Augustine's conversion. Yet Mallarmé's spiritual book is a modern, printed artifact whose perfection lies partly in its mechanical reproduction, where "typography becomes a rite." Mallarmé even frowned on italic type (modeled by Renaissance printers on manuscript calligraphy) as being too much like handwriting.[14] For him, it would seem, the codex symbolized less the idiosyncratic person than an idealized poetic self.

Mallarmé's remarks on the book as an alter ego were later echoed by Georges Poulet in an essay entitled "Phenomenology of Reading" (1969). Citing a Mallarmé story that features an empty room with a book lying on a table, a mere object, Poulet compares books to animals in cages waiting for a buyer to deliver them from objecthood: "They wait. Are they aware that an act of man might suddenly transform their existence? They appear to be lit up with that hope. Read me, they seem to say." For Poulet, one of many in a long line of writers to have invested the physical book with human qualities (Petrarch treated his cherished volumes of Cicero as personal friends), the book is virtually alive: "I realize that what I hold in my hands is no longer just an object, or even simply a living thing. I am aware of a rational being, of a consciousness; the consciousness of another. . . ."[15]

In recent decades, many theorists have further attested the book's centrality to Western notions of the subject by attacking precisely such "logocentric" equations of self and text. About the same time that Poulet professed to find appealing subjectivities in books, Jacques Derrida was denouncing the "metaphysics of presence" that had haunted Western ideas about writing for more than two millennia, ever since writing (as reified speech) had been equated with subjectivity: "From Plato and Aristotle on, scriptural images have regularly been used to *illustrate* the relationship between reason and experience, perception and memory," always under the assumption that writing as a known quality could represent the mysterious psyche. Derrida further noted that Freud, in a characteristically modern turn, instead equated the psyche with writing as a sign of the *unknown*, the enigmatic, using "metaphorical models which are borrowed not from spoken language or from verbal forms, nor even from phonetic writing, but from a script which is never subject to, never exterior and posterior to, the spoken word. . . ." And if "what we believe we know under the name of writing" remains "enigmatic," this raises a new question: "Not if the psyche is indeed a kind of text, but: what is a text, and what must the psyche be if it can be represented by a text?"[16]

Deconstruction has been likened to a neutron bomb that eliminates the human subject from the text (or book) and leaves only empty structures standing. In addition to banishing the subject from the text, poststructuralism also exploded the book itself as a literary object. According to Derrida, "the idea of the book," a largely medieval legacy, implied self-contained and totalized orders of myth, ideology, and culture ("The idea of the book is the idea of a totality . . ."), whereas writing (*écriture*) was an open field of signs having in principle no stable, predetermined meanings, and defying codification under a transcendental subject.[17] The idea of the book had enabled the Middle Ages to canonize and attribute to a single divine Author the diverse writings collected in Scripture, and likewise to codify the so-called "books" of nature, history, and the self.

A further challenge to the book came from Roland Barthes, who declared (in 1971) that literary criticism should shift its attention away from the "work" and toward the "text"; that is, away from the discrete unit of library shelf space occupied by the book—finite, self-contained, and traditionally full of intrinsic meaning—to the open field of signs unconstrained by old-fashioned kinds of closure or significance.[18] But just as Derrida seemed to ignore how the medieval book, as the product of an often decentralized scribal culture, anticipated certain characteristics of *écriture*, Barthes, in assuming the book's typographical integrity, failed to recognize that his more porous "text" had already existed in the Middle Ages by virtue of the same scribal culture, and that the discrete and self-contained "work" from which he would free it was largely a historical product of the printing press.

Nonetheless, these theoretical moves eerily anticipated the practical challenges to the book brought on by the personal-computer revolution of the 1980s, when desktop publishing began to rival the traditional system of book production and sales, and when hypertext promised (or threatened) to replace the physical book itself with a worldwide network of electronic texts that challenged every norm of traditional book culture, from copyright laws to obscenity codes. In some ways, the computer, and the PC in particular, may actually reinforce the identification of self with text that in different forms has shaped the evolution of Western subjectivity since the dawn of literacy. At the same time, however, the electronic word weakens the link between the individual and the printed book that has lasted for five hundred years, and the link between the individual and the codex that stretches back for some fifteen hundred, thus challenging traditional book-based concepts of the self as well.[19]

It is no small irony that writing—which Plato denounced in the early days of Western literacy as an alien technological threat to man's

essential being (reason, memory, the soul)—is often held up today in
the form of the codex book as a symbol of the "human" qualities supposedly threatened by newer technologies, especially the computer. As
Richard Lanham observes in a recent collection of essays (available in
both print and hypertext), the codex has long been regarded as essential
to Western culture and to certain ideas about the self. But the electronic word reduces the codex book to being an obsolete "container"
of texts that can be stored, transmitted, and used in other ways. As a
result, "our assumption that the book is the natural and only vehicle
for a written text has been irreparably shaken," and with it certain notions of the self that have long been associated with the book. For many
people, the codex is not only a precious cultural object, but also a repository of the self. In Lanham's hyperbolic paraphrase of such attitudes, "The book itself is sacred. . . . The codex book creates the vital
central self. The codex book defines human reason. Our cultural vitals
are isomorphic with the codex book. Its very feel and heft and look and
smell are talismanic. We must have an agency of the federal govern-
ment to protect it."[20] For Lanham, the question is not whether the
codex ultimately can be saved (it cannot), but whether the sort of experience and the kind of self traditionally associated with it are available
by other textual means. But what if the written word in its ghostly electronic form no longer provides a coherent center for a culture increasingly rapt in its oral and visual sensorium of TV, MTV, video games,
and movies? And what if instead of books or texts we happen to model
ourselves and our inner lives on the media and machines of a postmodern era?

## Changing Our Minds

Thomas Hobbes, one of the prophets of modernity, wrote sanguinely
in *Leviathan* (1651) that "NATURE . . . is by the *Art* of man, as in many
other things, so in this also imitated, that it can make an Artificial Animal." For Hobbes, "*Automata* (Engines that move themselves by springs
and wheels as doth a watch) have an artificial life," while living beings
are essentially machines: "For what is the *Heart* but a *Spring*; and the
*Nerves*, but so many *Strings* . . . ?"[21] Hobbes's mechanistic language was
not unusual at the time, when it was being adopted even by thinkers

still committed to an older cosmology.[22] The mechanistic bent of the age is illustrated by the history of the word "engine." Ultimately derived from Latin *ingenium* (wit, genius), the English word referred to both mental powers and mechanical devices from its first appearance (around 1300), but by the seventeenth century its mechanical sense had returned to psychology, now as a *metaphor*. Thus a 1633 play refers to "the engine of [the] brain," where "engine" means not "wit" but something more mechanical; and a 1664 treatise on natural philosophy specifies the animal spirits as "the chief Engine of Sight."[23]

The mental tropes spun off by the Industrial Revolution show especially well that psychology often follows technology. Steam power inspired many psychic metaphors still used today, of which "to blow off steam" is the most common.[24] Steam metaphors turn up even in the Romantic poets, those supposed enemies of industrialism. Shelley, who was fascinated by actual steam engines, wrote (in 1820) of the "self-impelling steam-wheels of the mind."[25] Victorian medical science adopted similar metaphors, as in an 1899 textbook that refers to the "shutting off of nervous steam."[26] The dynamo, another symbol of nineteenth-century industrial pride, exerted a more subtle power as a moral and psychological trope.[27] In 1892 George Meredith evoked another writer's "whirring dynamo of a brain," and the critic Edward Dowden wrote (in 1904) of how "any stream of moral electricity worked from a dynamo of the will."[28] In the twentieth century, the boiler and the dynamo lost some of their prestige to a new symbol of mechanical power, the internal combustion engine, as embodied in the ubiquitous automobile. The inroads of industrialism into popular psychology are nowhere clearer than in the many automotive expressions that came into vogue during the 1920s and that are still used today, from "all revved up" to "missing on a cylinder."[29]

Around the turn of the century, the founders of psychoanalysis were also using technical metaphors to describe their new science of the mind. Some of their favorite terms are "mechanism," "apparatus," "energy," "inertia," "excitation," "discharge," "condensation," "displacement," "resistance," and (perhaps their most important legacy) "repression."[30] Whereas Freud devoted his early efforts to "explaining mental phenomena in physiological and chemical terms," his collaborator Josef Breuer favored "parallels between the nervous system and electrical installations."[31] For example, in a treatise on hysteria that he coauthored with Freud (1893–95), Breuer likened cerebral activity "to a telephone line through which there is a constant flow of galvanic current. . . . Or better, let us imagine a widely-ramified electrical system for lighting and the transmission of motor power. . . ."[32] Clearly, scientific and mechanical analogies shaped the concepts and vocabulary of psychoanalysis as much as, if not more than, textual metaphors such as the palimpsest or writing tablet that hearkened back to a more humanistic or spiritual past.

Between about 1850 and 1925, other mental metaphors inspired by the modern visual media, especially photography and the movies, further altered our self-concepts and psychological language.[33] The photographic camera has been used metaphorically for the human eye since at least the 1930s and is derived from the older camera obscura, used figuratively in the same sense.[34] Although the camera can also stand for the entire psyche or self ("I am a camera," wrote Christopher Isherwood, "with its shutter open, quite passive, recording, not thinking"[35]), it is the images it produces that have been most thoroughly appropriated by psychology. The word "photograph" took on a psychological sense already in the 1860s, as did "snapshot" about a century later.[36] Although the phrase "mental picture" predates photography by a few years, it rapidly acquired photographic connotations as painting lost its documentary role to the camera.[37] And although the phrase "photographic memory" is not attested until 1940, by the turn of the century photography was already synonymous with exact mental recall and even with the "automatic" working of the unconscious mind ("A negative of a street scene, taken unconsciously when I was absorbed in other thoughts, rose in my memory with not a feature blurred . . .").[38] A century later, color photography sets the standard of mental imagery, as when scenes from an imaginary vacation are likened to "a loop of Kodachrome film in my mind."[39]

Modern medical imaging, beginning with the X ray, also helped to weaken the book as a metaphor of selfhood by offering powerful new representations of the human interior. At the end of the nineteenth century, the X ray seized the popular imagination by probing the inner recesses of the human body, a modern scientific counterpart to the all-seeing eye of God imagined by a more theological age.[40] Thomas Mann suggested as much in *The Magic Mountain* (1924), where the doctor who X-rays Hans Castorp offers his patient a copy of the photograph, saying that it reveals "the secrets of your bosom."[41] Here the book of the heart is replaced by a chest X ray.

Compared with the various forms of still photography, the motion picture has left an even wider trail of popular psychological metaphor. In a few cases, film has inspired or reinforced textual metaphors, as with "clichéd" characters or "scripted" behavior.[42] But its main legacy to popular thought and speech has been a host of visual tropes, from "take" (a synonym for viewpoint, as in, "What's your take on that?") and "flashback" (used of personal memories) to "slow motion" (applied to either perception or memory) and "montage" (similar applications).[43] Film, along with audiotape and videotape, has also popularized the metaphor of the "replay," now commonly heard in reference to memories, fantasies, and personal experience in general.[44] Movie and video metaphors have even redefined the novel; no longer are literary characters and their inner lives necessarily constructed from textual metaphor like those that seemed essential to Virginia Woolf. Instead, the conscious or unconscious mind is a machine that cannot always be turned off: "I lay awake for a while, doing an involuntary replay of that horrible dream. . . ."[45] Similarly, the author of a recent memoir recalls long-past events so fresh in his mind that (in a metaphor from televised sports) "they have the quality of instant replay."[46]

Lewis Lapham has described how film and other visual media tend to reduce the role of words in the cultural sensorium: "Instead of narrative we have montage, and our perceptions being tuned to the surfaces of film rather than to the structures of print, we tell one another stories not by lining up rows of words but by making connections . . . between the film loops stored in our heads. Words define themselves not as signs of a specific meaning but as symbols bearing lesser or greater weights of cinematic association, and history becomes a form of film criticism."[47] Not only personal memory and cultural history, but also science is reconceived in cinematic terms, at least on a popular level. For example, in his book *Wonderful Life* (1989), Stephen Jay Gould imagines the possibility of "replaying" the "tape" of evolution, a video metaphor based on the film allusion in his title, to illustrate the argument that species evolve as they do because of cascading contingencies that would never repeat themselves again in precisely the same way if we *could* "replay the tape."[48] Thus we are invited to imagine human biological history as part of a movie that might have had a very different plot.

Even the word "evolution," originally referring to an unrolled scroll and one of several textual metaphors adapted to biology (e.g., the "fossil record"), becomes synonymous here with the rolling of a videotape or film.[49]

But movie metaphors, which belong to a mechanical age, are themselves losing ground to computer metaphors, which are based on the preeminent symbol of high-technology culture. Especially with the arrival of the aptly (or ominously) named "personal computer" in millions of offices and homes, many people now regularly talk about themselves in electronic terms as they "access" their "hard drives" or "erase" their "screens." The computer-brain metaphor has even entered popular iconography. For example, to illustrate an article on computers ("Can Machines Think?"), the cover of *Time* magazine recently pictured the human head as a circuit board, an image that is worlds apart from the late medieval portraits of people holding heart-shaped books.[50]

The mind-as-computer is not just a popular trope of the Information Age; it reflects a model of the human brain that is widely held in various branches of science. For example, the field of cognitive psychology began adopting a computer model of the brain around 1970, just when computers themselves were assuming an extensive role in society but well before the advent of the PC. A recent study by Gerd Gigerenzer and Daniel Goldstein has demonstrated "the commonplace usage of computer terminology in the cognitive psychological literature since 1972," a tendency that has become nearly universal today: "How natural it seems for present-day psychologists to speak of cognition in terms of *encoding, storage, retrieval, executive processes, algorithms,* and *computational cost.*"[51] The "cybernetic brain" is even more deeply entrenched in the new field of evolutionary psychology, where, as N. Katherine Hayles remarks in her recent book *How We Became Posthuman,* "the model (or metaphor) of computation provides the basis for a wholesale revision of what counts as human nature."[52] And, according to Edwin Hutchins, "the last 30 years of cognitive science can be seen as attempts to remake the person in the image of the computer."[53] The spread of the mind-computer metaphor from research specialists to laypeople can be tracked by the rapid movement of a term such as "hard-wired" from computer technology in the late sixties, to brain and neural research in the early seventies, to popular accounts of the mind or brain just a few years later, and finally to popular speech, where reference to "hard-wired" gender or personality traits is now commonplace.[54] As another recent commentator, Mark Kingwell, puts it, computer metaphors "have trickled down to the rest of us in the form of a pervasive, unnoticed modeling of our cultural selves as wired."[55]

Like older metaphors of the engine or dynamo, the newer ones reflect the omnipresent power of computer technology itself. "It is no accident," writes Vivian Sobchack, "that in our now dominantly electronic (and only secondarily cinematic) culture, many human beings describe and understand their minds and bodies in terms of computer systems and programs (even as they still describe and understand their lives as movies)."[56] Kingwell likewise points to the shaping force of a high-tech environment on our psychological concepts and vocabulary: "In an age of inescapable image- and information-driven technologies like television and the Internet, the idea that our brains are running various kinds of cultural software, which can be altered and copied and spread by the file transfer protocols we call the media, is enormously seductive—even, we might say, natural."[57]

Of course, the computer metaphors that many people blithely or even unwittingly apply to themselves are anything but "natural"—at least no more so than the book metaphors used in earlier times. Ironically, the original "computer" was a human math whiz (Swift's *Tale of a Tub* [1704] mentions "a very skillful *Computer*"); only in the nineteenth century was the term applied to the mechanical calculator, and, in the 1940s, to its electronic successor.[58] As with "engine," then, the word's technical sense has returned to psychology as a metaphor. The curious life cycle of this term has been recently noted by John Searle: "As commercial computers have become such an essential part of our lives, the word 'computer' has shifted in meaning to mean 'machinery designed by us to use for computing,' and, for all I know, we may go through a change of meaning so that people will be said to be computers only in a metaphorical sense."[59]

A transparent metaphor that many people nonetheless treat as a solid reality, a facticity, the mind-computer model may owe as much to rhetoric as to science. According to Gigerenzer and Goldstein, who traced the origins of the mind-computer metaphor in cognitive psychology to the early 1970s, "The evidence provided for projecting the machine into the mind is"—in many cases—"mainly rhetorical."[60]

Kingwell concurs that today the computer metaphor is "a matter of currently dominant scientific vocabulary, rather than some fact of the matter about the world." Indeed, "on closer inspection the computer metaphor breaks down."[61] In some cases, the computer-brain model even borrows its terminology from other domains, including textuality. For example, "erase" comes from manuscript culture, and "encode" (one of the terms cited by Gigerenzer and Goldstein) is originally a book metaphor, from "codex." The way in which psychic metaphors have evolved and metamorphosed suggests that, in our centuries-long attempt to describe (let alone explain) the human mind or consciousness, we have been playing a kind of shell game, using one metaphor after another to contain this elusive entity.

Besides shared vocabulary, the mind-computer metaphor has other continuities with the older model of the mind as a text. In conceptual terms, it depends on the realization that "computers are symbol-manipulation devices in addition to being numerical calculators."[62] And, in practical terms, computers are often used for textual functions once confined to the written (or printed) page, from word-processing and database searching to e-mail. But the computer, especially the PC, has much closer affinities with the visual media than traditional forms of the written word. It resembles a television set and, like television, is designed mainly to display visual images. As such, the computer inherits the aura of the *screen* from TV and the movies (as well as radar), superseding these as cultural icon and catch-all metaphor in the post-textual, post-industrial age. As the intellectual historian and social critic Ivan Illich summarizes the matter, "The book has now ceased to be the root-metaphor of the age; the screen has taken its place."[63]

One of the most telling signs of this critical change is how both scientific and literary authors continue to *invoke* textual metaphors for the mind while actually *using* video or computer ones, as if these now come more naturally. For example, an article entitled "Palimpsest or Tabula Rasa: Developmental Biology of the Brain," published in 1993 by the *Journal of the American Academy of Psychoanalysis,* seemed to pose a choice between two textual metaphors but actually abandoned both in preference to computer tropes (a "hard-wired" brain, "synaptic circuits," etc.).[64] A similar thing happens to the metaphor of writing and erasure announced in the title of Gore Vidal's recent memoir *Palimpsest* (1995). At the outset, Vidal pictures himself "erasing some but not all

of the original while writing something new over the first layer of text."
From time to time, Vidal reverts to his title metaphor, but his imagery
of writing and erasure often gives way to other tropes. For example,
"As I replay the ancient tapes of memory, I begin to see the story from
quite a new angle." And, "If it were possible, I would like to reedit all
the tapes, but they are now so fragile with age that they would probably
turn to dust. . . ." The reference to "seeing" the story from a certain
"angle" and a later remark on film as "a sort of miracle, and a powerful
aid to memory" suggest Vidal's reliance on movie or videotape metaphors.[65] The mixed metaphors of memory are symptomatic of the century's end, when visual and electronic media have largely eclipsed the
older textual imagery for the mind, memory, and emotion.

While psychology often mimics technology, it also has a way of lag-
ging behind the latest developments and of keeping older metaphors
in circulation even as new ones arrive. Long after the steam engine has
disappeared from the scene, we still use it to describe our feelings or
behavior. The tendency of obsolete technologies to remain alive (or
at least dormant) as symbols, images, or metaphors has been dubbed
"iconographic inertia."[66] This inertia attends the book as well and textuality in general, which continue to provide us with useful terms and
concepts for ourselves and our inner lives, even as the age of the book
seems to be coming to a close. Well into the new century, we will
doubtless continue to invoke "character," "impressions," and other
traces of the old textual self that goes back to the beginnings of Western civilization. But this conception of the self has a limited future
when the technology on which it is based, the printed book, may soon
become as much a symbol of the past as the manuscript codex is nowa-
days.[67] Postmodern culture still pays homage to the old ideal, as in the
slogan of a recent literacy campaign, "Find Yourself in a Book." But
when these words flash onto the TV screen for a few seconds during a
station break, they ironically signal not only the book's demise as an
actual medium for understanding ourselves and the world, but also its
loosening hold as a symbol in our collective imagination.

# *Abbreviations*

| | |
|---|---|
| *CCSL* | *Corpus Christianorum, Series Latina* |
| *CHB* | *Cambridge History of the Bible* |
| *CSEL* | *Corpus Scriptorum Ecclesiasticorum Latinorum* |
| Douay | Douay-Rheims (Bible) |
| *DMLBS* | *Dictionary of Medieval Latin from British Sources* |
| *DS* | *Dictionnaire de Spiritualité* |
| EETS | Early English Text Society<br>· OS Original Series<br>· ES Extra Series<br>· SS Supplemental Series |
| FOC | Fathers of the Church |
| KJV | King James Version (Bible) |
| LCL | Loeb Classical Library |
| LOF | A Library of Fathers of the Holy Catholic Church |
| *MED* | *Middle English Dictionary* |
| MGH | Monumenta Germaniae Historica |
| NPNF | A Select Library of the Nicene and Post-Nicene Fathers |
| *OED* | *Oxford English Dictionary* (2nd ed.) |
| *OLD* | *Oxford Latin Dictionary* |

| | |
|---|---|
| OTP | *The Old Testament Pseudepigrapha* |
| PG | *Patrologia Graeca* |
| PL | *Patrologia Latina* |
| PMLA | *Publications of the Modern Language Association* |
| RSV | Revised Standard Version (Bible) |
| SC | *Sources Chrétiennes* |
| SE | *The Standard Edition of the Works of Sigmund Freud* |

# Notes

INTRODUCTION

1. Stevens, 265–67, offers a useful overview of the heart in medieval psychology.

2. Beaulieu, 311.

3. See Le Goff, 21–23.

4. Bernard Silvester, *Cosmographia*, 2.14.111–15; ed. Barach and Wrobel, 69; trans. Wetherbee, 125.

5. Marti, 2, asserts that the "post-medieval 'repression' of the body" remains the focus of study, at the expense of the Middle Ages themselves.

6. Curtius, 302–47.

7. Derrida, *Of Grammatology*, 15.

8. See Vance, 6–11; Gellrich, 157–66; Carruthers, 48–49, and passim; and Hamburger, *Nuns as Artists*, esp. 126–27, 163.

9. See Dinshaw, esp. 7–14.

10. On the medieval self, see Morris; Benton; and Bynum, *Jesus as Mother*, 82–109. For commentary on early modern selfhood studies, see Patterson, esp. 93–101; and Aers.

CHAPTER ONE

1. See Havelock, *Muse*, esp. chap. 10. The perceived superiority of alphabetic script goes back at least to Vico. For useful summary and discussion, see Chartier, 6–24.

2. Havelock, *Muse*, 113.

3. *Iliad* 6.169.

4. Pindar, *Olympian Odes*, 10.2–3 (*"phrenos . . . gegraptai"*). Examples of the classical metaphor are listed in Curtius, 304–10; and Kittel, 1:770. For discussion,

see Nieddu; Svenbro, 197–206; and Crane, 10–12. On the date of the Pindar quotation, see Svenbro, 200, with refs.

5. See Harris, 66–93, and, commenting on this metaphor in particular, 109.

6. For example, Euripides, *Trojan Women*, 662 ("*anaptuxo phrena*"), cited by Curtius, 304n. On tablets, scrolls, and other ancient writing media, see *CHB* 1:30–66.

7. Aeschylus, *Prometheus Bound*, 789 ("*mnemosin deltois phrenon*").

8. Aeschylus, *Agamemnon*, 801, trans. Lattimore, 59. On this passage, see Rose, 2:58–59.

9. Aeschylus, *Libation Bearers*, 450 (Loeb trans.).

10. Aeschylus, *Eumenides*, 275 (Loeb trans.).

11. Cf. Crane, 11–12, using "heart" to render *phrenes*.

12. See Onians, 23–40; and Bremmer, 62–63.

13. Homer, *Iliad*, 16.481, as translated in Onians, 26.

14. Onians, 29.

15. Onians, 28.

16. Onians, 67–68.

17. Cited in Liddell, Scott et al., s.v. *phren*, 2 ("heart").

18. Svenbro, 199–202.

19. See Snell, 1–22; Bremmer, 53–63; Taylor, 118.

20. See Onians, 23, 28–29; Bremmer, 63; Stevens, 265–66; and citations in Liddell, Scott et al., s.v. *kardia*, I.

21. *OLD*, s.v. *cor*, 2, cites examples of the heart as a repository for "*sententia*," "*praecepta*," and the like, but not for knowledge figured expressly as "writing." On the heart in classical doctrines of memory, see Carruthers, 48–49; and Small, 131–36.

22. Crane, 11.

23. The *psychē*, although etymologically connected with breathing, did not have a distinct bodily location (Bremmer, 21). "Plato's view . . . requires some conception of the mind as a unitary space" (Taylor, 119).

24. Small, 132.

25. Plato, *Theaetetus*, 194c–e ("*psuches kear*," "*kerou*").

26. See Havelock, *Preface*, 253 n. 44. On memory as writing in the Greek philosophers, see Yates, chap. 2.

27. Aristotle, *De memoria et reminiscentia*, 452a17–22. See discussion in Yates, 32–35.

28. Aristotle, *De anima*, 3.4, 429b32–430a2.

29. Plato, *Phaedrus*, 275a, 276a.

30. Crane, 253 (citing coinage along with writing).

31. Derrida, "Plato's Pharmacy, I," in *Dissemination*, 65–119. For briefer remarks, see *Of Grammatology*, 15.

32. Nehamas and Woodruff, introduction to *Phaedrus*, xxxv (summarizing Derrida's argument).

33. Plato, *Gorgias*, 524d–525a, trans. W. D. Woodhead in Hamilton and Cairns (eds.), 305.

34. Plato, *The Republic*, 10, 614d.

35. See Bettencourt, 98–99, and n. 47; also Liddell, Scott et al., s.v. *chartes*.

36. See *OLD*, s.v. *cor*; and Ovid, *Amores*, 1.2.7 ("*haeserunt tenues in corde sagittae*"); Plautus, *Persa*, 25 ("*sagitta Cupido cor meum transfixit*").

37. Pseudo-Cicero, *Ad C. Herennium de ratione dicendi (Rhetorica ad Herennium)*, 3.17.30. Further examples in Yates, chap. 1; and Carruthers, 16–32. For less technical usage, see also *OLD*, s.v. *scribo*, 2a (citing Terence, *Andria*, 283).

38. Quintilian, *Institutes*, 1.1.36 ("*impressa animo rudi*").

39. Cicero, *Letters to Atticus*, 10.6.1, cited in *OLD*, s.v. *explico*, 8.

40. Cicero, *De officiis*, 3.19.76 (changing translator's "unfold" to "unroll").

41. Seneca, *Epistle*, 72.1 (changing translator's "unrolled" to "unfolded").

42. See *OLD*, s.v. *reuoluo*, 2b (scroll), 2c (mind).

43. For examples and extensive analysis, see articles on "Heart" (or "*Kardia*") in Buttrick, 2:549–50; Bromiley, 2:650–53; Balz and Schneider, 2:249–51; and Kittel, 1:770. See also the useful critical survey of the biblical heart, relative to English literature, in Erickson, chap. 1.

44. See Breasted, 254–55, 260–64; Brandon, 28–29; and, for writing on the heart, Piankoff, 45 (citing the Lansing and Ani papyri). See also Small, 134–36, on heart and memory in Egyptian texts.

45. On these writing media, see *CHB* 1:32–35.

46. Ezekiel 11.19, 36.26.

47. "The heart is conceived as a tablet on which these Divine words shall be inscribed" (Hertz, 771). Cf. Deut. 4.9, 11.18, and the associated metaphor of the "circumcised" heart at 10.16.

48. Cf. Exod. 32.16; Deut. 10.2.

49. See Furnish, 183.

50. See Philo, *Legum allegoriae*, 3.38.115; Philo, *Quaestiones et solutiones in Exodum*, 2.115; and, for commentary, Bromiley, 2:650; and *DS* 2:2287.

51. Philo, *De specialibus legibus*, 4.26.137, referring to Deut. 6.6, 8, which enjoins both wearing phylacteries and keeping the Law in the heart.

52. Philo, *De specialibus legibus*, 4.28.149. Josephus, *Jewish Antiquities*, 4.210–11, likewise refers to a law written in the "soul" (*psychē*).

53. Philo, *Quis rerum divinarum heres*, 59.294.

54. See also Liddell, Scott et al., s.v. *kharakter*, II.3–4.

55. Philo, *De specialibus legibus*, 1.20.106–7.

56. *DS* 2:2287.

57. *Dictionary of Paul and His Letters*, 766; and Brown, *The Body and Society*, 35. See also Stacey, 194–97.

58. On the biblical and classical sources of Paul's terms, see Eden, 51 n. 12.

59. 1 Cor. 14.25; cf. 1 Cor. 4.5 ("purposes of the heart").

60. For commentary on the Greek text, with variants and probable sources, see Furnish, 180–83.

61. Plummer, 81, compares Plato, *Phaedrus*, 276c.

62. See Stacey, 194.

63. For example, Romans 7.25. For a clarifying discussion, see Brown, *The Body and Society*, 46–49.

64. See *OLD*, s.v. *cor*.

65. See Furnish, 183.

66. Curtius, 310–11, collects examples of biblical writing metaphors. See also *DS* 9:942–47 ("Livre de Vie").

67. See Brandon, 28–30, on Egypt; and Solmsen on the "Tablets of Zeus."

68. Ps. 51.1; Acts 3.19; Col. 2.14; cf. Rev. 3.5.

69. On ink, see refs. in Plummer, 81; and Furnish, 182.

70. Examples cited in *OTP* 1:889 n. 12d.

71. *Testament of Abraham* (Recension A), 12.8, 12–13, 17, *OTP* 1:889. For information on dating, see the editor's introduction, 874–75.

72. Erickson, 50.

73. *2 Enoch* 53.2–3 (Recension J), *OTP* 1:180 (on dating, see 94–95).

74. For a survey of patristic exegesis, including allegory, see *CHB* 2:155–83. Paul employs typology in Gal. 4.24–26, among other places. For a critical history, see Auerbach. Robertson, 286–317, discusses allegory in Paul and Augustine but stresses medieval developments.

75. Chrysostom, *Homiliae in Johannem*, 32.3, *PG* 59:187, trans. NPNF, ser. 1, 14:114.

76. Eusebius, *De martyribus Palestinae*, 13.7–8, *PG* 20:1515–16, trans. NPNF, ser. 2, 1:355.

77. Jerome, *Epistolae*, 31.2 ("*epistolam pectoris*"), *PL* 22:445, trans. NPNF, ser. 2, 6:45; and *Epistolae* 9, *PL* 22:342, trans. NPNF, ser. 2, 6:11.

78. Jerome, *Commentarii in Abacuc*, 1.2 (Habakkuk 2.2), *PL* 25:1290.

79. See Hausherr, 32, 92; and Spidlík, 77, 103–7, 242–47, 284.

80. Brown, *The Body and Society*, 229.

81. Basil, *Epistolae*, 2.2 (to Gregory), *Opera* 3:101, trans. FOC 13:6. Here the site of inscription varies between "heart" (*kardia*) and "soul" (*psychē*).

82. See also *DS* 8:1578, for several loci where Basil treats sin as inward writing (though not as a book).

83. See also citations listed in *DS* 4:1805–6; and Lampe, s.v. *kardia* (B), *plax*, and *chartes*.

84. Rufinus, *Historia monachorum*, 1, *PL* 21:403, cited by Brown, *The Body and Society*, 229.

85. Cassian, *Collationes*, 1.17, *SC* 42:98. Cf. *Collationes* 14.10, *SC* 54:195, where studying Scripture is said to shape the mind (*mens*) into a semblance of the Ark of the Covenant containing the two tablets of the Law.

86. Nilus of Ancyra, *Epistulae*, 3.129, *PG* 79:444 ("*charten . . . kardias*"). See also John Climacus, *Scala paradisi*, 1, *PG* 88:632 ("*kardiais . . . chartais*"), trans. Luibheid-Russell, 74.

87. Athanasius, *Vita Antonii*, 55.7–12, ed. Bartelink, 112, trans. Gregg, 72–73.

88. John Climacus, *Scala paradisi*, 4, *PG* 88:701, trans. Luibheid-Russell, 105 (and cited by Spidlík, 247). John's treatise opens by evoking inscription on "the tablets of the spirit" (*plakes pneumatikai; Scala* 1, col. 633, trans. 74). For an early illustration of this metaphor, see John Rupert Martin, 25–26, with fig. 32.

89. *DS* 8:1577–78 (s.v. "Jugement") cites book and writing metaphors in various patristic authors, including Origen and Basil. For additional loci in Origen, see *Commento* (ed. Cocchini), 1:81 n. 36. And for the influence of Origen's textual metaphors on other patristic authors, see *Encyclopedia of the Early Church* 1:457 (s.v. "Judgment").

90. Origen, *Commentarii in epistolam ad Romanos*, 2.10, *PG* 14:894, trans. (Italian) Cocchini, 1:81.

91. Origen, *Commentarii in epistolam ad Romanos*, 9.41, *PG* 14:1242, trans. (Italian) Cocchini, 2:146.

92. Tablets could hold "about fifty words a side, and a multiple set of tablets, as many as ten in a codex form, was commonly used" (Harris, 194).

93. On dates for the adoption of the codex by Christians, see Roberts and Skeat, chap. 8.

94. See Brown, *The Body and Society*, 163–64.

95. Origen, *In Numeros Homiliae*, 2.2, *PG* 12:592, trans. *SC* 194:85. Cited by Brown, *The Body and Society*, 165–66.

96. Origen, *Commentarii in epistolam ad Romanos*, 9.41, *PG* 14:1242–43, trans. (Italian) Cocchini, 2:147.

97. Brown, *The Body and Society*, 161.

98. Ambrose, *De Spiritu sancto*, 3.3.13a–14, *CSEL* 79:156–57, trans. NPNF, ser. 1, 10:137–38 (altering "table" to "tablet").

99. Ambrose, *Epistolae*, 63.5 (= Maurist edition 73.5), *CSEL* 82.2:144 ("*corrupta atque interlita*"), trans. FOC 26:465. On the inscribed heart and the Fall, see Jager, *The Tempter's Voice*, 64–65.

100. Ambrose, *Epistolae*, 63.3, *CSEL* 82.2:143–44, trans. FOC 26:464.

101. Ambrose, *Explanatio Psalmorum XII*, 1.52, *CSEL* 64:44–45, trans. (Italian)

Pizzolato, 105 (glossing Psalm 1.5, "Therefore the wicked will not stand in the judgment").

102. For example, *"uide ne deleas et scribas atramento flagitia tua."*

103. Augustine, *Confessions*, 6.3, describes Ambrose reading silently. See my next chapter, including n. 31.

104. On *liber*, see Arns, 103–6; and Holtz.

105. On the continuing use of scrolls among late-fourth-century patristic authors, see Roberts and Skeat, 24.

CHAPTER TWO

1. On Augustine's language theory, see Vance, chaps. 1–2; Colish, chap. 1; and Jackson. On Augustine's "theory of reading," see Stock, *Augustine*. Brown, *Augustine*, chap. 23, is also useful.

2. Vance, 34.

3. Augustine, *Sermon on Matthew 11.25–26*, 6 (*"magnus liber"*), ed. Morin, 360, trans. Howe, 224, cited in Jeffrey, 14.

4. Time as a recited psalm, *Confessions* 11.28; history as a poem, *De civitate Dei* 11.18, *De vera religione* 22.42; God as a book, *Confessions* 13.15.

5. Augustine, *Enarrationes in Psalmos*, 103.1.8. See Jager, *The Tempter's Voice*, 70–71.

6. See *Confessions* 13.15, *"retia,"* and commentary by Morrison, 30. For later elaborations, see Claudius of Turin (c. 800) as cited in Smalley, 1; and Leclercq, "Aspects spirituels," 68 n. 25.

7. Taylor, 128–29, credits Augustine with "discovering" interiority, without, however, citing Paul as a source.

8. Parenthetical citations to the *Confessions* refer to the Latin and English editions cited in the bibliography, with occasional minor changes in Warner's translation.

9. Brown, *Augustine*, 169.

10. In the *Confessions*, the term *cor* occurs 188 times, including *cor meum* (71), *cor nostrum* (9), and *praecordia* (3). Together *recordari* and *recordatio* add 37 instances. The heart appears in the work's opening and closing chapters, in the first paragraph of six other books (four times as *cor meum*), and in two more opening chapters as a cognate verb of memory: 1.1 (*cor nostrum*), 2.1 (*recordari*), 5.1 (*cor*), 6.1 (*cordis mei*), 7.1 (*cor meum*), 8.1 (*cor, recorder*), 9.1 (*cor meum*), 10.1 (*corde meo*), 12.1 (*cor meum*). As a concordance, I have used Cooper, Ferrari et al.

11. After *cor, pectus* is the most common, occurring 17 times, sometimes in close connection with *cor* (e.g., *Conf.* 6.1–2, 7.2).

12. O'Donnell, 2:13. Eliade, 6:236. See bibliography in Peza, 13–14.

13. *Conf.* 10.3, cited in Eliade, 6:236.

14. Freccero, 36.

15. Vance, 10, 31.

16. See citations and commentary in Colish, 50–54; and O'Donnell, 3:77–78.

17. *De doctrina christiana* 3.34.48 (Green, 182–85).

18. *De spiritu et littera* 17.30 (trans., 96).

19. *Epistolae* 31.2 (*"vos in cordibus eorum scriptos"*), *PL* 33:122, trans. NPNF, ser. 1, 1:258, cited by Brown, *Augustine*, 158–59.

20. *De spiritu et littera* 17.48 (*"impressum," "deletum"*), changing "blotted out" in the English translation to "erased" in accord with Augustine's tablet metaphor. See also *Enarrationes in Psalmos* 57.1.

21. *Conf.* 5.6, with similar wordplay on *cor* and *recordatio* in 9.12, 10.8. See Carruthers, 172.

22. *Conf.* 10.14–15 (*"imagines inpressas," "recordarer"*), with reference to *recordatio* in 10.14. *Conf.* 10.16 treats memory as writing (*"inprimitur . . . in memoria," "in memoria conscribebat"*), though without alluding to the heart. On Augustine and ancient memory theory, see Coleman, 95–98; and Stock, *Augustine*, 15.

23. Stock, *Augustine*, 13.

24. *Conf.* 10.35 (*". . . praeciderim et a meo corde dispulerim"*). See also *Conf.* 11.2 (*"circumcise my lips"*), discussed in Vance, 6–11.

25. Augustine, *De spiritu et littera*, 8.13 (orig. emphasis).

26. Vance, 8 (orig. emphasis).

27. Ps. 38.2 (Vulg. 37.3), *"sagittae tuae infixae sunt mihi"*; Ovid, *Amores*, 1.2.7; Plautus, *Persa*, 25.

28. *Conf.* 9.2 (*"Sagittaveras tu cor nostrum caritate tua, et gestabamus verba tua transfixa visceribus . . ."*).

29. See *OLD*, s.v. *uiscus*, 3b–c.

30. For example, citations in Riehle, 47–48; and Bernard of Clairvaux, *Sermones in laudibus Virginis Matris*, 4.11, in *Opera* 4:57. Augustine, *De spiritu et littera*, 16.28, evokes God's finger (*digitus dei*) writing on the heart, also a phallic image.

31. Carruthers, 170–73, untangles this passage from a century of misinterpretation, showing that Augustine contrasts two kinds of reading, *meditatio* (silent) and *lectio* (vocal), of which Ambrose here practices the former.

32. "This kind of reading, an ability to see beyond the material appearance of letters to their sources of meaning, is figured for Augustine in Ambrose's 'silent reading'" (Gellrich, 117).

33. For example, "I cried out as I read this with my outward eye and inwardly recognized its truth. . . . And in the next verse how my heart cried out from its depths!" (*Conf.* 9.4).

34. Henri-Jean Martin, 59. For details of the codex revolution, see Chartier, 18–20, and scholarship cited in the next note.

35. See Roberts and Skeat, chaps. 9–10; Gamble, 49–66; and, for a briefer review of hypotheses, Johannot, 32–35.

36. Stock, *Augustine*, 382 n. 89; although, as Morrison, 28–32, shows, scroll metaphors in the *Confessions* are not as "rare" as Stock, 377 n. 15, suggests.

37. See Gamble, 235–36.

38. See Roberts and Skeat, plate 6; and Johannot, 63–68. For early symbolic use of the book, including the codex, see Courcelle, 158–60.

39. For examples and superb commentary, see Morrison, 28–32, on which I depend here. See also Holtz on the scroll and the codex in Augustine.

40. Platonic scrolls, *Conf.* 7.20. In the passage on Ambrose reading (6.3), the key word is *paginas*, which Morrison, 166 n. 194, interprets as referring to the columns of a scroll (cf. *"voluminum evolveret"* in same chapter), although elsewhere Augustine uses *paginis* of a codex (*Conf.* 8.6). Carruthers, 92, states that in classical Latin, *pagina* referred to wax writing tablets.

41. *Conf.* 4.10 (*"glutine amore"*), 9.3 (*"evoluti sunt dies illi"*), 13.15 (*"caelum enim plicabitur ut liber . . ."*).

42. Morrison, 30, also noting Augustine's contrast of "the hide scroll of the firmament with the grass scroll of human flesh." But the body as "scroll" also points to hermeneutical issues. On the textual sense of *retia*, see also *OLD*, s.v. *rete*, 1e.

43. *Conf.* 8.12 (*"aperirem codicem," "posueram codicem," "codicem clausi"*).

44. Freccero, 36. See Marti, 57, on textual "centers."

45. For objections, see Roberts and Skeat, 50; and Gamble, 239–40 (noting that Greeks, Romans, and Jews practiced the *sortes* with scrolls). For the *sortes* in patristic times, see Courcelle, 143–54.

46. See examples in *DS* 2:2282. On the "bodily" aspect of the codex, see also Camille, in Frese and O'Keeffe, esp. 36–46.

47. Cf. *Conf.* 1.13 (*"lumen cordis mei"*). In *Conf.* 8.12 there is also a hint of bodily correlation in the way that Augustine's *"oculi"* meet the *"capitulum"* (from *caput*, "head").

48. See Mellinkoff, 36.

49. See Johannot, 43–52.

50. On Augustine's terminology in this passage, see Holtz, 110–11.

51. On publication, see *Conf.* 10.3, as quoted below; and refs. in Brown, *Augustine*, 304; and Morrison, 28–29.

52. For example, *Conf.* 8.4 (Victorinus). On Augustine's chest complaint, see Brown, *Augustine*, 109–10; and Vance, 26. See also Jager, "Speech and the Chest," esp. 846–47.

53. Brown, *The Body and Society*, 388.

54. *Retractiones* 2.32.1, *CSEL* 36:137–38, trans. FOC 60:130.

55. Stock, *Augustine*, 16.

56. See Poulet as quoted below in chap. 9.

57. See Vance, 2; Bloch, 47; and Stock, *Augustine*, 15. Brown, *Augustine*, 210, refers to Augustine's sense of "the unknown and the unknowable in human character."

58. Augustine, *Epistolae*, 31.2 ("... *in nostra corda transcripsimus*"), *PL* 33:122, trans. NPNF, ser. 1, 1:258.

59. Vance, 28.

60. *Conf.* 11.28, cited by Vance, 37.

61. Stock, *Augustine*, 16.

62. Augustine, *De civitate Dei*, 20.14, *CCSL* 48:724, trans. Dods, 733.

63. Kierkegaard, *Journals* IV A 164, ed. Hong, 1:450 (no. 1030).

64. Jeffrey, 16.


CHAPTER THREE

1. On the material book as a secret, self-enclosed object, see Camille, in Frese and O'Keeffe, 40–41, 52. On the heart as a "book of secrets" (*liber occultorum*), see Gellrich, 162–64.

2. Saenger, "Silent Reading," 384.

3. See Clanchy, 105.

4. Illich, 3–4.

5. See Morris and the more recent assessments in Benton; and Bynum, *Jesus as Mother*, 82–109.

6. On Latin autobiography, see Spence.

7. Benedict of Nursia, *Regula*, Prologus 1 ("*aurem cordis tui*"), 9.10 ("*ex corde recitanda*"), 48.15 ("*accipiant omnes singulos codices*"), *CSEL* 75:1, 56, 117, trans. Mc-Cann, 7, 51, 113. On monastic memory culture, see Leclercq, *The Love of Learning*, 18–22, 89–93; and Carruthers, 170–73. On the chant, see refs. in Gellrich, 87.

8. See refs. in Smalley, 1–2.

9. Gregory, *Moralia*, 4 (preface), 19.12.20, 24.8.16, *PL* 75:633, 76:109, 295, trans. LOF 1:177–78, 2:411, 3:61.

10. Alcuin, *Epistolae*, 83 ("*pectoris arcana cartis*"), 167 ("*per cartas loqui potuissent et necessaria proferre in cor alterius*"), in MGH, *Epistolae Karolini Aevi*, 4/2:126, 275. Cited in Bolton, 14, 15.

11. Alcuin, *Adversus Elipandum Toletanum*, 2.14, *PL* 101:270 ("*Rade ... tabulis tui cordis*"). Cited in Bolton, 20 (quoted here in altered form).

12. Pseudo-Jerome, *Breviarium in psalmos*, 81, *PL* 26:1062–63. For authorship and dating, see Dekkers, 218, no. 629 (with refs.).

13. See *OLD*, s.v. *plico*, 1b, for classical use with scrolls. According to Rouse, 2–3, the term implies a codex by the twelfth century. However, Bernard of Clairvaux, *Sermones ad clericos de conversione*, 2.3 (*Opera* 4:73), as quoted later in this chapter, still applies the related term *replicare* (unfold) to the scroll.

14. See Bede, *Explanatio Apocalypsis*, 3.20, *PL* 93:193, "*quasi in expansione librorum*" (glossing Rev. 20.12), where *expansio* implies "scrolls" (cf. *DMLBS*, s.v. *expandere*, 3b).

15. Hraban Maur, *Enarrationes in epistolas beati Pauli*, 7.14, *PL* 111:1581, quoting Origen, *Commentarii in epistolam ad Romanos*, 9.41, *PG* 14:1242, as cited in chap. 1. On Origen at Fulda, see Wallace-Hadrill, 337.

16. Aachen, Cathedral Treasury, Gospel Book of Otto III, fol. 15v, ed. and reprod. in Beissel, 5 ("HOC AUGUSTE LIBRO TIBI COR DEUS INDUAT OTTO"), plate II, trans. Beckwith, 106. The facing illumination (16r) shows the emperor with a scroll extended across his chest (Beissel, plate III; Beckwith, fig. 87).

17. See Curtius, 315–21; Singleton, 37–42; and Gellrich, 157–64. See also Leclercq, "Aspects spirituels," which gives many examples and offers the following taxonomy of twelfth-century book metaphors: *liber conscientiae, liber cordis*, and *liber experientiae*.

18. Richard of St. Victor, *De judiciaria potestate in finali et universali judicio*, *PL* 196:1182.

19. Richard of St. Victor, *Sermo in festo sancti Augustini* (= Pseudo-Hugh of St. Victor, *Sermones*, 99), *PL* 177:1205–6, as reattributed by Glorieux, 70.

20. Richard (or Hugh) of St. Victor, *Commentarius in Nahum*, 42, *PL* 96:726. On the disputed attribution of this work, see Baron.

21. For glossed Bibles and their page layout, see De Hamel.

22. Peter of Blois, *Sermones*, 65, *PL* 207:754, quoting Jer. 17.9 (Vulg. 17.8), and substituting *profundum* for *pravum*.

23. See *DMLBS*, s.v. *fasciculus*, 1d.

24. Augustine, *De civitate*, 20.14, as discussed above, chap. 2.

25. On the *pecia* system of book copying, see Pollard, and the essays collected in Bataillon et al.

26. Durham Cathedral MS B.IV.12, fols. 37v–38v, ed. and trans. Rouse, 5–7 (Latin), 8–9 (English).

27. Cf. the Anglo-Norman bishop Herbert de Losinga (c. 1050–c. 1119), who opens a letter to a fellow churchman as follows: "While writing this letter, I have dipped my pen not into my ink-horn, but into my heart [*non cornu sed in corde calamum intinxi*]." Letter 13, ed. Anstruther, 22, trans. Goulburn and Symonds, 1:288.

28. Peter Comestor, *Sermo de libro vitae* (= Pseudo-Hildebert of Lavardin, *Sermones ad diversos*, 102), *PL* 171:814–18, cited by Curtius, 318–19, reattributed by

Glorieux, 63–64. Cf. the similar passage in Peter Comestor, *Sermones*, 6 (*"In nativitate Domini"*), *PL* 198:1740.

29. A related scribal trope is the *compunctio cordis*, discussed by Carruthers in Frese and O'Keeffe, 2, 19, 21–23.

30. *De claustro animae*, 4.33, *PL* 176:1170, emending *liber generationis* to *liber rationis* based on subsequent references. Cited in Curtius, 320 (as Hugh of Folieto); on this monastic genre, see Hamburger, *Nuns as Artists*, 157, with refs.

31. Pseudo-Bernard, *De interiori domo*, 18, *PL* 184:523. Reattributed in Glorieux, 71.

32. Pseudo-Bernard, *De interiori domo*, 15, *PL* 184:520.

33. Hugh of St. Victor(?), *De unione corporis et spiritus*, *PL* 177:293 (closely resembling Pseudo-Bernard, *De interiori domo*, 15, as cited earlier).

34. Peter Comestor, *Sermones*, 6, *PL* 198:1741 (*". . . tam a clerico quam a laico"*); and *Sermo de libro vitae* (= Pseudo-Hildebert of Lavardin), *PL* 171:815 (*"nos qui litteras non didicimus, nec scribere scimus . . ."*).

35. Bernard of Clairvaux, *Sermo ad clericos de conversione*, 2.3, *Opera* 4:73 (with *revolvitur, replicatur,* and *evoluta* suggesting a scroll). Saïd's translation, *Sermons on Conversion*, 34, does not emphasize the scroll imagery. A parchment and erasure metaphor later in the same sermon (*Ad clericos* 15.28; *Opera* 4:102–4), is discussed by Carruthers in Frese and O'Keeffe, 19–20.

36. On dating, see Mellinkoff, 29–30.

37. Pseudo-Hugh of St. Victor, *Miscellanea*, 3.66, *PL* 177:675. On the authenticity of this work, see Glorieux, 70.

38. See Hendrix, esp. 196–97.

39. Another elaborate scribal metaphor appears in Hugh's gloss on Psalm 45.1 (Vulg. 44.2), *Opera omnia* 2:115v–116r.

40. Hugh of St. Cher, *De doctrina cordis*, 6, ed. Hendrix, 183–85. Subsequent citations are parenthetical and refer to page.

41. For examples, see Schiller's plates, 5:588 (no. 708a), 597 (no. 726), 605–6 (nos. 743–45).

42. Paris, Bibliothèque nationale, MS fr. 403, fol. 40v, ed. Breder, 47 (*"Ceo que li livre sunt overt signefie que tutes les consciences seront apertes coment il 'averont' les commandemenz Deu 'gardé'"*).

43. For a higher ratio of books to persons, see Breslau (Wroclaw), University Library, MS I Qu. 19, fol. 118r, as reprod. in Schiller's plates, 5:597 (no. 726).

44. On the "book of experience" in particular, see Leclercq, "Aspects spirituels," 70–72. The *liber experientiae* sometimes stands for other figurative books, such as the "record" of history. See *DMLBS*, s.v. *liber*, 13.

45. Guibert, *Liber quo ordine sermo fieri debeat*, *PL* 156:26, trans. Miller, 50

(slightly altered), cited in Curtius, 318. Guibert probably has in mind a codex, although a few lines earlier he figures the four senses of Scripture as four scrolls (*rotis*) on which "each sacred page is rolled" (*PL* 156:25, trans. Miller, 49).

46. Guibert, *Liber quo ordine sermo fieri debeat*, *PL* 156:28, trans. Miller, 51. Quoted in Morris, 67.

47. Alan of Lille, *Ars praedicandi*, 3, *PL* 210:118, trans. Evans, 29.

48. On Cistercian book metaphors, see Bynum, *Jesus as Mother*, 78–79; and Verdeyen and Fassetta, eds., Bernard of Clairvaux, *Sermons sur le Cantique*, tome 1 (= *SC* 414), 100 n. 1.

49. Bernard, *Sermones super Cantica Canticorum*, 3.1, *Opera* 1:14, trans. Walsh, 16.

50. Isaac of Stella, *Sermones*, 29.13, *SC* 207:176–77.

51. Guigo II, *Scala claustralium*, 8, *SC* 163:98–100, trans. Colledge and Walsh, 75–76. Bynum, *Jesus as Mother*, 79, cites this passage.

## CHAPTER FOUR

1. Andreas Capellanus indicates his aim "to instruct" (*docere*) his audience (*De amore*, Praefatio, ed. and trans. Walsh, 30–31). Dante, *Inferno*, 5.127–38. Some of Chaucer's amorous letters are listed in Jager, *The Tempter's Voice*, 243 n. 4. *Sir Gawain and the Green Knight* 1515 ("*tyxt*"), ed. Andrew and Waldron, 263.

2. Ovid, *Ars amatoria*, 3.621–26.

3. Alan of Lille, *De planctu naturae*, prose 5 ("*librum ... experientiae*"), ed. Wright 2:474, trans. Sheridan, 154, cited in Curtius, 316.

4. Constance of Angers, letter, 239.9–10, 13–14, 17–18, in Baudri de Bourgueil, *Oeuvres poétiques*, 345, trans. Dronke, 88, cited in Nichols, "An Intellectual Anthropology," 84.

5. Nichols, "An Intellectual Anthropology," 84.

6. Constance, letter, 239.15, ed. Abrahams, 347, trans. Dronke, 89, cited in Nichols, "An Intellectual Anthropology," 84.

7. Bernard of Clairvaux, *Epistolae*, 116, in *Opera* 7:296, trans. James (as letter 119), 181 (slightly modified).

8. Bernard, *Sermones in laudibus Virginis Matris*, 4.11, in *Opera* 4:57, trans. Saïd and Perigo, *Four Homilies*, 57.

9. See Camille in Frese and O'Keeffe, 41.

10. Dinshaw, 9.

11. Heloise, letter 4, ed. Truci, 174, trans. Radice, 133 (as letter 3), with alterations. See also Heloise's reflections on writing and the mind and heart (*animus, cor*) at the beginning of letter 6, ed. Truci, 226, 228, trans. Radice, 159 (as letter 5).

12. Jean de Meun's translation of Heloise, letter 4, ed. Beggiato, 1:110 (English translation based on Radice, 133).

13. Abelard, *Historia calamitatum*, 6, ed. Truci (as letter 1), 26, trans. Radice, 67.

14. Sordello, "Tant m'abellis lo terminis novels," 15–17, 74–79, ed. and trans. Wilhelm, 42–47.

15. Folquet de Marseille, "En chantan m'aven a membrar," 8–10, ed. Stronski, 27 (with modern French trans., 122).

16. New York, Pierpont Morgan Library MS 819, fol. 59r, discussed by Rieger, 399–400, with reproduction (386) and catalog entry (407, no. 16).

17. Nichols, "Portraits of Poets." My thanks to the author for providing me with a typescript of this unpublished lecture.

18. Rieger, 399 (and 400, on *"signes de renvoi en rouge"*).

19. Morgan MS 819, fol. 63r, as discussed by Rieger, 399.

20. Petrarch, *Canzoniere* (= *Rime sparse*), 96.5–6, ed. and trans. Durling, 198–99.

21. *Le Roman de la Rose* 4334, 4336–40, ed. Lecoy, 1:134, trans. Dahlberg, 95. The metaphor of an interior notebook is more explicit in Chaucer, *The Romaunt of the Rose* 4796–4801, ed. Benson, 737.

22. *Roman* 13235–38, ed. Lecoy, 2:153, trans. Dahlberg, 229.

23. *Roman* 13469–83, ed. Lecoy, 2:160, trans. Dahlberg, 232–33.

24. *Roman* 19599–606, ed. Lecoy, 3:89, trans. Dahlberg, 323. The metaphor is from Alan de Lille, *De planctu naturae*, prose 5.

25. *Roman* 20667–68, ed. Lecoy, 3:121, trans. Dahlberg, 338.

26. Dante, *La vita nuova*, 1, ed. Barbi, 3–4, trans. Reynolds, 29.

27. On Dante's book metaphors and their (often scholastic) sources, see Curtius, 326–32; Singleton, 37–42, 127–29; and Gellrich, 139–66 (passim).

28. Singleton, 28; see also 37–38.

29. Dante, *La vita nuova*, 2, ed. Barbi, 8, trans. Reynolds, 30.

30. See *Enciclopedia Dantesca*, s.v. *ricordare* (cf. *cuore*).

31. Dante, *La vita nuova*, 2, ed. Barbi, 6, trans. Reynolds, 29. Mazzotta, 150 (with refs.).

32. Dante, *La vita nuova*, 39, "Lasso! per forza di molti sospiri," lines 11–16, ed. Barbi, 98, trans. Reynolds, 96.

33. Augustine, *Confessions*, 8.6 (*". . . parturitione novae vitae"*).

34. Singleton, 35.

35. Dante, *La vita nuova*, 28, ed. Barbi, 77, trans. Reynolds, 79, cited by Singleton, 34.

36. Dante, *La vita nuova*, 29, ed. Barbi, 77, trans. Reynolds, 80.

37. Dante, *La vita nuova*, 29, ed. Barbi, 78, trans. Reynolds, 81.

38. Boccaccio, *Amorosa visione*, 45.10–15 (*". . . aprirmi il petto, e dentro poi scrivesse / là in mezzo 'l core . . ."*), ed. and trans. Hollander, 182–83.

39. On women as writers and scribes, see Schibanoff, esp. 194–97.

40. On the heart as a gift, see Camille, 113.

41. On individuality and medieval scripts, signatures, and seals, see Clanchy, 98–99.

42. See Huot, 298, and plate 18. "Arrow" and "pen" were synonymous since antiquity; see *OLD*, s.v. *calamus* 2, 6.

43. Petrarch, *Canzoniere*, 127.5–10, ed. and trans. Durling, 248–49, lineation added ("... *la storia trovo scritta / in mezzo 'l cor che sì spesso rincorro / co la sua propria man de' miei martiri ...*").

44. Freccero, 34. For more on how Petrarch imagines the self in terms of literary activity, especially in the *Secretum*, see Stock, "Reading, Writing, and the Self."

45. Petrarch, *Secretum*, 3, ed. Bigi, 638 ("*de medio experientie libro michi videris excerpsisse*"), trans. Draper, 136–37 (modified).

46. On Charles's frequent book and reading metaphors, see Fein, 104–7.

47. Charles d'Orléans, *Ballade*, 8.1–5, ed. and trans. Purcell, 30–31. Other verses quoted: 9–12, 14.

48. Charles d'Orléans, *Rondeau*, 33, lines 1–6, ed. Purcell, 99 (my trans.).

49. For heraldry, see Boutell, 63, citing the Douglas coat-of-arms (*ante* 1330), as illustrated in plate 3 (no. 3). Sauvy, 47–48, dates the birth of the visual image to c. 1450.

50. For illustrated examples, see Higgins, 40, 92, and 147.

51. Chantilly, Musée Condé, MS 564 (formerly 1047), fol. 11v. Full text and score in Reaney, 1–9. Also in Greene, 1–2, with notes (145).

52. For example, a copy (c. 1410–15) of Jean de Meun's *Testament*, as reprod. in Dutschke, 1:33, item EL 26 A 3, art. 2 (and fig. 8).

53. Clara d'Anduza, "En greu esmai ...," lines 26–27, ed. and trans. Bogin, 130–31.

54. Paris, Bibliothèque nationale, MS Rothschild 2973, "Mort he mercy ..." (no. 10, fol. 12v–13r, 14v–15r), ed. Thibault-Fallows, 18–19. The illustration (in which Cupid shoots the lady rather than the male lover) forms the volume's frontispiece; see discussion by Jean Porcher, in Thibault-Fallows, xv–xvi. Color images in Thibault-Fallows, frontispiece; and Camille, 116.

55. "De mon povoir vous veul complaire ..." (no. 39, fol. 56v–57r), in Thibault-Fallows, 79–80, line 4.

56. "Faites-moy sçavoir de la belle ..." (no. 43, fol. 62v–64v), in Thibault-Fallows, 87–88, lines 1–2, 12.

57. Jean's ecclesiastical appointments are detailed by Porcher in Thibault-Fallows, xvii–xx.

58. "Faites-moy sçavoir de la belle ..." (no. 43), Thibault-Fallows, 87–88,

line 3. Cf. *"crudel martire"* in "Mort he mercy ..." (no. 10), Thibault-Fallows, 18–19, line 7.

59. Pesaro, Biblioteca Oliveriana, MS 1144 (lute scores, c. 1500, with poems and other late-sixteenth-century additions). For dating, contents, ownership, and two illustrations, see Rubsamen; for a codicological analysis (with corrections to Rubsamen) and another illustration, see Fallows; and Thibault-Fallows, plate 1. The other heart-shaped Pesaro volume is MS 1145 (poetry anthology, c. 1550).

60. See Fallows, 14–15; and, for transcripts of these notations, Saviotti, 234.

61. See the detailed chronology in Fallows, 10–15, who notes (14), that "changes in Tempesta's hand suggest compilation over a long period."

CHAPTER FIVE

1. For a recent discussion, with useful references, see Beaulieu.

2. Bynum, *Holy Feast*, 212.

3. Lochrie, 13–14 (see also 15).

4. Curtius, 311–12, quoting *Crowns of Martyrdom* (*Peristephanon*) 10.1119. On the saint's body as a "text" in Prudentius, see further in Frese and O'Keeffe, ix–xi.

5. Prudentius, *Crowns*, 9.13–16, 56–58.

6. Prudentius, *Crowns*, 9.60, 63, 69–72, 79–82, 90.

7. Derrida, *Of Grammatology*, 101–40, uses the phrase in discussing Lévi-Strauss, "A Writing Lesson." For a critical résumé, see Goldberg, 57–107.

8. "Whatever commandment the prisoner has disobeyed is written upon his body by the Harrow" (Kafka, "In the Penal Colony," 144).

9. Prudentius, *Crowns*, 9.10 ("*imago*"), 1.1 ("*Scripta sunt caelo ...*"), 1.74 ("*fama ... extinguitur*").

10. Prudentius, *Crowns*, 3.136–40.

11. See *DS* 2:1023–46.

12. Pseudo-Anselm, *Meditatio*, 10, *PL* 158:762 ("*apertio ... revelavit nobis divitias*," etc.). Bernard, *Sermones super Cantica*, 61.3–4 (= pt. II), *Opera* 2:150–51 ("*vulnerum Domini recordabor*," "*Patet arcanum cordis per foramina corporis*"). Þe *Wohunge of Ure Lauerd*, 283 ("... trewe luue lettres"). See Riehle, 48.

13. Christ's heart wound traditionally resulted from the soldier's lance (John 19.34).

14. Anonymous, *I Fioretti di San Francesco*, 2.3, ed. Bonino, 182, trans. Brown, 1450.

15. The popularity of the *Legenda* has somewhat overshadowed its often dubious quality as hagiography, as well as its numerous local versions or variants. See Reames.

16. Jacobus de Voragine, *Legenda aurea,* 36, ed. Graesse, 157, trans. Ryan, 1:142–43.

17. See Lightbown, 2:67.

18. Vincent of Beauvais, *Speculum historiale,* 10.57; *Speculum quadruplex* 4:388, col. 1.

19. See further examples and source material in Bynum, *Holy Feast,* 210–12, 255–57; and Beaulieu.

20. Capgrave, *The Life of St. Katharine of Alexandria* (Arundel MS), 3.13.580–81 ("enprended . . . / on-to hir herte"), 4.5.493 ("emprended with-inne hir entrayle"), ed. Horstmann, 205, 277. Cf. *The Golden Legend,* trans. Ryan, 2:334–41. Catherine's iconography often includes books, and one Flemish painting (now lost) even depicts her with a heart-shaped volume that implies writing on her heart; see below, chap. 7.

21. Bernard, *Sermones in laudibus Virginis Matris,* 4.11, in *Opera* 4:57, as quoted more fully above in chap. 4.

22. See Dinshaw, 9.

23. Gertrude of Helfta, *Legatus divinae pietatis* (= *Le Héraut*), 2.4.1, ed. Doyère, *SC* 139:242, trans. Barratt, 109.

24. Bynum, *Holy Feast,* 211 (and further refs., 257, 406 n. 50). See also Hamburger, *Nuns as Artists,* 178, with refs.

25. On writing as a fetish in the Middle Ages, see Camille, in Frese and O'Keeffe, 36–46.

26. Bynum, *Holy Feast,* 174 (exchange of hearts). On heart/book imagery in Catherine's iconography, see Bianchi, 1:112–14, 172, 175–76. On Catherine's heart and wounds, see *DS* 2:328–29, 332.

27. For background, see *DS* 10:576–88.

28. Guerin, 6:168.

29. Puccini, 58–59.

30. The similarity is noted by Chiarini, 30. Réau, 3/2:888, notes that Maria's visions "*rappellent celles de sainte Thérèse.*" On Sagrestani, see refs. in Turner, 27:521–22. I am indebted to Marlene Villalobos Hennessy for calling my attention to the Sagrestani painting.

31. Augustine, *Confessions,* 9.2, as discussed above in chap. 2. See also chap. 4, n. 42.

32. For background on Suso, see *DS* 7:234–57; and Hamburger, "The Use of Images."

33. Suso, *Briefbüchlein,* no. 11, ed. Bihlmeyer, 391–93, trans. Edward, 2:201–2.

34. On authorship, see Hamburger, "The Use of Images," 22.

35. Suso, *Leben,* 15, ed. Bihlmeyer, 40, trans. Edward, 1:38.

36. Suso, *Leben,* 4, ed. Bihlmeyer, 15–16, trans. Edward, 1:13–14.

37. *DS* 7:246.

38. Suso, *Leben*, 4, ed. Bihlmeyer, 16, trans. Edward, 1:14.

39. Suso as "minnesinger," Edward, 1:xlvi.

40. Lochrie, 14, 15.

41. Wattenbach, 187, mentions "*Wachstafeln*" under "*Urkunden.*"

42. See Wattenbach, 219; Glenisson and Holtz, 27–30 (with illustr.); *OLD*, s.v. *ferrum*, 2b.

43. Suso, *Horologium sapientiae*, 2.7.13–14 (quoting 2 Cor. 3.3), ed. Künzle, 596–97, trans. Colledge, 321 (altering "knife" to "iron stylus").

44. For an illustration and discussion, see Hamburger, *Nuns as Artists*, 178–80.

45. Several of these illustrations are reproduced in Bihlmeyer, figs. 4, 6, 10, 11, although poorly. One is sharply reproduced by van Os, 160 (fig. 72).

46. Suso, *Leben*, 45, ed. Bihlmeyer, 154–55, trans. Edward, 1:143. See also the account of Suso's devotion to Christ's name in *Zusätze zum Briefbüchlein*, ed. Bihlmeyer, 393–95, trans. Edward, 2:203–4.

47. On the "Charter of Christ," see Rubin, 306–8.

48. Suso, *Büchlein der Ewigen Weisheit*, 3 ("... büch mines gekrúzgeten libes"), ed. Bihlmeyer, 209, trans. Edward, 2:14.

49. See Hamburger, "The Use of Images," 43.


CHAPTER SIX

1. Sheingorn, 38.

2. Atkinson, 129, in a chapter discussing affective piety in general. On "prayer of the heart," see Saenger, "Books of Hours," as cited below.

3. Peter Comestor, *Sermo 6* ("*In nativitate domini*"), *PL* 198:1741.

4. Parkes, 560, 572, 565. For further background on lay literacy, see Clanchy, chap. 7.

5. Parkes, 563, with specific examples of books used by the laity, 565–70.

6. Wyclif, *De veritate sacrae scripturae*, 6, ed. Buddensieg, 1:108, cited in Tresko, 177. "The *liber* is the meaning or the truth of which the *codex* is a sign; it is the metaphysical reality of which the *codex* has the form but not the actuality" (Tresko, 175).

7. Tresko, 177, mentions *imitatio*.

8. This and subsequent quotations are from Pecock, *Repressor*, 1.5, ed. Babington, 1:25–26 (text modernized).

9. Babington, in Pecock, *Repressor*, introduction, 1:xxii.

10. See Babington's biographical summary in Pecock, *Repressor*, introduction, 1:xxxi–lvii.

11. For example, Thomas à Kempis, *Imitatio Christi*, 3.2, describes an interiority centered on the heart (*cor*).

12. Kempis, *Imitatio*, 3.3.20–21 ("*Scribe verba mea in corde tuo et pertracta diligenter . . .*"), ed. Lupo, 139, trans. Creasy, 57.

13. Kempis, *Imitatio*, 3.4.20–21, ed. Lupo, 143, trans. Creasy, 59.

14. Kempis, *Imitatio*, 3.43.16, ed. Lupo, 244, trans. Creasy, 102. "Reader" translates *intellector*, punning on *lector* (reader).

15. Biggs, ed., *The Imitation of Christ*, lxxix (audience), lxxiv (translation).

16. On vernacular versions of *De doctrina cordis*, see refs. in Hamburger, *Nuns as Artists*, 266 n. 77.

17. A female audience is also specified by one of the manuscript colophons: "Here endith a tretice made to religious wommen which is clepid the doctrine of the hert" (Cambridge, Trinity College Library MS B.14.15, quoted by Candon, ed., *The Doctrine of the Hert*, xiii).

18. *The Doctrine of the Hert* 3, ed. Candon, 99 (text modernized).

19. *The Doctrine of the Hert* 3, ed. Candon, 100.

20. The devotional book of the heart also has a feminine aspect in a fourteenth-century French play where the empress of Rome vows to praise the Virgin from a book she will write in her own heart—"*en mon cuer tel livre, / . . . en escripray*" (*Miracles de Nostre Dame*, no. 27, lines 1297–98, ed. Paris and Robert, 4:285).

21. Þe *Wohunge of Ure Lauerd*, 283 ("to reden trewe luue lettres"); see Riehle, 48. Rolle *Meditations on the Passion* (Text II), ed. Allen, *English Writings*, 36, lines 285–86 (text modernized). On the "Charter of Christ," see Rosemary Woolf, 210–14, and Rubin, 306–8. Henry Suso also likens Christ's body to a book, as cited in chap. 5.

22. See *DS* 2:1023–51.

23. Gertrude of Helfta, *Legatus divinae pietatis*, 2.4.1, ed. Doyère, *SC* 139:242, trans. Barratt, 109 (quoted more fully above, chap. 5).

24. Cited in Philippe de Mézières, *Le livre de la vertu du sacrement de mariage*, 2.26, ed. Williamson, 214.

25. John Howden, *Philomena*, 3.491.2, ed. Blume, 43. Cf. Pseudo-Augustine, *Liber meditationum*, 36, PL 40:931 ("*Scribe digito tuo in pectore meo dulcem memoriam . . .*"), cited in Brown, *Religious Lyrics*, 274–75.

26. *Meditations on the Life and Passion of Christ*, ed. D'Evelyn, lines 884, 1061–62, 1415, 2243 (text modernized). Cf. line 695, "Herte, write wiþ loue-lettre."

27. Brown, ed., *Religious Lyrics*, 114–19, 274–75 (no. 91, lines 1–8; text modernized). Further citations (by line) appear parenthetically. For other manuscripts and editions, see Wells, *Second Supplement*, 1078; Brown and Robbins, *Index*, no. 1761.

28. For example, "with loue bandes bynde þou so me / þat I be neuer de-

parted fro the" (lines 85–86; see also 80, 82, 84) The verb *binden* is attested for bookbinding from 1395 (*MED*, s.v. *binden*, 2c). On theological bookbinding metaphors, see Ahern.

29. On blood/ink, see Marti, 53; and Rubin, 307.

30. Augustine, *Confessions*, 9. 2. Rosemary Woolf, 164–66, discusses wounds and writing in this and other Middle English lyrics.

31. D'Evelyn, *Meditations*, 89–90.

32. Bath, Longleat MS 29, fol. 147r, quoted in Brown, ed., *Religious Lyrics*, 114 (text modernized). For the other citation, see *The Wheatley Manuscript*, ed. Day, ix, where cross marks in the manuscripts are also described.

33. Philippe de Mézières, *Le livre de la vertu du sacrement de mariage*, 2.26, ed. Williamson, 213–15, as expanded slightly in the appended French translation. (Latin text: "*O bone Jhesu, scribe in corde meo vulnera tua preciosissimo sanguine tuo ut semper cognoscam quid desit michi legam, senciam et intelligam dolorem et amorem tuum, bone Jhesu*").

34. On *ruminatio*, see Leclercq, *The Love of Learning*, 90; and Carruthers, 164–69.

35. Saenger, "Books of Hours," 145–46, with subsequent quotations from 144–46, 153, 154.

36. *Dies Irae*, lines 13–14, ed. Connelly, 254 ("*Liber scriptus . . . / In quo totum continetur*").

37. Pseudo-Bernard, *De interiori domo*, 18, *PL* 184:523, cited more fully above, chap. 3.

38. See Clanchy, esp. chap. 8.

39. See Chaucer, *Canterbury Tales*, III.1318, 1364 (Friar's Tale). Hahn and Kaeuper, 71, 74, cite surviving documentary evidence.

40. Wells, *Manual*, 385–87 (item 7.25); with additional MSS cited in *MED*, Plan and Bibliography, 66 (s.v. *PMor.*).

41. *Poema morale* 100 (devils), 113, 117–18, ed. and trans. Morris, 164–67.

42. Wells, *Manual*, 385.

43. *Cursor Mundi* (Cotton MS), 26727–29, ed. Morris, 1502 (text modernized).

44. Lewis and McIntosh, *A Descriptive Guide*, 1, 4 (dating).

45. *The Pricke of Conscience*, lines 5444–55, 5490, ed. Morris, 148–49 (text modernized).

46. *Imitatio* 3.43.8, ed. Lupo, 244, trans. Creasy, 102 (modified).

47. *Imitation of Christ* 3.48.8 (text modernized), ed. Biggs, 118 (editor's brackets), noting the misconstrued Latin (200n).

48. In the *Towneley Plays* (Wakefield), no. 30 (Judgment), the devils refer to "rentals" (line 196, ed. Stevens and Cawley, 1:406). In the *York Plays*, no. 48 (The Judgment Day), sinners complain of clearly "wreten" sins (line 132, ed.

Smith, 501). In the *Chester Mystery Cycle*, no. 24 (The Judgment), an angel cites a "Good accompt" (line 35, ed. Lumiansky and Mills, 1:439, with note, 2:354–55). And in the *N-Town Play*, sins can be "rede" off the foreheads of sinners, where they are "wretyn with letteris blake" (lines 77, 92, 96, ed. Spector, 1:412).

49. *Everyman* 104, 133–37 (altering *and* to *if*, and *year* to *years*), 187, 503, trans. Cawley, 210–12, 221.

50. See Terret, 1:100–1, with plate 26 (Michael stands directly to the left of the weighing of souls). Terret cites the *Dies Irae* in connection with this image, but also a pseudo-Bernardine passage implying a more individualized and interiorized book.

51. The same motif appears in a now fragmentary fresco of the Last Judgment at the Musée des Augustins de Toulouse. See Mesplé, 115–16 (with fig. 6).

52. See Tenenti, 103, illustration ("*Ecce peccata tua*"); Durliat, 96–97, one of the best recent articles on the Albi fresco; and Mâle, *La Cathédrale d'Albi*, 135–36.

53. Ariès, *Essais*, 34–35, trans. Ranum, 32–33 ("passport" rendering *pièce d'identité*). For more detailed commentary on these books as signs of "individualism," see Biget, 34–41.

54. Biget, 35.

55. Durliat, 100–1, thus dates the fresco and even suggests the stylistic influence of Rogier van der Weyden, the same Flemish master who most influenced the Master of Sainte Gudule.

CHAPTER SEVEN

1. For convenience I have chosen the shortest of the artist's several designations, the main variant of which is the Master of the View of Sainte Gudule (or Gudula). Bénézit, *Dictionnaire*, 7:101, identifies him as Valentin van Orley, but few scholars agree. For bibliography, see Friedländer, *Early Netherlandish Painting*, 4:62–63, 79–80, 85–86, 90, 99–100 (and *Supplements*, 12); Comblen-Sonkes, 125–27; Barbara Lane, 232–34; and Catheline Périer-D'Ieteren, in Turner, 20:780–81. The two paintings are *Young Man Holding a Book* (50.145.27), New York, The Metropolitan Museum of Art; and *Portrait of a Young Man* (2612), London, The National Gallery. The London painting is catalogued by Davies, *The National Gallery*, 2:202–7 (no. 62), now updated by Campbell, 346–53. No detailed catalog description exists for the New York painting, but I have been kindly shown its archives by Veronique Sintobin, a member of the curatorial staff. For color reproductions, see Bauman, 40; and Campbell, 347 (London portrait only).

2. See Panofsky, 1:346.

3. Catheline Périer-D'Ieteren, in *Dictionnaire des peintres belges*, 2:671–72. See also Toussaint and Dijkstra, 539–40, as quoted below.

4. Sterling, 9.

5. Nathalie Toussaint and Jellie Dijkstra, in *Les Primitifs flamands*, 540, 539.

6. Schneider, 6, 9.

7. For example, Friedländer, *Early Netherlandish Painting*, 4:80 (nos. 76–77, titles); Davies, *The National Gallery*, 2:203; Bauman, 41; Nicole Véronee-Verhaegen, in *Les Primitifs flamands*, 229; and Campbell, 350.

8. Nicole Véronee-Verhaegen, in *Les Primitifs flamands*, 229.

9. On the heart in fifteenth-century devotional psychology, see Saenger, "Books of Hours," 145–46.

10. Gertrude of Helfta, *Legatus divinae pietatis*, 2.4.1, ed. Doyère, *SC* 139:242.

11. "Ihesu þat hast me dere I-boght," line 29, ed. Brown, *Religious Lyrics*, 115.

12. For the history of these liturgical elements, see Jungmann, 1:454–55 (*Dominus sit in corde tuo*), 2:210–13 (*Sursum corda*), 2:218–26 (*Unde et memores*). On the formula of the Consecration, see Jungmann, 2:194–201.

13. Lamentations 3.41 ("*levemus corda nostra cum manibus ad Dominum in caelos*").

14. Rubin, 63 ("efficacy"); Hardison, 64–65 ("focus," "suspended"); Saenger, "Books of Hours," 153 ("especially"). For more on the Elevation, see Jungmann, 2:206–10; and Rubin, 55–82, 131–34, 155–63, and figs. 1, 7, 9, 19. Cf. Camille, 111, on an amorous "*elevatio* of the heart" in a fourteenth-century ivory carving.

15. "Welcome, Lord, in forme of bred" (Gurney lyric, c. 1400), lines 9–10, in Robbins, 374 (text modernized), cited by Rubin, 161 (as "Robbins 1939a" but actually "1939b").

16. Infrared study of underdrawings in the London portrait reveals that the artist emphasized the book by eliminating several human figures in the space above it. See Ainsworth, "Northern Renaissance Drawings," fig. 9 (reprod. in Campbell, 349).

17. For example, *Missale sarum*, Canon, 615–18. For the history of this practice, see Jungmann, 1:452–54, 2:210, 308, 351.

18. On *fractio hostiae* and *apertio Scripturae*, see de Lubac, 82–83. On the Eucharist as "food of the heart," see Rubin, 38 (quoting James of Vitry).

19. The Virgin and Child are more sharply detailed in Rogier van der Weyden's *Altarpiece of the Seven Sacraments*, reproduced in Bauman, 41, as a likely source for the Master of Sainte Gudule.

20. See Rubin, 135–39.

21. For example, van de Castyne, 327 ("*le personnage portraituré reparaît au second plan, servant la messe au moment de l'offertoire*").

22. See Jungmann, 2:210–14; and Rubin, 57.

23. Beaulieu, 310. Cf. Philippians 2.10 (*"in nomine Iesu omne genu flectat"*).

24. *Oratio Manassae* 11, ed. Weber, *Biblia sacra,* 1909. See further in Curtius, 137–38.

25. See detail reproduced in Bauman, 41.

26. *Thesaurus linguae Latinae,* s.v. *diptychum.*

27. See Mellinkoff, 36. For round-topped (and round-sided) wax tablets, see figures in Glenisson and Holtz, 30–31, and 41 (medallion no. 2).

28. See Johannot, 43–46.

29. Peter Comestor, *Sermo de libro vitae* (= Pseudo-Hildebert of Lavardin, *Sermones ad diversos* 102), *PL* 171:814–18.

30. Davies, *The National Gallery,* 2:204, and Bauman, 40, deem this hypothesis only "possibly" true, but Campbell, 352, seems to think it more probable. For examples of such diptychs, see van Os, 116–17 (pl. 36), and other folding icons, passim.

31. Cf. the folding heart-shaped altarpiece produced about a century later by Lucas Cranach the Younger, for a Protestant patron, as discussed and illustrated in Hamburger, *Nuns as Artists,* 171–73.

32. Paris, Bibliothèque nationale, Latin MS 10536, catalogued and described in Leroquais, 1:337–38 (no. 157).

33. Jean Porcher, in Thibault-Fallows, xxii, describes the cordiform book in the London painting as *"Coeur simple, comme les heures à l'usage d'Amiens."* Campbell, 348, reproduces the cordiform prayer book as an analogue to the book in the London portrait. Cf. Bauman, 41 (apparently unaware of Paris, Latin MS 10536), "a prayer book might just as well have a heart shape—indicative of passionate devotion."

34. Notre-Dame des Victoires au Sablon. On the sitter as scribe, see van Bastelaer and van de Castyne, both summarized and discussed in Davies, *The National Gallery,* 2:205–207; and Campbell, 352.

35. Davies, *The Early Netherlandish School,* 115 n. 8.

36. Van de Castyne, 326, 328.

37. Campbell, 350.

38. Saenger, "Books of Hours," 155–56.

39. Peter Comestor, *Sermo de libro vitae* (= Pseudo-Hildebert of Lavardin, *Sermones ad diversos* 102), *PL* 171:815.

40. Durham Cathedral MS B.IV.12, fols. 37v–38v, ed. and trans. Rouse, 7 (Latin), 9 (English).

41. Kempis, *Imitatio,* 3.3.20–21, ed. Lupo, 139, trans. Creasy, 57.

42. *Miracles de Nostre Dame,* no. 27, lines 1297–98, ed. Paris and Robert, 4:285 (*"en mon cuer tel livre, / . . . en escripray"*).

43. Ambrose, *Explanatio Psalmorum XII,* 1.52, *CSEL* 64:45.

44. Pseudo-Bernard, *De interiori domo,* 18, *PL* 184:523.

45. Pseudo-Bernard, *De interiori domo*, 15, *PL* 184:520.

46. *Everyman* 136, ed. Cawley, 5.

47. See Ps. 40.8 (= Vulg. 39.9, *"legem tuam in medio cordis mei"*); Prov. 4.21.

48. Petrarch, *Secretum*, 3 (*"de medio experientie libro"*), ed. Bigi, 638, trans. Draper, 137 (modified).

49. Van Bastelaer, 18; Davies, *The National Gallery*, 2:203–204; Campbell, 350.

50. Campbell, 349.

51. Peter of Blois, *Sermones*, 65, *PL* 207:754, quoting Jer. 17.9 (= Vulg. 17.8), and substituting *profundum* for *pravum*.

52. Hugh of St. Cher, *De doctrina cordis*, 6, in Hendrix, 185.

53. Schneider, 9 (emphasis added).

54. Guigo II, *Scala claustralium*, 8, *SC* 163:100, trans. Colledge and Walsh, 76.

55. Augustine, *Confessions*, 10.1 (see also fig. 1).

56. Petrarch, *Secretum*, 3, ed. Bigi, 638, trans. Draper, 137 (modified).

57. Dante, *La vita nuova*, 1, ed. Barbi, 3–4, trans. Reynolds, 29.

58. See Jeffrey, 16, discussing Augustine's book metaphor for self-understanding in *The City of God*, 20.14.

59. The seminal article is Friedländer, "Die Brüsseler Tafelmalerei," esp. 317–20.

60. Arndt, 17 (*". . . un nom imaginaire, à défaut d'une identité réelle"*).

61. On the concept of "authorship" in art history, see Moxey, chap. 3, esp. 57–59.

62. For example, Nathalie Toussaint and Jellie Dijkstra, in *Les Primitifs flamands*, 540, equating the master's handling of drapery with *"une signature"*; and Catheline Périer-D'Ieteren, in *Dictionnaire des peintres belges*, 2:671–72, replete with scribal metaphors (*"une écriture incisive,"* etc.).

63. For this theory, see Beard; and, for rebuttal, Davies, *The National Gallery*, 2:204.

64. See Campbell, 352.

65. See van Bastelaer, 17 (London portrait); and van de Castyne, 327 (both paintings; quoted above, n. 21, on the New York portrait).

66. Schneider, 12.

67. Montaigne, *Essais*, "Au Lecteur" (*"C'est moy que je peins. . . . Je suis moy-mesmes la matiere de mon livre . . ."*), ed. Villey-Saulnier, 1:3, trans. Cohen, 23; and *Essais*, 3.9 (*"luy seul jouyssoit de ma vraye image, et l'emporta. C'est pourquoy je me deschiffre moy-mesme, si curieusement"*), ed. Villey-Saulnier, 2:983 n. 4, as trans. by Taylor, 183.

68. Summers, in Preziosi, 133.

69. Catheline Périer-D'Ieteren, in *Dictionnaire des peintres belges*, 2:671.

70. The Master of the Embroidered Foliage (fl. 1495–1500), *Saints Jerome and Catherine*, known to have been at the Perdoux Gallery, Paris, in 1936. See Fried-

länder, 4:87 (Supp. 131), and plate III. The archives of the Metropolitan Museum of Art, New York, contain a larger photo of the Catherine painting, kindly shown to me by Veronique Sintobin. In the Saint Catherine, according to Campbell, 346, "the sitter's hand and book are copied" from the London portrait. On Catherine's inscribed heart, see Capgrave, as cited above in chap. 5.

## CHAPTER EIGHT

1. Trithemius, *De laude scriptorum*, 6; Arnold/Behrendt, 60–61 (trans. modified), where *imprimere* and related terms denote mechanical printing (see esp. chap. 7; Arnold/Behrendt, 64–65).

2. The scholarly studies that I have found most helpful for this chapter include Erickson, Heffernan, Kiefer, Taylor, and Stevens.

3. Cave, 85 (omitting emphasis on "living").

4. Greenblatt, 84. *New England Primer*, ed. Ford, 66 (orig. emphasis), with heart/book emblem; see also 69, 78, 81 (lessons "by Heart").

5. Greenblatt, 86, 96.

6. On the "heart" as conscience in the seventeenth century, see Kiefer 115–16; and Stevens, 271.

7. Kiefer, 106.

8. Pecke, "Cordial Prayer," line 4, in *Parnassi Puerperium*, 97; Harvey, *Schola cordis*, preface ("The Learning of the Heart"), line 4 (punctuation modernized in both texts).

9. Nashe, *Christ's Teares*, 179 (spelling modernized). *OED*, s.v. *diary*, sb., 1.

10. Donne, *Sermons*, 9:237 (spelling modernized), cited by Heffernan, 21.

11. See *OED*, s.v. *pocket-book*, with 1617 quotation referring to "a manuall or pocket-booke, . . . a pectorall or bosome-booke."

12. Carpenter, *The Conscionable Christian*, 41, 45 (spelling and punctuation modernized), as cited by Kiefer, 113, who likens the scribal work of conscience to "a spiritual biography."

13. See *OED*, s.v. *character*, sb., 10, 11, attesting the ethical sense of *character*, as applied to external features that betoken inner qualities, or inner qualities themselves, from about 1600. For medieval precedents, see *DMLBS*, s.v. *character*, 4.

14. Watson, "The Day of Judgment Asserted," ed. Nichols, 5:463–65, cited by Erickson, 220.

15. Harvey, *Schola cordis*, 105, ode 26, st. 1, lines 5–8 (spelling modernized).

16. Harvey, *Schola cordis*, 105, epigram 26, line 4; 107, ode 26, stanza 6, line 6.

17. Burton, *The Anatomy of Melancholy*, 776, cited in Kiefer, 113 (spelling modernized).

18. Downame, *The Christian Warfare*, 379 (spelling modernized), as quoted in Kiefer, 113.

19. Watson, *God's Anatomy*, 6 (spelling modernized), as quoted in Erickson, 46.

20. Watson, *God's Anatomy*, 10–11 (spelling modernized), as quoted in Erickson, 46–47.

21. Acts 1.24, 15.8. See above, chap. 1, n. 79.

22. See *OED*, s.v. *key*, sb.[1], 6b.

23. See *OED*, s.v. *character*, sb., 4c.

24. Donne, *Sermons*, 9:237 (spelling and punctuation modernized; my emphasis).

25. See *OED*, s.v. *interline*, v.[1] Donne also uses expressly typographical terms in comparing Elizabeth Drury's soul to a book translated to heaven "in a far fairer print" ("The Second Anniversarie," line 314, ed. Milgate, 50).

26. For example, Pseudo-Hugh of St. Victor, *Miscellanea*, 3.66, *PL* 177:675, as cited in chap. 3. Kiefer, 115, cites John Hughes (1622), on the two "parts" or "volumes" of man's inner book.

27. Donne, *Sermons*, 1:303, line 81, cited in *OED*, s.v. *middle age*, sb., 2.

28. Donne, *Pseudo-Martyr*, preface, sig. B2v (modernized), cited in Carey, 14.

29. Herrick, "To His Conscience," ed. Martin, 357 (spelling modernized).

30. Herbert, "Judgement," lines 5, 13, ed. Hutchinson, 187–88 (modernized). For more about writing on the heart in Herbert, see Heffernan, 43–57.

31. Fish, 158. Toliver, 190, refers to a persona "acutely aware of his singularity and its incriminating history. . . ."

32. Fletcher, *Licia*, Sonnet 6 ("My love amaz'd did blush her selfe to see"), lines 9–10, ed. Berry, 84. See also Donne, "The Dampe," line 4: "When they shall finde your Picture in my heart," ed. Gardner, 49.

33. Francis Rous, *Thule; or Vertues Historie*, 2.8.109–12, ed. Crossley, 145 (spelling modernized).

34. Shakespeare, Sonnet 24.1–2, 6–8, ed. Evans (altering "stell'd"). Play texts, and act, scene, and line numbers also follow this edition (with brackets removed).

35. Sidney, *Astrophil and Stella*, Sonnet 1, lines 7, 14, ed. Ringler, 165 (spelling modernized).

36. Spenser, *Amoretti*, Sonnet 1 ("Happy ye leaves . . ."), lines 1, 8, ed. Oram, 600 (spelling modernized).

37. John Wilson, "You Heralds of my Mistresse heart," in *Cheerfull Ayres*, 1:94 (spelling modernized). Aphra Behn, "A Voyage to the Isle of Love," line 34, ed. Todd, 103.

38. Curtius, 332–40, catalogs some of Shakespeare's book metaphors. See further in Kiefer, chaps. 7, 8.

39. Shakespeare, *Romeo and Juliet*, 1.3.81–88. For Shakespeare on "reading" persons in general, see *OED*, s.v. *read*, v., 10b (1604), 10c (1590).

40. Shakespeare, *Twelfth Night*, 1.4.13–14, 24; 1.5.223–29.

41. Cervantes, *Don Quixote*, part 3, chap. 16 (*"eternamente escrito en mi memoria"*), ed. Allen, 1:199, trans. Cohen, 120.

42. Lafayette, *La Princesse de Clèves* (*"une grande impression dans son coeur"*), ed. Magne, 37, trans. Mitford-Tancock, 53.

43. Lafayette, *La Princesse de Clèves*, 121, trans., 127.

44. For example, Lafayette, *La Princesse de Clèves*, 163 (*"impressions dans son coeur"*), trans., 164.

45. Lafayette, *La Princesse de Clèves*, 199–200, trans., 196.

46. Fielding, *Amelia*, vol. 2, bk. 6, chap. 6, ed. Battestin, 252. Writing on the heart is also invoked to authenticate love letters: "I need not sign this Letter, otherwise than with that Impression of my Heart which I hope it bears . . ." (vol. 4, bk. 10, chap. 8, 443).

47. Erickson, 188. On the heart in Richardson's novels in general, see Erickson's superb chapter 5.

48. Richardson, *Clarissa* (3rd ed., 1751), vol. 1, letter 3, 18; vol. 2, letter 39, 264.

49. Richardson, *Pamela* (vol. 2, "Tuesday Morning, the Sixth Day of my Happiness"), ed. Sabor, 467.

50. Richardson, *Sir Charles Grandison*, vol. 4, letter 9, ed. Harris, 2:312.

51. Richardson, *Sir Charles Grandison*, vol. 6, letter 24, ed. Harris, 3:91.

52. See Erickson, 195.

53. Hawthorne, *The Scarlet Letter*, chap. 23, 255 (this "stigma" being "no more than the type of what has seared his inmost heart").

54. A search of the Chadwyck-Healey *Literature Online* database of *Eighteenth-Century Fiction (1700–1780)* for the word "impression" turned up 109 hits in 41 works for "heart" (within ten words), and 81 hits in 37 works for "mind."

55. Richardson, *Sir Charles Grandison*, vol. 4, letter 18, ed. Harris, 2:357 (omitting the original emphasis on *prepared*).

56. Montaigne, *Essais*, 3.9, as cited above in chap. 7. Poulet, *Études*, 1:32.

57. Erickson, 75–78, citing Burton and Harvey. See further examples in Stevens, 269–70.

58. Stevens, 273.

59. See Erickson, 4; Stevens, 265–66; and LeGoff.

60. Descartes, *Les Passions de l'âme*, art. 32, ed. Rodis-Lewis, 90. In article 33, Descartes denies that the heart is the seat of the passions. For analysis, see Stevens, 268–69, noting that for Descartes the pineal gland was not the exclusive seat of the soul but the site of mind-body interaction.

61. On the Counter-Reformation heart, see Stevens, esp. 271–72.

62. Marti, 2.

63. Shakespeare, Sonnets 59.2, 5, 8; 108.1–2; 122.1–2, 5. Stevens, 265–67, discusses Shakespeare's head/heart equivocation.

64. Shakespeare, *Hamlet*, 1.1.2. Cf. Polonius to Laertes, "And these few precepts in thy memory / Look thou character" (1.3.58–59), where the textual and ethical senses of "character" coincide. For a detailed study of books and textual metaphor in *Hamlet*, see Sanders, 57–87.

65. Shakespeare, *Hamlet*, 1.5.91, 97–103.

66. Hobbes, *Leviathan*, 3.42, ed. Macpherson, 545 (punctuation modernized), cited by Erickson, 17. Johnson, *Rasselas*, chap. 22, ed. Kolb, 86 ("that universal and unalterable law with which every heart is originally impressed"). Derrida, *Of Grammatology*, 17, cites passages from Rousseau.

67. Hooker, *Of the Laws of Ecclesiastical Polity*, 1.6.1, ed. Kebel, 1:217.

68. Locke himself never actually used the term *tabula rasa*, which appears in Latin translations of Aristotle used by medieval scholastics. See references in Hooker, *Laws*, ed. Hill, 1:492; and Taylor, 165, citing Cudworth.

69. Locke, *Essay*, 2.1.1, 2.1.2, ed. Nidditch, 104.

70. Locke, *Essay*, 2.1.15, ed. Nidditch, 112.

71. Erickson, 214 (citing a rare use of "heart" language in Locke).

72. Taylor, 166, 167 (original emphasis).

73. See Kernan, 48–55.

74. Eisenstein, 1:262.

75. Ong, 131–32.

76. See Tanner, ed., *Pride and Prejudice*, introduction, 9–13.

77. On Locke in Sterne's novel, see Butt and Carnall, 432, 444–46.

78. So called by Butt and Carnall, 456–57.

79. Johnstone, *Chrysal*, bk. 1, chap. 2 (1:8–9; original emphasis); further citations are parenthetical and refer to page.

80. Cf. Locke, *Essay*, 2.27.9, ed. Nidditch, 335 ("consciousness always accompanies thinking, and 'tis that, that makes every one to be, what he calls *self*," and "in this alone consists *personal Identity* . . .").

CHAPTER NINE

1. On palimpsests, see Roberts and Skeat, 16–18; and Reynolds and Wilson, 174–77.

2. Browning, *Aurora Leigh*, 1.824–32, ed. Reynolds, 195–96.

3. De Quincey, "The Palimpsest of the Human Brain," in *Suspiria de Profundis*, pt. 2, ed. Masson, 13:346, with further citations from 347, 349.

4. Sully, 364, also comparing the "dream-inscription" to "some letter in cipher."

5. Freud, *The Interpretation of Dreams*, 4, *SE* 4:135.

6. Freud, *The Interpretation of Dreams*, 6(I), *SE* 5:500–501. Frieden, 46, notes Freud's citation of Sully.

7. Freud, "A Note upon the 'Mystic Writing-Pad,'" *SE* 19:225–32, with citations from 229, 230–31.

8. Wharton, *The House of Mirth*, 1.5, 2.3, ed. Benstock, 69, 204; see also 2.1 (185), referring to the "grooves" and "impressions" of thought.

9. Woolf, *To the Lighthouse*, 3.4, 169. Similarly, James "[turns] back among the many leaves which the past had folded in him . . ." (3.8, 185).

10. Woolf, *To the Lighthouse*, 1.9, 51. Although Cam imagines James as "the lawgiver, with the tablets of eternal wisdom laid open on his knee" (3.4, 168), these "tablets" are open and external rather than inward and concealed. Nussbaum, 740–43, discusses Woolf's metaphor of "reading" other minds.

11. Lorenz, 262 ("I have called it '*Pragung*' in German, which I purpose [*sic*] to translate into English by the term 'imprinting'"), cited in *OED*, s.v. *imprinting*, sb., 2; and Ostow, citing a 1970 study in a 1992 letter ("It is as though . . . the ego were indeed a palimpsest").

12. Lacan, "The Agency of the Letter . . . ," in *Écrits*, 147 ("What the psychoanalytic experience discovers in the unconscious is the whole structure of language"); "The Function and Field of Speech . . . ," in *Écrits*, 50.

13. Mallarmé, "Le Livre, Instrument Spirituel," ed. Mondor and Jean-Aubry, trans. Cook, as rpt. in Hazard Adams (quoted here with minor corrections).

14. Planche, 788.

15. Poulet, "Phenomenology of Reading," 54, rpt. in Hazard Adams, 1213.

16. Derrida, "Freud and the Scene of Writing," in *Writing and Difference*, 199. For discussion, see Christopher Lane, esp. 110.

17. Derrida, *Of Grammatology*, 18.

18. Barthes, "From Work to Text."

19. For illuminating comments on the age of the codex, see Chartier, "Representations of the Written Word," esp. 20–24.

20. Lanham, 8, 154. See Birkerts for a recent and widely noted example of lament.

21. Hobbes, introduction, *Leviathan*, ed. Macpherson, 81 (spelling modernized).

22. See Taylor, 164.

23. *OLD*, s.v. *ingenium*; *OED*, s.v *engine*, sb., 7b, 10b (spelling modernized).

24. For numerous examples, see *OED*, s.v. *steam*, sb., 7d.

25. Shelley, letter to Maria Gisborne (1820), as cited in *OED*, s.v. *steam*, sb., 17.

26. See *OED*, s.v. *steam*, sb., 7d (Allbutt quot.).

27. The classic essay on dynamo symbolism is Henry Adams, *The Education*, chap. 25 ("The Dynamo and the Virgin").

28. Quotations cited in *OED*, s.v. *dynamo*, sb., 1b.

29. See *OED*, s.v. *rev*, v., 2; and *cylinder*, sb., 6 (1932 quot.); and, for an iconographic equivalent, see Wright, as cited in n. 50, below. For other industrial or technical terms adapted to popular psychology, see *OED*, s.v. *screw*, sb.[1], 3b ("a screw loose," attested since 1810); and *gear*, sb., 7a ("out of gear," attested since 1849).

30. The psychoanalytic concept of "repression" (*Verdrängung*) first appeared in an 1893 paper on hysteria coauthored by Freud and Breuer (as *verdrängt*, "repressed"); see *SE* 2:10, with editor's note, and further references in *SE* 14:16n, 143–45.

31. James Strachey, introduction to Breuer and Freud, *Studies on Hysteria*, *SE* 2:xxiv. For more on the Freud's psychic metaphors and their development, see Yovell.

32. Breuer, in Breuer and Freud, *Studies on Hysteria*, 3.2, ed. Strachey, *SE* 2:193.

33. The phonograph also supplied new psychic metaphors. For example, "Their small talk ... flew back and forth over little grooves worn in the thin upper surface of the brain ..." (Porter, "Pale Horse, Pale Rider," 279–80).

34. See *OED*, s.v. *camera*, 3d (*camera-eye*, etc.), 3a (1878 quot.), 4a (1822 quot.).

35. Isherwood, *Goodbye to Berlin*, 13.

36. See *OED*, s.v. *photograph*, v., 2; *snap-shot*, sb., 2a. Cf. *daguerrotype*, 3 (1858 quot.).

37. Searching the CD-ROM version of the *OED* for the phrase "mental picture" yielded fourteen quotations of which all but the first postdate the invention of photography: 1832, 1865, 1894, 1909, 1934, 1936, 1943, 1949, 1958 (2 quots.), 1964, 1972, 1976 (2 quots.). The twenty-four examples of the phrase "mental picture" similarly postdate photography, except for the first attested use (1668).

38. Stevenson and Osbourne, *Wrecker*, chap. 10, 189, cited in *OED*, s.v. *negative*, sb., 8a. *OED*, s.v. *photographic*, 1c. Cf. *mental photograph*, with one citation from 1903 (*OED*, s.v. *psychometer*, 1). Thomas, *Lewis Carroll*, 267, cites an 1850 sermon that uses photographic metaphors ("image," "focus") for "mental pictures" of forbidden sexuality.

39. Gray, 160.

40. For a superb history of this subject, see Kevles.

41. Mann, *The Magic Mountain*, 5.2 (215), where the German edition has "*die Geheimnisse Ihres Busens*" (302), cited in Kevles, 79.

42. See *OED*, s.v. *cliché*, 3; and *script*, sb., 5c.

43. See *OED*, s.v. *flashback*, sb., 2 ("a revival of the memory of past events"); *montage*, 3 (1941 quot.); and *slow*, a., 14a (1973 quot.). See also *Webster's Third*, s.v.

*flashback*, n., 1c ("a past incident recurring vividly in the mind"); and *take*, n., 5 ("an act or the action of taking something in mentally").

44. See *OED*, s.v. *replay*, sb., 3.

45. Canaway, *The Willow-Pattern War*, chap. 15, 152–53, cited in *OED*, s.v. *replay*, sb., 3.

46. Styron, 74. Cf. a witness to an execution referring to memory as "my mental videotape," *New York Times*, 22 February 1996, A14.

47. Lapham, 12.

48. Gould, 287–89, using "replay" and "tape" in reference to both film and biology. Gould sometimes mixes textual and video metaphors (e.g., ". . . any *replay*, altered by an apparently insignificant *jot or tittle* at the outset" [289, my emphasis]).

49. See *OED*, s.v. *evolution* (etymology); Cicero, *De officiis*, 3.19.76 (see above, chap. 1). *OED*, s.v. *hominoid*, attests "fossil records" (1949); and, s.v. *progressionist*, 2, "geological record" (1867).

50. Wright, cover story in *Time*, 25 March 1996 (with an interior photo, 52–53, illustrating the older metaphor of the mind as an "engine"). A more recent *Newsweek* cover story on human memory contained a full-page illustration (Cowley and Underwood, 48) of a human head swathed in photographic film (the mind as camera), but the article itself features mainly computer analogies (RAM, hard drive, etc.) despite the disclaimer "Brains are different from computers, but the analogy can be helpful" (50).

51. Gigerenzer and Goldstein, 138.

52. Hayles, 242–43.

53. Hutchins, 363, in a chapter offering a valuable critique of cognitive science.

54. See *OED*, s.v. *hard-wired*.

55. Kingwell, 85 (discussing meme theory).

56. Sobchack, 85.

57. Kingwell, 84.

58. Swift, *A Tale of a Tub*, 7, ed. Davis, 92. See *OED*, s.v. *computer*, 1, 2.

59. Searle, 38 (col. 2).

60. Gigerenzer and Goldstein, 137.

61. Kingwell, 89.

62. Gigerenzer and Goldstein, 136.

63. Illich, 3.

64. Nelson, who, apart from a few verbal (but not strictly textual) tropes (e.g., "discourse," "chatter," [530]), refers to a "hard-wired" brain (526–27, 534) and "synaptic circuits" (529), noting that "electrical activity is our surrogate for 'experience'" (529). Compare Ostow's unqualified palimpsest meta-

phor, cited above in n. 11. Greenberg and Leiderman, in a 1966 article, claim to "update" Freud's writing pad with a tape-recorder analogy.

65. Vidal, 6 ("erasing . . . while writing"), 9 ("Palimpsest time"), 31–32 ("re-play, "reedit"), 47 ("miracle"). See also the mixed metaphors cited above in n. 48.

66. Baker, 40.

67. Unless a new "electronic book" prolongs the life of the codex. For technical details, see Jacobson and Comiskey. News articles appeared in the *New York Times*, 8 April and 2 July 1998.

# Works Cited

Abelard, Peter. *Historia calamitatum.* Edited by Nada Cappelletti Truci. *Abelardo ed Eloisa: Lettere,* 2–118. Turin: Einaudi, 1982. Translated in Radice, 57–106.

Adams, Hazard, ed. *Critical Theory since Plato.* New York: Harcourt, 1971.

Adams, Henry. *The Education of Henry Adams.* 1907. Edited by Ernest Samuels and Jayne N. Samuels. *Henry Adams: Novels, Mont Saint Michel, The Education,* 715–1192. New York: The Library of America, 1983.

Aers, David. "A Whisper in the Ear of Early Modernists; or, Reflections on Literary Critics Writing the 'History of the Subject.'" In *Culture and History, 1350–1600: Essays on English Communities, Identities and Writing.* Edited by David Aers, 177–202. Detroit: Wayne State University Press, 1992.

Aeschylus. *Aeschylus.* Edited and translated by Herbert Weir Smyth. LCL. 2 vols. London: Heinemann, 1926.

———. *Oresteia.* Translated by Richmond Lattimore. Chicago: University of Chicago Press, 1953.

Ahern, John. "Binding the Book: Hermeneutics and Manuscript Production in *Paradiso* 33." *PMLA* 97 (1982): 800–9.

Ainsworth, Maryan Wynn. "Northern Renaissance Drawings and Underdrawings: A Proposed Method of Study." *Master Drawings* 27 (1989): 5–38.

Alan of Lille. *Ars praedicandi. PL* 210:109–35. Translated by Gillian R. Evans. *The Art of Preaching.* Kalamazoo: Cistercian Publications, 1981.

———. *De planctu naturae.* Edited by Thomas Wright. *The Anglo-Latin Satirical Poets and Epigrammatists of the Twelfth Century,* 2:429–522. Roll Series 59. London: Longman and Trübner, 1872. Translated by James J. Sheridan. *The Plaint of Nature.* Toronto: Pontifical Institute of Mediaeval Studies, 1980.

Alcuin of York. *Adversus Elipandum Toletanum* (Against Elipandus). *PL* 101: 243–300.

———. *Epistolae.* Edited by Ernest Dümmler. Monumenta Germaniae Historica. *Epistolae Karolini Aevi,* 4/2:1–493. Berlin: Weidmann, 1895.

Alighieri, Dante. *La Divina Commedia.* Edited by C. H. Grandgent. Revised by Charles S. Singleton. Cambridge: Harvard University Press, 1972.

———. *La vita nuova.* Edited by Michele Barbi. Florence: Società Dantesca Italiana, 1907. Translated by Barbara Reynolds. *La Vita Nuova.* Penguin: Harmondsworth, 1969.

Ambrose. *De spiritu sancto.* Edited by Otto Faller. *CSEL* 79. Vienna: Tempsky, 1964. Translation, *Of the Holy Spirit.* NPNF, ser. 1, vol. 10.

———. *Epistolae.* Edited by Otto Faller and Michael Zelzer. *CSEL* 82 (in 4 pts.). Vienna: Hoelder, Pichler, Tempsky, 1968–96. Translated by Mary M. Beyenka. *Saint Ambrose, Letters.* FOC 26. New York: Fathers of the Church, 1954.

———. *Explanatio Psalmorum XII.* Edited by M. Petschenig. *CSEL* 64. Vienna: Tempsky, 1919. Reprint, New York: Johnson, 1962. Translated by Luigi Franco Pizzolato. *Commento a dodici Salmi.* 2 vols. Milan: Biblioteca Ambrosiana, 1980.

Andreas Capellanus. *De amore.* Edited and translated by P. G. Walsh. *Andreas Capellanus on Love* (Latin and English). London: Duckworth, 1982.

Anonymous. *I Fioretti di San Francesco* (The Little Flowers of St. Francis). Edited by Guido Davico Bonino. 2nd ed. Turin: Einaudi, 1968. Translated by Raphael Brown. *St. Francis of Assisi: Writings and Early Biographies.* Edited by Marion A. Habig, 1267–1530. 3rd rev. ed. Chicago: Franciscan Herald Press, 1973.

Ariès, Philippe. *Essais sur l'histoire de la mort en occident: du moyen age à nos jours.* Paris: Seuil, 1975. Translated by Patricia M. Ranum. *Western Attitudes toward Death: From the Middle Ages to the Present.* Baltimore: Johns Hopkins University Press, 1974.

Aristotle. *On Memory and Recollection.* Translated by W. S. Hett. LCL, *Aristotle,* vol. 8:285–313. Rev. ed. London: Heinemann, 1957.

———. *On the Soul.* Translated by W. S. Hett. LCL, *Aristotle,* vol. 8:1–203. Rev. ed. London: Heinemann, 1957.

Arndt, Karl. "Les Maîtres anonymes et leurs problèmes." *Primitifs flamands anonymes: Maîtres aux noms d'emprunt des Pays-Bas méridionaux du XVᵉ et du début du XVIᵉ siècle,* 17–24. Bruges: Ville de Bruges, 1969.

Arns, Evaristo. *La technique du livre d'après saint Jérôme.* Paris: Boccard, 1953.

Athanasius. *Vita Antonii.* Edited by G. J. M. Bartelink. *Vita di Antonio.* Fondazione Lorenzo Valla: Mondadori, 1974. Translated by Robert C. Gregg. *The Life of Anthony.* New York: Paulist, 1980.

Atkinson, Clarissa W. *Mystic and Pilgrim: The Book and the World of Margery Kempe.* Ithaca, N.Y.: Cornell University Press, 1983.

Auerbach, Erich. "Figura." In *Scenes from the Drama of European Literature: Six Es-*

*says,* translated by Ralph Manheim and Catherine Garvin, 11–76. 1959. Reprint, Gloucester, Mass.: Peter Smith, 1973.

Augustine. *Confessions.* Edited by Martinus Skutella, revised by H. Juergens and W. Schaub. *Confessionum libri xiii.* Stuttgart: Teubner, 1981. Translated by Rex Warner. *The Confessions of St. Augustine.* New York: New American Library, 1963.

――――. *De civitate Dei.* Edited by Bernard Dombart and Alphonse Kalb. *CCSL* 47–48. Turnhout: Brepols, 1955. Translated by Marcus Dods et al. *The City of God.* New York: Modern Library, 1950

――――. *De doctrina Christiana.* Edited and translated by R. P. N. Green. *On Christian Doctrine.* Oxford: Clarendon, 1995.

――――. *De spiritu et littera.* Edited by Charles Urba and Joseph Zycha. *CSEL* 60:155–229. Translation. *On the Spirit and the Letter.* NPNF, ser. 1, vol. 5.

――――. *De vera religione.* Edited by Klaus-Detlef Daur. *CCSL* 32:169–260. Translated by John H. S. Burleigh. *Of True Religion.* In *Augustine: Earlier Writings,* 218–83. Philadelphia: Westminster, 1953.

――――. *Enarrationes in Psalmos.* Edited by Eligius Dekkers and Johannes Fraipont. *CCSL* 38–40. Translation, *Expositions on the Book of Psalms.* 6 vols. LOF, vols. 24, 25, 30, 32, 37, 39. Oxford, 1847–57.

――――. *Epistolae.* *PL* 33:61–1162. Translated by J. G. Cunningham. *Letters.* NPNF, ser. 1, vol. 1:209–593. New York: Scribner's, 1907.

――――. *Retractiones.* Edited by Pius Knöll. *CSEL* 36. Vienna: Tempsky, 1902. Translated by Sister Mary Inez Bogan. *The Retractions.* FOC 60. Washington: Catholic University of America Press, 1968.

――――. *Sermon on Matthew 11.25, 26.* Latin text edited by D. Germani Morin. *Miscellanea Agostiniana* 1:356–67. Rome: Vatican, 1930. Translated by Quincy Howe, Jr. *Selected Sermons of St. Augustine,* 219–34. New York: Holt, Rinehart and Winston, 1966.

Austen, Jane. *Pride and Prejudice.* 1813. Edited by Tony Tanner. Harmondsworth: Penguin, 1972. Reprint, 1987.

Baker, Nicholson. *The Size of Thoughts: Essays and Other Lumber.* New York: Random House, 1996.

Balz, Horst, and Gerhard Schneider, eds. *Exegetical Dictionary of the New Testament.* 3 vols. Grand Rapids: Eerdmans, 1990–93.

Baron, R. "Richard de Saint-Victor est-il l'auteur des commentaires de Nahum, Joël, Abdias?" *Revue benedictine* 68 (1958):118–22.

Barthes, Roland. "From Work to Text." (Orig. "De l'oeuvre au texte," 1971.) Translated by Josué V. Harari. *Textual Strategies: Perspectives in Post-Structuralist Criticism,* 73–81. Edited by Josué V. Harari. Ithaca, N.Y.: Cornell University Press, 1979.

Basil of Caesarea. *Epistolae.* In *Opera omnia,* vol. 3. Paris, 1839. Translated by Sister Agnes Clare Way. *Saint Basil: Letters.* FOC 13. New York: Fathers of the Church, 1951.

Bataillon, Louis J., Bertrand G. Guyot, and Richard H. Rouse, eds. *La Production du livre universitaire au moyen âge: exemplar et pecia.* Paris: Centre National de la Recherche Scientifique, 1988.

Baudri de Bourgueil. *Les Oeuvres poétiques.* Edited by Phyllis Abrahams. Paris: Champion, 1926.

Bauman, Guy. "Early Flemish Portraits, 1425–1525." *The Metropolitan Museum of Art Bulletin* 43.4 (Spring 1986).

Beard, Charles R. "A Problem Solved: A Portrait of Louis XI." *The Connoisseur* 87 (1931): 274–76.

Beaulieu, Marie Anne Polo de. "La Légende du coeur inscrit dans la littérature religieuse et didactique." In *Le "Cuer" au moyen âge (Réalité et Senefiance),* 299–312. Aix-en-Provence: Centre Universitaire d'Études et de Recherches Médiévales d'Aix, 1991.

Beckwith, John. *Early Medieval Art: Carolingian, Ottonian, Romanesque.* Rev. ed. London: Thames and Hudson, 1969.

Bede, the Venerable. *Explanatio Apocalypsis.* PL 93:129–206.

Behn, Aphra. *Poetry.* Edited by Janet Todd. Columbus: Ohio State University Press, 1992.

Beissel, Stephan. *Die Bilder der Handschrift des Kaisers Otto im Münster zu Aachen.* Aachen: Barth, 1886.

Benedict of Nursia. *Regula.* Edited by Rudolph Hanslik. *CSEL* 75. Vienna: Hoelder, Pichler, Tempsky, 1960. Translated by Justin McCann. *The Rule of Saint Benedict.* London: Burns and Oates, 1952.

Bénézit, Emmanuel. *Dictionnaire critique et documentaire des peintres, sculpteurs, dessinateurs et graveurs.* Rev. ed. 10 vols. Paris: Gründ, 1976.

Benton, John F. "Consciousness of Self and Perceptions of Individuality." *Renaissance and Renewal in the Twelfth Century,* edited by Robert L. Benson and Giles Constable, 263–95. Cambridge: Harvard University Press, 1982.

Bernard of Clairvaux. *Four Homilies in Praise of the Virgin Mother.* In *Magnificat: Homilies in Praise of the Blessed Virgin Mary.* Translated by Marie-Bernard Saïd and Grace Perigo, 1–58. Cistercian Fathers Series 18. Kalamazoo: Cistercian Publications, 1979.

———. *The Letters of St. Bernard of Clairvaux.* Translated by Bruno Scott James. London: Burns and Oates, 1953.

———. *On the Song of Songs I.* Translated by Kilian Walsh. Cistercian Fathers Series 4. Kalamazoo, Mich.: Cistercian Publications, 1977.

———. *Sancti Bernardi Opera.* Edited by Jean Leclercq, C. H. Talbot, and

H. M. Rochais. 8 vols. in 9 pts. Rome: Editiones Cistercienses, 1957–77.

———. *Sermons sur le Cantique*. Translated by Paul Verdeyen and Raffaele Fassetta. Tome 1. SC 414. Paris: Cerf, 1996.

———. *Sermons on Conversion*. Translated by Marie-Bernard Saïd. Cistercian Fathers Series 25. Kalamazoo: Cistercian Publications, 1981.

Bernard Silvester. *Cosmographia*. Edited by Carl Sigmund Barach and Johann Wrobel. *De mundi universitate libri duo sive Megacosmus et Microcosmus*. Innsbruck: Wagner'schen Universitaets-Buchhandlung, 1876. Translated by Winthrop Wetherbee. *The Cosmographia of Bernardus Silvestris*. New York: Columbia University Press, 1973.

Bettencourt, Stephanus Taveres. *Doctrina ascetica Origenis*. Studia Anselmiana 16. Vatican City: Libreria Vaticana, 1945.

Bianchi, Lidia, et al. *Iconografia di S. Caterina da Siena*. Vol. 1. *L'Immagine*. Rome: Città Nuova Editrice, 1988.

Bible (Douay-Rheims). *The Holy Bible translated from the Latin Vulgate*. New York: Pustet, 1912.

——— (Greek). *The Greek New Testament*. Edited by Kurt Aland, Matthew Black et al. 3rd ed. Stuttgart: United Bible Societies, 1983.

——— (RSV). *The New Oxford Annotated Bible with the Apocrypha, Expanded Edition*. Edited by Herbert G. May, Bruce M. Metzger. New York: Oxford University Press, 1977.

——— (Septuagint). *Septuaginta, id est Vetus Testamentum Graece iuxta LXX interpretes*. Edited by Alfred Rahlfs. 2 vols. Stuttgart: Privilegierte, 1935.

——— (Vulgate). *Biblia sacra iuxta vulgatam versionem*. 3rd ed. Edited by Robertus Weber, Bonifatius Fischer et al. Stuttgart: Deutsche Bibelgesellschaft, 1983.

Biget, Jean-Louis. *La Cathédrale d'Albi*. 2nd. ed. Albi: Centre du documentation pedagogique du Tarn, 1984.

Birkerts, Sven. *The Gutenberg Elegies: The Fate of Reading in an Electronic Age*. Boston: Faber, 1994.

Bloch, R. Howard. *Etymologies and Genealogies: A Literary Anthropology of the French Middle Ages*. Chicago: University of Chicago Press, 1983.

Boccaccio, Giovanni. *Amorosa visione: Bilingual edition*. Translated by Robert Hollander et al. Hanover, N.H.: University Press of New England, 1986.

Bogin, Meg (Magda). *The Women Troubadours*. 1976. Reprint, New York: Norton, 1980.

Bolton, W. F. *Alcuin and Beowulf: An Eighth-Century View*. New Brunswick, N.J.: Rutgers University Press, 1978.

Boutell, Charles. *Boutell's Heraldry*. Revised by J. P. Brooke-Little. London: Frederick Warne, 1978.

Brandon, S. G. F. *The Judgment of the Dead: An Historical and Comparative Study of the Idea of a Post-Mortem Judgment in the Major Religions.* London: Weidenfeld and Nicolson, 1967.

Breasted, James Henry. *The Dawn of Conscience.* New York: Scribner's, 1935.

Breder, Günter. *Die Lateinische Vorlage des altfranzösischen Apokalypsenkommentars des 13.Jahrhunderts* (Paris, B. N., MS. Fr. 403). Münster, Westphalia: Aschendorff, 1960.

Bremmer, Jan. *The Early Greek Concept of the Soul.* Princeton: Princeton University Press, 1983.

Bromiley, Geoffrey W. et al., eds. *The International Standard Bible Encyclopedia.* 4 vols. Rev. ed. Grand Rapids: Eerdmans, 1979–1988.

Brown, Carleton, and Rossell Hope Robbins. *The Index of Middle English Verse.* New York: Columbia University Press, 1943.

Brown, Carleton, ed. *Religious Lyrics of the XIVth Century.* Revised by G. V. Smithers. Oxford: Clarendon, 1952.

Brown, Peter. *Augustine of Hippo: A Biography.* 1967. Reprint, Berkeley: University of California Press, 1969.

————. *The Body and Society: Men, Women and Sexual Renunciation in Early Christianity.* New York: Columbia University Press, 1988.

Browning, Elizabeth Barrett. *Aurora Leigh.* 1857. Edited by Margaret Reynolds. Athens: Ohio University Press, 1992.

Burton, Robert. *The Anatomy of Melancholy.* 1621. Reprint, Amsterdam: Da Capo, 1971.

Butt, John, and Geoffrey Carnall. *The Mid-Eighteenth Century.* The Oxford History of English Literature, vol. 8. Oxford: Clarendon, 1979.

Buttrick, George A., et al., eds. *The Interpreter's Dictionary of the Bible.* 4 vols. Nashville: Abingdon, 1962. *Supplement,* 1976.

Bynum, Caroline Walker. *Holy Feast and Holy Fast: The Religious Significance of Food to Medieval Women.* Berkeley: University of California Press, 1987.

————. *Jesus as Mother: Studies in the Spirituality of the High Middle Ages.* Berkeley: University of California Press, 1982.

*The Cambridge History of the Bible.* Edited by P. R. Ackroyd, C. F. Evans et al. 3 vols. Cambridge: Cambridge University Press, 1963–70.

Camille, Michael. *The Medieval Art of Love: Objects and Subjects of Desire.* London: Laurence King, 1998.

Campbell, Lorne. *The Fifteenth Century Netherlandish Schools.* London: The National Gallery, 1998.

Canaway, W. H. *The Willow-Pattern War.* London: Hutchinson, 1976.

Capgrave, John. *The Life of St. Katharine of Alexandria.* Edited by Carl Horstmann. EETS OS 100. London: Kegan Paul, Trench, Trübner, 1893.

Carey, John. *John Donne: Life, Mind and Art.* 1981. Reprint, London: Faber, 1990.

Carpenter, Richard. *The Conscionable Christian.* London, 1623.

Carruthers, Mary J. *The Book of Memory: A Study of Memory in Medieval Culture.* Cambridge: Cambridge University Press, 1990.

Cassian, John. *Collationes.* Edited by E. Pichery. *Jean Cassien: Conférences. SC* 42, 54, 64. Paris: Éditions du Cerf, 1955, 1958, 1959.

Cave, Terence. *The Cornucopian Text: Problems of Writing in the French Renaissance.* Oxford: Clarendon, 1979.

Cervantes, Miguel de. *Don Quijote de la Mancha.* Edited by John Jay Allen. 2nd ed. 2 vols. Madrid: Cátedra, 1980. Translated by J. M. Cohen. *The Adventures of Don Quixote.* Harmondsworth: Penguin, 1950. Reprint, 1988.

Charles d'Orléans. *The Poems of Charles of Orleans.* Edited and translated by Sally Purcell. Cheadle, Cheshire: Fyfield, 1973.

Chartier, Roger. *Forms and Meanings: Texts, Performances, and Audiences from Codex to Computer.* Philadelphia: University of Pennsylvania Press, 1995.

Chaucer, Geoffrey. *The Riverside Chaucer.* 3rd ed. Edited by Larry D. Benson. Boston: Houghton Mifflin, 1987.

*The Chester Mystery Cycle.* Edited by R. M. Lumiansky and David Mills. EETS SS 3, 9. London: Oxford University Press, 1974, 1986.

Chiarini, Marco. "Nota in margine a una mostra." *Antichità viva* 18.4 (1979): 28–30.

Chrysostom, John. *Homiliae in Johannem. PG* 50:23–482. Trans. NPNF, ser. 1, vol. 14.

Cicero. *De officiis.* Edited and translated by Walter Miller. LCL, *Cicero,* vol. 21. London: Heinemann, 1913.

———. *Letters to Atticus.* Edited and translated by E. O. Winstedt. 3 vols. LCL, *Cicero,* vols. 22–24. London: Heinemann, 1912–18.

Clanchy, M. T. *From Memory to Written Record, England, 1066–1307.* Cambridge: Harvard University Press, 1979.

Coleman, Janet. *Ancient and Medieval Memories: Studies in the Reconstruction of the Past.* Cambridge: Cambridge University Press, 1992.

Colish, Marcia L. *The Mirror of Language: A Study in the Medieval Theory of Knowledge.* Rev. ed. Lincoln: University of Nebraska Press, 1983.

Comblen-Sonkes, Micheline. *Guide bibliographique de la peinture flamande du XVᵉ siècle.* Brussels: Centre national de recherches "Primitifs flamands," 1984.

Connelly, Joseph, ed. and trans. *Hymns of the Roman Liturgy.* London: Longmans, 1957.

Cooper, Rodney H., Leo C. Ferrari et al., eds. *Concordantia in libros XIII confessionum S. Aurelii Augustini.* 2 vols. Hildesheim: Olms-Weidmann, 1991.

Courcelle, Pierre. *Les Confessions de Saint Augustin dans la tradition littéraire: Antécédents et postérité.* Paris: Études augustiniennes, 1963.

Cowley, Geoffrey, and Anne Underwood. "How Memory Works." *Newsweek* 131, no. 24 (15 June 1998): 48–54.

Crane, Gregory. *The Blinded Eye: Thucydides and the New Written Word.* London: Rowman & Littlefield, 1996.

*Cursor Mundi: A Northumbrian Poem of the XIVth Century.* Edited by Richard Morris. Part 5. EETS OS 68. London: Oxford University Press, 1878. Reprint, 1966.

Curtius, Ernst Robert. *European Literature and the Latin Middle Ages.* Translated by Willard R. Trask. Princeton: Princeton University Press, 1953.

Davies, Martin. *The Early Netherlandish School.* 3rd ed. London: The National Gallery, 1968.

———. *The National Gallery, London* (= *Les Primitifs flamands, I. Corpus de la peinture des anciens Pays-Bas méridionaux au quinzième siècle,* no. 3). 2 vols. Antwerp: De Sikkel, 1953–54.

*De claustro animae. PL* 176:1017–1182.

De Hamel, Christopher. *Glossed Books of the Bible and the Origins of the Paris Booktrade.* Woodbridge, Suffolk: Brewer, 1984.

Dekkers, Eligius. *Clavis patrum latinorum.* 3rd ed. Steenbrugge: Abbey of St. Pierre, 1995.

De Quincey, Thomas. *The Collected Writings of Thomas de Quincey.* Edited by David Masson. 14 vols. Edinburgh: Adam and Charles Black, 1889–90.

Derrida, Jacques. *Dissemination.* Translated by Barbara Johnson. Chicago: University of Chicago Press, 1981.

———. *Of Grammatology.* Translated by Gayatri Chakravorty Spivak. Baltimore: Johns Hopkins University Press, 1976.

———. *Writing and Difference.* Translated by Alan Bass. Chicago: University of Chicago Press, 1978.

Descartes, Réné. *Les Passions de l'âme.* 1649. Edited by Geneviève Rodis-Lewis. Paris: Vrin, 1955.

D'Evelyn, Charlotte. "'Meditations on the Life and Passion of Christ': A Note on its Literary Relationships." In *Essays and Studies in Honor of Carleton Brown,* 79–90. 1940. Reprint, Freeport, N.Y.: Books for Libraries, 1969.

*Dictionary of Medieval Latin from British Sources.* Edited by R. E. Latham et al. London: Oxford University Press, 1975–.

*Dictionary of Paul and His Letters.* Edited by Gerald F. Hawthorne, Ralph P. Martin, and Daniel G. Reid. Downers Grove, Ill.: InterVarsity, 1993.

*Le Dictionnaire des peintres belges du XIV<sup>e</sup> siècle à nos jours.* Edited by Carine Dechaux, Brigitte de Patoul et al. 3 vols. Brussels: De Boeck-Wesmael, 1995.

*Dictionnaire de Spiritualité ascétique et mystique, doctrine et histoire.* Edited by Marcel Viller et al. 17 vols. Paris: Beauschesne, 1937–95.

Dinshaw, Carolyn. *Chaucer's Sexual Poetics.* Madison: University of Wisconsin Press, 1989.

*The Doctrine of the Hert.* Edited by Sister Mary Patrick Candon. Doctoral dissertation. New York: Fordham University, 1963. Reprint, Ann Arbor: UMI, 1998.

Donne, John. *The Elegies and the Songs and Sonnets.* Edited by Helen Gardner. Oxford: Clarendon, 1965.

—————. *The Epithalamions, Anniversaries and Epicedes.* Edited by W. Milgate. Oxford: Clarendon, 1978.

—————. *Pseudo-Martyr.* London, 1610. Reprint, New York: Scholars' Facsimiles and Reprints, 1974.

—————. *The Sermons of John Donne.* Edited by George R. Potter and Evelyn M. Simpson. 10 vols. Berkeley: University of California Press, 1953–62.

Downame, John. *The Christian Warfare.* London, 1604. Reprint, Norwood, N.J.: Johnson, 1974.

Dronke, Peter. *Women Writers of the Middle Ages: A Critical Study of Texts from Perpetua (†203) to Marguerite Porete (†1310).* Cambridge: Cambridge University Press, 1984.

Durliat, Marcel. "Le Jugement dernier de la cathédrale d'Albi." *Congrès archéologique de France, 140ᵉ session (1982),* 92–101. Paris: Société française d'archéologie, 1985.

Dutschke, C. W., et al., eds. *Guide to Medieval and Renaissance Manuscripts in the Huntington Library.* 2 vols. San Marino, Calif.: Huntington Library, 1989.

Eden, Kathy. "The Rhetorical Tradition and Augustinian Hermeneutics in *De doctrina christiana.*" *Rhetorica* 8 (1990): 45–63.

Eisenstein, Elizabeth. *The Printing Press as an Agent of Change: Communications and Cultural Transformations in Early-Modern Europe.* 2 vols. New York: Cambridge University Press, 1979.

Eliade, Mircea, ed. *The Encyclopedia of Religion.* 16 vols. New York: Macmillan, 1987.

*Enciclopedia Dantesca.* Edited by Umberto Bosco. 6 vols. Rome: Istituto dell'Enciclopedia Italiana, 1970–78.

*Encyclopedia of the Early Church.* Edited by Angelo Di Berardino. Translated by Adrian Walford. 2 vols. New York: Oxford University Press, 1992.

Erickson, Robert A. *The Language of the Heart, 1600–1750.* Philadelphia: University of Pennsylvania Press, 1997.

Euripides. *Trojan Women* (= *The Daughters of Troy*). Translated by Arthur S. Way. LCL, *Euripides,* vol. 1:351–459. London: Heinemann, 1912.

Eusebius. *De martyribus Palestinae. PG* 20:1457–1520. Trans. NPNF, ser. 2, vol. 1.

Everyman. Edited and translated by A. C. Cawley. *Everyman and Medieval Miracle Plays,* 205–34. New York: Dutton, 1959.

Fallows, David. "15th-Century Tablatures for Plucked Instruments: A Summary, A Revision and a Suggestion." *The Lute Society Journal* 19 (1977): 7–33.

Fein, David A. *Charles d'Orléans.* Boston: Twayne, 1983.

Fielding, Henry. *Amelia.* 1752. Edited by Martin C. Battestin. Middletown, Conn.: Wesleyan University Press, 1983.

Fish, Stanley E. *Self-Consuming Artifacts: The Experience of Seventeenth-Century Literature.* Berkeley: University of California Press, 1972.

Fletcher, Giles. *Licia, Or Poemes of Love.* 1593. Edited by Lloyd E. Berry. *The English Works of Giles Fletcher, the Elder,* 55–132. Madison: University of Wisconsin Press, 1964.

Folquet de Marseille. Edited by Stanislaw Stronski. *Le Troubadour Folquet de Marseille: Édition critique.* Cracow: Oslawski, 1910.

Freccero, John. "The Fig Tree and the Laurel: Petrarch's Poetics." *Diacritics* 5 (1975): 34–40.

Frese, Dolores Warwick, and Katherine O'Brien O'Keeffe, eds. *The Book and the Body.* Notre Dame: University of Notre Dame Press, 1997.

Freud, Sigmund. *The Standard Edition of the Complete Psychological Works of Sigmund Freud.* Edited and translated by James Strachey et al. 24 vols. London: Hogarth, 1953–74.

Frieden, Ken. *Freud's Dream of Interpretation.* Albany: SUNY, 1990.

Friedländer, Max J. "Die Brüsseler Tafelmalerei gegen den ausgang des 15. Jahrhunderts." *Belgische Kunstdenkmäler.* Edited by Paul Clemen. 2 vols. Munich: Bruckmann, 1923. 1:309–20.

———. *Early Netherlandish Painting.* 14 vols. and *Supplements.* Edited by Nicole Véronee-Verhaegen. Translated by Heinz Norden. Leyden: Sijthoff, 1967–1976.

Furnish, Victor Paul, trans. and comm. *The Anchor Bible: II Corinthians.* Garden City, N.Y.: Doubleday, 1984.

Gamble, Harry Y. *Books and Readers in the Early Church: A History of Early Christian Texts.* New Haven: Yale University Press, 1995.

Gellrich, Jesse M. *The Idea of the Book in the Middle Ages: Language Theory, Mythology, and Fiction.* Ithaca, N.Y.: Cornell University Press, 1985.

Gertrude of Helfta. *Legatus divinae pietatis* (= *Le Héraut*): Books 1–2. *Gertrude d'Helfta: Oeuvres Spirituelles,* vol. 2. Edited by Pierre Doyère. *SC* 139. Paris: Cerf, 1968. Translated by Alexandra Barratt. *The Herald of God's Lovingkindness: Books One and Two.* Cistercian Fathers Series 35. Kalamazoo: Cistercian Publications, 1991.

Gigerenzer, Gerd, and Daniel G. Goldstein. "Mind as Computer: Birth of a Metaphor." *Creativity Research Journal* 9 (1996): 131–44.

Glenisson, Jean, and Louis Holtz. *Le Livre au moyen âge.* Paris: CNRS, 1988.

Glorieux, Palémon. *Pour revaloriser Migne: Tables rectificatives. Mélanges de science religieuse* 9 (1952): cahier supplémentaire.

Goldberg, Jonathan. *Writing Matter: From the Hands of the English Renaissance.* Stanford: Stanford University Press, 1990.

Gould, Stephen Jay. *Wonderful Life: The Burgess Shale and the Nature of History.* New York: Norton, 1989.

Gray, Spalding. *Impossible Vacation.* New York: Knopf, 1992.

Greenberg, Ramon, and P. H. Leiderman. "Perceptions, the Dream Process and Memory: An Up-to-Date Version of Notes on a Mystic Writing Pad." *Comprehensive Psychiatry* 7 (1966): 517–23.

Greenblatt, Stephen. *Renaissance Self-Fashioning: From More to Shakespeare.* Chicago: University of Chicago Press, 1980.

Greene, Gordon K., ed. *French Secular Music: Manuscript Chantilly, Musée Condé 564 (First Part, Nos. 1–50).* Polyphonic Music of the Fourteenth Century, ed. Kurt von Fischer and Ian Bent, vol. 18. Monaco: Éditions de l'Oiseau-Lyre, 1981.

Gregory (the Great). *Moralia in Iob. PL* 75:509–1162, 76:9–782. Translated by J. Bliss et al. *Morals on the Book of Job.* 3 vols. LOF. Oxford: Parker, 1845–1850.

Guerin, Paul, ed. *Les Petits Bollandistes: vies des saints de l'ancien et du nouveau testament. . . .* 7th ed. 17 vols. Bar-le-Duc: Typographie des Celestins, 1874–1900.

Guibert de Nogent. *De vita sua. PL* 156:837–962. Edited by John F. Benton. Translated by C. C. Swinton Bland. *Self and Society in Medieval France: The Memoirs of Abbot Guibert of Nogent.* New York: Harper, 1970.

———. *Liber quo ordine sermo fieri debeat. PL* 156:21–32. Translated by Joseph M. Miller. "Guibert de Nogent's *Liber quo ordine sermo fieri debeat:* A Translation of the Earliest Modern Speech Textbook." *Today's Speech* 17.4 (November 1969): 45–56.

Guigo II. *Scala claustralium.* Edited and translated by Edmund Colledge and James Walsh. *SC* 163:81–123. Paris: Cerf, 1970. English translation by Edmund Colledge and James Walsh. *The Ladder of Monks: A Letter on the Contemplative Life, and Twelve Meditations.* Kalamazoo: Cistercian Publications, 1981. 65–86.

Hahn, Thomas, and Richard W. Kaeuper. "Text and Context: Chaucer's Friar's Tale." *Studies in the Age of Chaucer* 5 (1983): 67–101.

Hamburger, Jeffrey F. *Nuns as Artists: The Visual Culture of a Medieval Convent.* Berkeley: University of California Press, 1997.

———. "The Use of Images in the Pastoral Care of Nuns: The Case of Heinrich Suso and the Dominicans." *The Art Bulletin* 71 (1989): 20–46.

Hardison, O. B. *Christian Rite and Christian Drama in the Middle Ages.* Baltimore: Johns Hopkins University Press, 1965. Reprint, 1969.

Harris, William V. *Ancient Literacy.* Cambridge: Harvard University Press, 1989.

Harvey, Christopher. *Schola cordis, or The Heart of it Selfe gone away from God . . . in 47 Emblems.* London, 1647.

Hausherr, Irénée. *Spiritual Direction in the Early Christian East.* Translated by Anthony P. Gythiel. Cistercian Studies Series 116. Kalamazoo: Cistercian Publications, 1990.

Havelock, Eric A. *The Muse Learns to Write: Reflections on Orality and Literacy from Antiquity to the Present.* New Haven: Yale University Press, 1986.

———. *Preface to Plato.* Cambridge: Harvard University Press, 1963.

Hawthorne, Nathaniel. *The Scarlet Letter.* 1850. Edited by Fredson Bowers. *The Centenary Edition of the Works of Nathaniel Hawthorne,* vol. 1. Columbus: Ohio State University Press, 1962. Reprint, 1971.

Hayles, N. Katherine. *How We Became Posthuman: Virtual Bodies in Cyberspace, Literature, and Informatics.* Chicago: University of Chicago Press, 1999.

Heffernan, Thomas. *Art and Emblem: Early Seventeenth-Century English Poetry of Devotion.* Renaissance Monographs 17. Tokyo: Sophia University, 1991.

Heloise. *Epistolae.* Edited by Nada Cappelletti Truci. *Abelardo ed Eloisa: Lettere.* Turin: Einaudi, 1982. Translated in Radice, 109–179.

Hendrix, Guido. "*De apercione cordis, De impedimentis* and *De custodia linguae:* Three Pseudo-Bernardine Texts Restored to Their True Author, Hugh of St. Cher." *Recherches de Théologie ancienne et médiévale* 48 (1981): 172–97.

Herbert, George. *The Works of George Herbert.* Edited by F. E. Hutchinson. Oxford: Clarendon, 1959.

Herbert de Losinga. *Epistolae.* Edited by Robert Anstruther. 1846. Reprint, New York: Burt Franklin, 1969. Translated by Edward M. Goulburn and Henry Symonds. *The Life, Letters, and Sermons of Bishop Herbert de Losinga.* 2 vols. Oxford: Parker, 1878. Vol. 1.

Herrick, Robert. *The Poetical Works.* Edited by L. C. Martin. Oxford: Clarendon, 1956.

Hertz, J. H., ed. *The Pentateuch and Haftorahs.* London: Soncino, 1987.

Higgins, Dick. *Pattern Poetry: Guide to an Unknown Literature.* Albany: SUNY, 1987.

Hobbes, Thomas. *Leviathan.* 1651. Edited by C. B. Macpherson. Harmondsworth: Penguin, 1981.

Holtz, Louis. "Les mots latins désignant le livre au temps d'Augustin." In *Les Débuts du codex,* edited by Alain Blanchard, 105–113. *Bibliologia* 9. Turnhout: Brepols, 1989.

Homer. *The Iliad.* Translated by A. T. Murray. LCL, 2 vols. London: Heinemann, 1924–25.

Hooker, Richard. *Of the Laws of Ecclesiastical Polity.* Edited by John Kebel. 7th ed. Revised by R. W. Church and F. Paget. 3 vols. 1888. Reprint, New York: Burt Franklin, 1970.

———. *Of the Laws of Ecclesiastical Polity: Commentary.* Edited by W. Speed Hill et al. 2 vols. Binghamton, N.Y.: Medieval and Renaissance Texts and Studies, 1993.

Howden, John. *Philomena.* Edited by Clemens Blume. *John Hovedens Nachtigallenlied über die Liebe unseres Erlösers und Königs Christus.* Leipzig: Reisland, 1930.

Hraban Maur. *Enarrationes in epistolas beati Pauli. PL* 111:1273–1616.

Hugh of St. Cher. *De doctrina cordis.* Selections (chaps. 6–8). Edited by Guido Hendrix. *Recherches de Théologie ancienne et médiévale* 48 (1981):172–97.

———. *Opera omnia.* 8 vols. Venice, 1732.

Hugh of St. Victor (?). *De unione corporis et spiritus. PL* 177:285–94.

Huot, Sylvia. *The Romance of the Rose and Its Medieval Readers: Interpretation, Reception, Manuscript Transmission.* Cambridge: Cambridge University Press, 1993.

Hutchins, Edwin. *Cognition in the Wild.* Cambridge: MIT Press, 1995.

Illich, Ivan. *In the Vineyard of the Text: A Commentary to Hugh's Didascalicon.* Chicago: University of Chicago Press, 1993.

Isaac of Stella. *Sermons.* Edited by Anselm Hoste. Translated by Gaston Salet. 3 vols. *SC* 130, 207, 339. Paris: Cerf, 1967–87.

Isherwood, Christopher. *Goodbye to Berlin.* London: Hogarth, 1939.

Jackson, B. Darrell. "The Theory of Signs in St. Augustine's *De Doctrina Christiana.*" *Revue des études augustiniennes* 15 (1969): 9–49. Reprint in Markus, 92–147.

Jacobson, J., B. Comiskey et al. "The Last Book." *IBM Systems Journal* 36 (1997): 457–63.

Jager, Eric. "The Book of the Heart: Reading and Writing the Medieval Subject." *Speculum* 71 (1996): 1–26.

———. "Speech and the Chest in Old English Poetry: Orality or Pectorality?" *Speculum* 65 (1990): 845–59.

———. *The Tempter's Voice: Language and the Fall in Medieval Literature.* Ithaca: Cornell University Press, 1993.

Jeffrey, David L. "The Self and the Book: Reference and Recognition in Medieval Thought." In *By Things Seen: Reference and Recognition in Medieval Thought,* edited by David L. Jeffrey, 1–17. Ottawa: University of Ottawa Press, 1979.

Jean de Meun. *Le lettere di Abelardo ed Eloisa nella traduzione di Jean de Meun.* Edited by Fabrizio Beggiato. 2 vols. Modena: Mucchi, 1977.

Jerome. *Commentarii in Abacuc. PL* 25:1273–1338.

———. *Epistolae. PL* 22:325–1224. Trans. NPNF, ser. 2, vol. 6.

Johannot, Yvonne. *Tourner la page: Livre, rites et symboles.* Aubenas d'Ardèche: Millon, 1988.

John Climacus. *Scala paradisi.* PG 88:632–1164. Translated by Colm Luibheid and Norman Russell. *The Ladder of Divine Ascent.* New York: Paulist Press, 1982.

Johnson, Samuel. *Rasselas and Other Tales.* Edited by Gwin J. Kolb. New Haven: Yale University Press, 1990.

Johnstone, Charles. *Chrysal; or the Adventures of a Guinea.* 4 vols. London, 1760–65.

Josephus, Flavius. *Jewish Antiquities.* Edited and translated by H. St. J. Thackeray et al. LCL. 6 vols. London: Heinemann, 1930–65.

Jungmann, Joseph A. *The Mass of the Roman Rite: Its Origins and Development (Missarum Sollemnia).* Translated by Francis A. Brunner. 2 vols. 1951, 1955. Reprint, Westminster, Md.: Christian Classics, 1986.

Kafka, Franz. "In the Penal Colony." Translated by Willa and Edwin Muir. *The Complete Stories,* edited by Nahum N. Glatzer, 140–67. New York: Schocken, 1971.

Kernan, Alvin. *Printing Technology, Letters, and Samuel Johnson.* Princeton: Princeton University Press, 1987.

Kevles, Bettyann Holtzmann. *Naked to the Bone: Medical Imaging in the Twentieth Century.* 1997. Reprint, Reading, Mass.: Addison Wesley Longman, 1998.

Kiefer, Frederick. *Writing on the Renaissance Stage: Written Words, Printed Pages, Metaphoric Books.* Newark: University of Delaware Press, 1996.

Kierkegaard, Søren. *Journals and Papers.* Edited by Howard V. Hong and Edna H. Hong. 7 vols. Bloomington: Indiana University Press, 1967–78.

Kingwell, Mark. "Viral Culture: A Fashionable Theory Takes the Self out of Consciousness." *Harper's Magazine* 298, no. 1787 (April 1999): 83–91.

Kittel, Gerhard. *Theological Dictionary of the New Testament.* Edited and translated by Geoffrey W. Bromiley. 9 vols. Grand Rapids: Eerdmans, 1964–74.

Lacan, Jacques. *Écrits: A Selection.* Translated by Alan Sheridan. New York: Norton, 1977.

Lafayette, Madame de. *La Princesse de Clèves.* 1678. Edited by Émile Magne. Paris: Droz, 1946. Translated by Nancy Mitford. Revised by Leonard Tancock. *The Princesse de Clèves.* Harmondsworth: Penguin, 1978. Reprint, 1988.

Lampe, G. W. H., ed. *A Patristic Greek Lexicon.* Oxford: Clarendon Press, 1961.

Lane, Barbara G. *Flemish Painting outside Bruges, 1400–1500: An Annotated Bibliography.* Boston: G. K. Hall, 1986.

Lane, Christopher. "Philosophy of the Unconscious: Vacillating on the Scene of Writing in Freud's *Project.*" *Prose Studies* 17 (1994): 98–129.

Lanham, Richard A. *The Electronic Word: Democracy, Technology, and the Arts.* Chicago: University of Chicago Press, 1993.

Lapham, Lewis H. "Notebook: Magic Lanterns." *Harper's Magazine* 294, no. 1764 (May 1997): 11–14.

Leclercq, Jean. "Aspects spirituels de la symbolique du livre au XII$^e$ siècle." *L'homme devant Dieu: Mélanges offerts au Père Henri de Lubac,* 63–72. Vol. 2 (*Du moyen âge au siècle des Lumières*). Paris: Aubier, 1964.

————. *The Love of Learning and the Desire for God: A Study of Monastic Culture.* Translated by Catharine Misrahi, 2nd ed. New York: Fordham University Press, 1977.

Le Goff, Jacques. "Head or Heart? The Political Use of Body Metaphors in the Middle Ages." Translated by Patricia Ranum. In *Fragments for a History of the Human Body: Part Three,* edited by Michel Feher, 12–26. New York: Zone, 1989.

Leroquais, Victor. *Les Livres d'heures manuscrits de la Bibliothèque Nationale.* 3 vols. Paris: Macon, 1927. *Supplément,* 1943.

Lévi-Strauss, Claude. "A Writing Lesson." In *Tristes Tropiques,* translated by John and Doreen Weightman, 294–304. 1974. Reprint, Harmondsworth: Penguin, 1992.

Lewis, Robert E., and Angus McIntosh. *A Descriptive Guide to the Manuscripts of the Prick of Conscience.* Oxford: Society for the Study of Mediaeval Languages and Literature, 1982.

Liddell, Henry George, and Robert Scott et al. *A Greek-English Lexicon.* 9th ed. with Supplement. Oxford: Clarendon, 1968.

Lightbown, Ronald. *Sandro Botticelli.* 2 vols. Berkeley: University of California Press, 1978.

*Literature Online. Eighteenth-Century Fiction (1700–1780).* Alexandria, Va.: Chadwyck-Healey, 1996–99.

Lochrie, Karma. *Margery Kempe and Translations of the Flesh.* Philadelphia: University of Pennsylvania Press, 1991.

Locke, John. *An Essay Concerning Human Understanding.* 1690. Edited by Peter H. Nidditch. Oxford: Clarendon, 1975.

Lorenz, Konrad Z. "The Companion in the Bird's World." *The Auk* 54 (1937): 245–71.

Lubac, Henri de. *Corpus mysticum: l'eucharistie et l'église au moyen âge: Étude historique.* 2nd ed. Paris: Aubier, 1949.

Mâle, Émile. *La Cathédrale d'Albi.* 1950. Reprint, Paris: Zodiaque, 1974.

Mallarmé, Stéphane. "Le Livre, Instrument Spirituel." 1895. *Oeuvres complètes,* edited by Henri Mondor and G. Jean-Aubry, 378–82. Paris: Gallimard, 1945. Translated by Bradford Cook. "The Book: A Spiritual Instrument." *Mallarmé: Selected Prose Poems, Essays, and Letters,* 24–29. Baltimore: Johns Hopkins University Press, 1956. Reprinted in Hazard Adams, 690–92.

Mann, Thomas. *Der Zauberberg.* 1924. Reprint, Berlin: Fischer, 1960. Translated by H. T. Lowe-Porter. *The Magic Mountain.* 1927. Reprint, New York: Knopf, 1945.

Markus, R. A., ed. *Augustine: A Collection of Critical Essays.* New York: Anchor-Doubleday, 1972.

Marti, Kevin. *Body, Heart, and Text in the Pearl-Poet.* Lewiston, N.Y.: Mellen, 1991.

Martin, Henri-Jean. *The History and Power of Writing.* Translated by Lydia G. Cochrane. Chicago: University of Chicago Press, 1994.

Martin, John Rupert. *The Illustration of the Heavenly Ladder of John Climacus.* Princeton: Princeton University Press, 1954.

Mazzotta, Giuseppe. *The World at Play in Boccaccio's Decameron.* Princeton: Princeton University Press, 1986.

*Meditations on the Life and Passion of Christ.* Edited by Charlotte D'Evelyn. EETS OS 158. London: Oxford University Press, 1921.

Mellinkoff, Ruth. "The Round-Topped Tablets of the Law: Sacred Symbol and Emblem of Evil." *Journal of Jewish Art* 1 (1974): 28–43.

Mesplé, Paul. "Heurs et malheurs de l'église des augustins." *La revue des arts* 2 (1952): 113–16.

*Middle English Dictionary.* Edited by Hans Kurath, Sherman M. Kuhn, Robert E. Lewis. Ann Arbor: University of Michigan Press, 1952–.

*Miracles de Nostre Dame par personnages.* Edited by Gaston Paris and Ulysse Robert. 8 vols. Société des anciens textes français. Paris: Firmin Didot, 1876–93.

*Missale sarum ad usum insignis et praeclarae ecclesiae.* Edited by Francis Henry Dickinson. Oxford: Parker, 1861–83.

Montaigne, Michel de. *Les Essais de Michel de Montaigne.* Edited by Pierre Villey and V.-L. Saulnier. 3rd ed. 2 vols. Paris: Presses Universitaires de France, 1978. Translated by J. M. Cohen. *Essays.* Harmondsworth: Penguin, 1958. Reprint, 1985.

Morris, Colin. *The Discovery of the Individual, 1050–1200.* 1972. Reprint, New York: Harper, 1973.

Morrison, Karl F. *Conversion and Text: The Cases of Augustine of Hippo, Herman-Judah, and Constantine Tsatsos.* Charlottesville: University of Virginia Press, 1992.

Moxey, Keith. *The Practice of Theory: Poststructuralism, Cultural Politics, and Art History.* Ithaca: Cornell University Press, 1994.

*The N-Town Play: Cotton MS Vespasian D. 8.* Edited by Stephen Spector. 2 vols. EETS SS 11–12. Oxford: Oxford University Press, 1991.

Nashe, Thomas. *Christ's Teares ouer Ierusalem.* Edited by Alexander B. Grosart. London: The Huth Library, 1883–84.

Nelson, Phillip G. "Palimpsest or Tabula Rasa: Developmental Biology of the Brain." *Journal of the American Academy of Psychoanalysis* 21 (1993): 525–37.

*The New-England Primer: A History of Its Origin and Development, with a Reprint of the Unique Copy of the Earliest Known Edition. . . .* Edited by Paul Leicester Ford. New York: Dodd, Mead, and Co., 1897.

Nichols, Stephen G., Jr. "An Intellectual Anthropology of Marriage in the Middle Ages." In *The New Medievalism,* edited by Marina S. Brownlee, Kevin Brownlee, and Stephen G. Nichols, 70–95. Baltimore: Johns Hopkins University Press, 1991.

———. "Portraits of Poets in Medieval Manuscripts." Unpublished lecture. 1990.

Nieddu, Gian Franco. "La metafora della memoria come scrittura e l'immagine dell'animo come *deltos.*" *Quaderni di storia* 19 (Jan.–Jun. 1984): 213–19.

Nilus of Ancyra. *Epistolae. PG* 79:81–582.

Nussbaum, Martha. "The Window: Knowledge of Other Minds in Virginia Woolf's *To the Lighthouse.*" *New Literary History* 26 (1995): 731–53.

O'Donnell, James J., ed. and comm. *Augustine: Confessions.* 3 vols. Oxford: Clarendon, 1992.

*The Old Testament Pseudepigrapha.* Edited by James H. Charlesworth. 2 vols. New York: Doubleday, 1983–85.

Ong, Walter J. *Orality and Literacy: The Technologizing of the Word.* London: Methuen, 1982.

Onians, Richard Broxton. *The Origins of European Thought about the Body, the Mind, the Soul, the World, Time, and Fate.* 2nd ed. Cambridge: Cambridge University Press, 1954.

Origen. *Commentarii in epistolam ad Romanos. PG* 14:837–1292. Italian translation by Francesca Cocchini. *Commento alla Lettera ai Romani.* 2 vols. Monferrato: Marietti, 1985–86.

———. *In Numeros homiliae. PG* 12:583–806. Translated by André Méhat. *Homélies sur les Nombres. SC* 194. Paris: Cerf, 1951.

Ostow, Mortimer. "The Palimpsest Phenomenon." *Journal of Clinical Psychopharmacology* 12 (1992): 301.

Ovid. *Amores.* Edited and translated by Grant Showerman. LCL, *Ovid,* vol. 1. London: Heinemann, 1914.

———. *The Art of Love, and Other Poems.* Edited and translated by J. H. Mozley. 2nd ed. Revised by G. P. Goold. LCL, *Ovid,* vol. 2. London: Heinemann, 1979.

*The Oxford English Dictionary.* 2nd ed. Edited by J. A. Simpson and E. S. C. Weiner. 20 vols. Oxford: Oxford University Press, 1989. CD-ROM version, 1992.

*Oxford Latin Dictionary.* Edited by P. G. W. Glare. Oxford: Clarendon, 1982.

Panofsky, Erwin. *Early Netherlandish Painting: Its Origins and Character.* 2 vols. Cambridge: Harvard University Press, 1953.

Parkes, M. B. "The Literacy of the Laity." In *The Mediaeval World,* edited by David Daiches and Anthony Thorlby. *Literature and Western Civilization,* 2:555–77. London: Aldous Books, 1973.

Patterson, Lee. "On the Margin: Postmodernism, Ironic History, and Medieval Studies." *Speculum* 65 (1990): 87–108.

Pecke, Thomas. *Parnassi Puerperium.* London, 1659.

Pecock, Reginald. *The Repressor of Over Much Blaming of the Clergy.* Edited by Churchill Babington. Rolls Series 19. 2 vols. London: Longman, 1860.

Peter of Blois. *Sermones. PL* 207:559–776.

Peter Comestor. *Sermones. PL* 198:1721–1844.

———. *Sermo de libro vitae* ( = Pseudo-Hildebert of Lavardin, *Sermones ad diversos* 102). *PL* 171:814–18.

Petrarch, Francesco. *Canzoniere.* In *Petrarch's Lyric Poems: The Rime sparse and Other Lyrics,* edited and translated by Robert M. Durling. Cambridge: Harvard University Press, 1976.

———. *Secretum: De secreto conflictu curarum mearum.* Edited by Emilio Bigi. *Opere di Francesco Petrarca,* 517–683. Milan: Mursia, 1963–79. Translated by William H. Draper. *Petrarch's Secret, or The Soul's Conflict with Passion.* 1911. Reprint, Norwood, Pa.: Norwood Editions, 1975.

Peza, Edgardo de la. *El significado de "cor" en San Agustin.* Paris: Études augustiniennes, 1962.

Philippe de Mézières. *Le Livre de la vertu du sacrement de mariage.* Edited by Joan B. Williamson. Washington: Catholic University of America Press, 1993.

Philo of Alexandria. *De specialibus legibus.* Edited and translated by F. H. Colson. *On the Special Laws.* LCL, *Philo,* vols. 7–8. London: Heinemann, 1937–39.

———. *Legum allegoria.* Edited and translated by F. H. Colson and G. H. Whitaker. *Allegorical Interpretation of Genesis 2–3.* LCL, *Philo,* vol. 1:139–484. London: Heinemann, 1929.

———. *Quaestiones et solutiones in Exodum.* Translated by Ralph Marcus. *Questions and Answers on Exodus.* LCL, *Philo,* Supplement, vol. 2:1–176. London: Heinemann, 1953.

———. *Quis rerum divinarum heres.* Translated by F. H. Colson and G. H. Whitaker. *Who Is the Heir of Divine Things.* LCL, *Philo,* vol. 4:269–447. London: Heinemann, 1932.

Piankoff, Alexandre. *Le "Coeur" dans les textes Égyptiens depuis l'Ancien jusqu'à la fin du Nouvel Empire.* Paris: Librairie Orientaliste Paul Geuthner, 1930.

Pindar. *Odes.* Edited and translated by John Sandys. LCL. Rev. ed. London: Heinemann, 1937.

Planche, Alice. *Charles D'Orléans ou la recherche d'un langage.* Paris: Champion, 1975.

Plato. *The Collected Dialogues.* Edited by Edith Hamilton and Huntington Cairns. Princeton: Princeton University Press, 1961. Reprint, 1987.

————. *Gorgias*. Edited and translated by W. R. M. Lamb. LCL, *Plato*, vol. 5:247–533. London: Heinemann, 1925.

————. *Laws*. Edited and translated by R. G. Bury. LCL, *Plato*, vols. 10–11. London: Heinemann, 1926.

————. *Phaedrus*. Edited and translated by Harold North Fowler. LCL, *Plato*, vol. 1:405–579. London: Heinemann, 1914.

————. *Phaedrus*. Edited and translated by Alexander Nehamas and Paul Woodruff. Indianapolis: Hackett, 1995.

————. *Republic*. Edited and translated by Paul Shorey. 2 vols. LCL, *Plato*, vols. 5–6. London: Heinemann, 1935–37.

————. *Theaetetus*. Edited and translated by Harold North Fowler. LCL, *Plato*, vol. 7:1–257. Rev. ed. London: Heinemann, 1928.

Plautus. *Persa* (The Persian). Edited and translated by Paul Nixon. LCL, *Plautus*, vol. 3:417–523. London: Heinemann, 1924.

Plummer, Alfred. *A Critical and Exegetical Commentary on the Second Epistle of St Paul to the Corinthians*. Edinburgh: Clark, 1915. Reprint, 1960.

*Poema morale* (A Moral Ode). Edited and translated by Richard Morris. *Old English Homilies and Homiletic Treatises of the Twelfth and Thirteenth Centuries*. EETS OS 29, 34. London: Trübner, 1868. Reprint, New York: Greenwood, 1969. 158–83.

Pollard, Graham. "The *Pecia* System in the Medieval Universities." In *Medieval Scribes, Manuscripts and Libraries: Essays Presented to N. R. Ker*, edited by M. B. Parkes and Andrew G. Watson, 145–61. London: Scolar, 1978.

Porter, Katherine Anne. "Pale Horse, Pale Rider." 1939. *The Collected Stories*, 269–317. New York: Harcourt, 1965.

Poulet, Georges. *Études sur le temps humain*. 4 vols. 1949–68. Reprint, Paris: Éditions du Rocher, 1976.

————. "Phenomenology of Reading." *New Literary History* 1 (1969): 53–68. Reprint, in Hazard Adams, 1213–22.

*The Pricke of Conscience (Stimulus Conscientiae): A Northumbrian Poem*. Edited by Richard Morris. Berlin: Asher, 1863.

*Les Primitifs flamands et leur temps*. Edited by Michel de Grand Ry et al. Louvain-la-Neuve: Jean-Pâques, 1994.

Prudentius. *Peristephanon Liber* (Crowns of Martyrdom). Edited and translated by H. J. Thomson. LCL, *Prudentius*, vol. 2:98–345. London: Heinemann, 1953.

Pseudo-Anselm. *Meditatio* 10. *PL* 158: 761–62.

Pseudo-Augustine. *Liber meditationum*. *PL* 40:901–42.

Pseudo-Bernard. *De interiori domo*. *PL* 184:507–52.

Pseudo-Cicero. *Ad C. Herennium de ratione dicendi (Rhetorica ad Herennium)*. Edited and translated by Harry Caplan. LCL, *Cicero*, vol. 1. London: Heinemann, 1954.

Pseudo-Hugh of St. Victor. *Miscellanea*. *PL* 177:469–900.

Pseudo-Jerome. *Breviarium in Psalmos*. *PL* 26:821–1270.

Puccini, Vincenzio. *The Life of St. Mary Magdalene of Pazzi, a Carmelite Nunn*. London, 1687.

Quintilian. *Institutio Oratoria*. Edited and translated by H. E. Butler. LCL, 4 vols. London: Heinemann, 1920–22.

Radice, Betty, trans. *The Letters of Abelard and Heloise*. Harmondsworth: Penguin, 1974.

Reames, Sherry L. *The Legenda aurea: A Reexamination of Its Paradoxical History*. Madison: University of Wisconsin Press, 1985.

Reaney, Gilbert, ed. *Early Fifteenth-Century Music*. Vol. 1. Corpus Mensurabilis Musicae, no. 11. Rome: American Institute of Musicology, 1955.

Réau, Louis. *Iconographie de l'art Chrétien*. 3 vols. in 6 parts. Paris: Presses Universitaires de France, 1955–59.

Reynolds, L. D., and N. G. Wilson. *Scribes and Scholars: A Guide to the Transmission of Greek and Latin Literature*. 2nd ed. Oxford: Clarendon, 1974.

Richard of St. Victor. *Commentarius in Nahum* (= Pseudo-Julian of Toledo). *PL* 96:705–58.

———. *De judiciaria potestate in finali et universali judicio*. *PL* 196:1177–86.

———. *Sermo in festo sancti Augustini* (= Pseudo-Hugh of St. Victor, *Sermones* 99). *PL* 177:1205–6.

Richardson, Samuel. *Clarissa; or, The History of a Young Lady*. 3rd ed. 1751. Reprint, New York: AMS, 1990.

———. *The History of Sir Charles Grandison*. 1753–54. Edited by Jocelyn Harris. 3 vols. London: Oxford University Press, 1972.

———. *Pamela; or, Virtue Rewarded*. 1740. 14th ed., 1801. Edited by Peter Sabor. London: Penguin, 1985.

Rieger, Angelica. "'Ins e.l cor port, dona, vostra faisso': Image et imaginaire de la femme à travers l'enluminure dans les chansonniers de troubadours." *Cahiers de civilisation médiévale, $x^e$–$xi^e$ siècles* 28 (1985): 385–415.

Riehle, Wolfgang. *The Middle English Mystics*. Translated by Bernard Standring. London: Routledge and Kegan Paul, 1981.

Robbins, Rossell Hope. "The Gurney Series of Religious Lyrics." *PMLA* 54 (1939): 369–90.

Roberts, Colin H., and T. C. Skeat. *The Birth of the Codex*. London: Oxford University Press, 1987.

Robertson, D. W., Jr. *A Preface to Chaucer: Studies in Medieval Perspectives*. Princeton: Princeton University Press, 1962.

Rolle, Richard. *English Writings of Richard Rolle, Hermit of Hampole.* Edited by Hope Emily Allen. Oxford: Clarendon, 1931.

*Le Roman de la Rose.* Edited by Félix Lecoy. 3 vols. Paris: Champion, 1973–82. Translated by Charles Dahlberg. *The Romance of the Rose.* Princeton: Princeton University Press, 1971.

Rose, H. J. *A Commentary on the Surviving Plays of Aeschylus.* 2 vols. Amsterdam: N. V. Noord-Hollandsche Uitgevers Maatschappij, 1957–58.

Rous, Francis. *Thule, or Vertues Historie.* 1598. Edited by J. Crossley. The Spenser Society, no. 23. 1878. Reprint, New York: Burt Franklin, 1967.

Rouse, Mary A., and Richard H. Rouse. "From Flax to Parchment: A Monastic Sermon from Twelfth-Century Durham." *New Science Out of Old Books: Studies in Manuscripts and Early Printed Books in Honour of A. I. Doyle.* Edited by Richard Beadle and A. J. Piper. London: Scolar, 1995. 1–13.

Rubin, Miri. *Corpus Christi: The Eucharist in Late Medieval Culture.* Cambridge: Cambridge University Press, 1991.

Rubsamen, Walter H. "The Earliest French Lute Tablature." *Journal of the American Musicological Society* 21 (1968): 286–99.

Rufinus. *Historia monachorum.* PL 21:387–462.

Saenger, Paul. "Books of Hours and the Reading Habits of the Later Middle Ages." In *The Culture of Print: Power and the Uses of Print in Early Modern Europe,* edited by Roger Chartier, translated by Lydia G. Cochrane, 141–73. Princeton: Princeton University Press, 1987.

———. "Silent Reading: Its Impact on Late Medieval Script and Society." *Viator* 13 (1982): 367–414.

Sanders, Eve Rachele. *Gender and Literacy on Stage in Early Modern England.* Cambridge: Cambridge University Press, 1998.

Sauvy, Anne. *Le miroir du coeur: Quatre siècles d'images savantes et populaires.* Paris: Cerf, 1989.

Saviotti, Alfredo. "Di un codice musicale del sec. xvi." *Giornale storico della letteratura italiana* 14 (1889): 234–53.

Schibanoff, Susan. "Botticelli's *Madonna del Magnificat:* Constructing the Woman Writer in Early Humanist Italy." *PMLA* 109 (1994): 190–206.

Schiller, Gertrud. *Ikonographie der christlichen Kunst.* 5 vols. in 7. Gütersloher: Gerd Mohn, 1966–1991.

Schneider, Norbert. *The Art of the Portrait: Masterpieces of European Portrait-Painting, 1420–1670.* Translated by Iain Galbraith. New York: Barnes and Noble, 1997.

Searle, John R. "I Married a Computer." *The New York Review* 46.6 (8 April 1999): 34–38.

*A Select Library of the Nicene and Post-Nicene Fathers of the Christian Church.* Edited by

Philip Schaff and Henry Wace. 1st ser., 14 vols. New York: The Christian Literature Company, 1886–90. 2nd series, 14 vols. New York: The Christian Literature Company, 1890–1900.

Seneca. *Epistulae morales.* Edited and translated by Richard M. Gummere. 3 vols. LCL, *Seneca*, vols. 4–6. London: Heinemann, 1917–25.

Shakespeare, William. *The Riverside Shakespeare.* Edited by G. Blakemore Evans. 2nd ed. Boston: Houghton Mifflin, 1997.

Sheingorn, Pamela. "'For God Is Such a Doomsman': Origins and Development of the Theme of the Last Judgment." In *Homo, Memento Finis: The Iconography of Just Judgment in Medieval Art and Drama,* edited by David Bevington, 15–58. Kalamazoo: The Medieval Institute, 1985.

Sidney, Sir Philip. *The Poems of Sir Philip Sidney.* Edited by William A. Ringler, Jr. Oxford: Clarendon, 1962.

Singleton, Charles S. *An Essay on the Vita Nuova.* 1949. Reprint, Baltimore: Johns Hopkins University Press, 1983.

*Sir Gawain and the Green Knight.* Edited by Malcolm Andrew and Ronald Waldron. *The Poems of the Pearl Manuscript,* 207–300. Berkeley: University of California Press, 1978.

Small, Jocelyn Penny. *Wax Tablets of the Mind: Cognitive Studies of Memory and Literacy in Classical Antiquity.* London: Routledge, 1997.

Smalley, Beryl. *The Study of the Bible in the Middle Ages.* 1952. Reprint, Notre Dame: University of Notre Dame Press, 1978.

Snell, Bruno. *The Discovery of the Mind: The Greek Origins of European Thought.* Translated by T. G. Rosenmeyer. 1953. Reprint, New York: Harper and Row, 1960.

Sobchack, Vivian. "The Scene of the Screen: Envisioning Cinematic and Electronic 'Presence.'" *Materialities of Communication.* Edited by Hans Ulrich Gumbrecht and K. Ludwig Pfeiffer. Translated by William Whobrey. Stanford: Stanford University Press, 1994. 83–106.

Solmsen, Friedrich. "The Tablets of Zeus." *Classical Quarterly* 38 (1944): 27–30.

Sordello. *The Poetry of Sordello.* Edited and translated by James J. Wilhelm. New York: Garland, 1987.

Spence, Sarah. *Texts and the Self in the Twelfth Century.* Cambridge: Cambridge University Press, 1996.

Spenser, Edmund. *The Yale Edition of the Shorter Poems of Edmund Spenser.* Edited by William A. Oram et al. New Haven: Yale University Press, 1989.

Spidlík, Tomás. *The Spirituality of the Christian East: A Systematic Handbook.* Translated by Anthony P. Gythiel. Cistercian Studies Series 79. Kalamazoo: Cistercian Publications, 1986.

Stacey, W. David. *The Pauline View of Man in Relation to its Judaic and Hellenistic Background.* London: Macmillan, 1956.

Sterling, Charles. "Le Maître de la Vue de Sainte-Gudule: Une enquête." *Bulletin des musées royaux des beaux-arts de Belgique* 23–29 (1974–1980): 9–28.

Stevens, Scott Manning. "Sacred Heart and Secular Brain." In *The Body in Parts: Fantasies of Corporeality in Early Modern Europe,* edited by David Hillman and Carla Mazzio, 263–82. New York: Routledge, 1997.

Stevenson, Robert Louis, and Lloyd Osbourne. *The Wrecker.* 1891. Reprint, New York: Scribner's, 1899.

Stock, Brian. *Augustine the Reader: Meditation, Self-Knowledge, and the Ethics of Interpretation.* Cambridge: Harvard University Press, 1996.

———. "Reading, Writing, and the Self: Petrarch and His Forerunners." *New Literary History* 26 (1995): 717–30.

Styron, William. "A Case of the Great Pox." *The New Yorker* 71, no. 28 (18 September 1995): 62–75.

Sully, James. "The Dream as a Revelation." *The Fortnightly Review,* n.s. 53 (1893): 354–65.

Summers, David. "'Form,' Nineteenth-Century Metaphysics, and the Problem of Art Historical Description." *Critical Inquiry* 15 (1989): 372–93. Reprint in *The Art of Art History: A Critical Anthology,* edited by Donald Preziosi, 127–42. Oxford: Oxford University Press, 1998.

Suso (Seuse), Heinrich. *Deutsche Schriften.* Edited by Karl Bihlmeyer. Stuttgart: Minerva, 1907. Reprint, 1961. Translated by Sister M. Ann Edward (from the edition by Nicholas Heller). *The Exemplar: Life and Writings of Blessed Henry Suso, O.P.* 2 vols. Dubuque: The Priory Press, 1962.

———. *Horologium sapientiae.* Edited by Pius Künzle. Freiburg: Universitätsverlag, 1977. Translated by Edmund Colledge. *Wisdom's Watch Upon the Hours.* FOC, Mediaeval Continuation, 4. Washington, D.C.: The Catholic University of America Press, 1994.

Svenbro, Jesper. *Phrasikleia: anthropologie de la lecture en Grèce ancienne.* Paris: Éditions la Découverte, 1988.

Swift, Jonathan. *A Tale of a Tub.* 5th ed. 1710. Edited by Herbert Davis. *A Tale of a Tub, with Other Early Works, 1696–1707.* Oxford: Blackwell, 1957.

Taylor, Charles. *Sources of the Self: The Making of the Modern Identity.* Cambridge: Harvard University Press, 1989.

Tenenti, Alberto. *La Vie et la mort à travers l'art du XV^e siècle.* Paris: Armand Colin, 1952.

Terret, Victor. *La Sculpture bourguignonne aux XII^e et XIII^e siècles, ses origines et ses sources d'inspiration: Autun.* 2 vols. Autun: Taverne et Chandioux, 1925.

*Thesaurus linguae Latinae.* Leipzig: Teubner, 1900–.

Thibault, Geneviève, and David Fallows, eds. *Chansonnier de Jean de Montchenu* (Bibliothèque nationale, Rothschild 2973 [I.5.13]). Paris: La Société Française de Musicologie, 1991.

Thomas à Kempis. *De Imitatione Christi libri quatuor.* Edited by Tiburzio Lupo. Vatican City: Libreria Editrice Vaticana, 1982. Translated by William C. Creasy. *The Imitation of Christ.* Macon, Ga.: Mercer University Press, 1989.

———. *The Imitation of Christ: The First English Translation of the "Imitatio Christi."* Edited by B. J. H. Biggs. EETS OS 309. Oxford: Oxford University Press, 1997.

Thomas, Donald. *Lewis Carroll: A Portrait with Background.* London: John Murray, 1996.

Toliver, Harold. *George Herbert's Christian Narrative.* University Park: Pennsylvania State University Press, 1993.

*The Towneley Plays.* Edited by Martin Stevens and A. C. Cawley. EETS SS 13, 14. Oxford: Oxford University Press, 1994.

Tresko, Michael. "John Wyclif's Metaphysics of Scriptural Integrity in the *De Veritate Sacrae Scripturae.*" *Dionysius* 13 (December 1989): 153–96.

Trithemius, Johannes. *De laude scriptorum* (In Praise of Scribes). Edited by Klaus Arnold. Translated by Roland Behrendt. Lawrence, Kan.: Coronado, 1974.

Turner, Jane, ed. *The Dictionary of Art.* 34 vols. New York: Grove, 1996.

van Bastelaer, René. "Note sur quelques peintures du maître anonyme dit 'de Sainte-Gudule.'" *Académie royale de Belgique, Bulletins de la classe des beaux-arts* 6 (1924): 16–25.

van de Castyne, Oda. "Autour de 'L'Instruction pastorale' du Louvre." *Revue belge d'archéologie et d'histoire de l'art* 5 (1935): 319–28.

van Os, Henk, et al. *The Art of Devotion in the Late Middle Ages in Europe, 1300–1500.* Translated by Michael Hoyle. Princeton: Princeton University Press, 1994.

Vance, Eugene. *Mervelous Signals: Poetics and Sign Theory in the Middle Ages.* Lincoln: University of Nebraska Press, 1986.

Vidal, Gore. *Palimpsest: A Memoir.* New York: Random House, 1995.

Vincent of Beauvais. *Speculum quadruplex; sive, Speculum maius.* 4 vols. Douai, 1624. Reprint, Graz, Austria: Akademische Druck-u. Verlagsanstalt, 1964–65.

Voragine, Jacobus de. *Legenda aurea.* Edited by Th. Graesse. *Legenda aurea vulgo historia lombardica dicta.* 3rd ed. Bratislava: Koebner, 1890; reprint, Osnabrück, 1969. Translated by William Granger Ryan. *The Golden Legend: Readings on the Saints.* 2 vols. Princeton: Princeton University Press, 1993.

Wallace-Hadrill, J. M. *The Frankish Church.* Oxford: Clarendon, 1983.

Watson, Thomas. "The Day of Judgment Asserted." Edited by James Nichols. *Puritan Sermons, 1659–1689.* 6 vols. 1844–45. Reprint, Wheaton, Ill.: Richard Owen Roberts, 1981. 5:459–70.

———. *Gods Anatomy upon Mans Heart.* London, 1649.

Wattenbach, Wilhelm. *Das Schriftwesen im Mittelalter.* 3rd ed. Leipzig: Hirzel, 1896.

*Webster's Third New International Dictionary of the English Language, Unabridged.* Edited by Philip Babcock Gove et al. Springfield, Mass.: Merriam, 1966.

Wells, John Edwin. *A Manual of the Writings in Middle English, 1050–1400.* New Haven: Connecticut Academy of Arts and Sciences, 1916. *Supplements* 1–9, 1919–52.

Wharton, Edith. *The House of Mirth.* 1905. Edited by Shari Benstock. Boston: St. Martin's, 1994.

*The Wheatley Manuscript.* Edited by Mabel Day. EETS OS 155. London: Oxford University Press, 1921.

Wilson, John. *Cheerfull Ayres or Ballads.* 3 vols. Oxford, 1660.

þe *Wohunge of Ure Lauerd.* Edited and translated by Richard Morris. *Old English Homilies and Homiletic Treatises of the Twelfth and Thirteenth Centuries.* EETS OS 29, 34. London: Trübner, 1868. Reprint, New York: Greenwood, 1969. 268–304.

Woolf, Rosemary. *The English Religious Lyric in the Middle Ages.* Oxford: Clarendon, 1968.

Woolf, Virginia. *To the Lighthouse.* 1927. Reprint, New York: Harcourt, 1989.

Wright, Robert. "Can Machines Think?" *Time* 147, no. 13 (25 March 1996): 50–58.

Wyclif, John. *De veritate sacrae scripturae.* Edited by Rudolf Buddensieg. 3 vols. London: Trübner, 1905–1907. Reprint, New York: Johnson, 1966.

Yates, Frances A. *The Art of Memory.* Chicago: University of Chicago Press, 1966.

*York Plays: The Plays Performed by the Crafts or Mysteries of York.* Edited by Lucy Toulmin Smith. 1885. Reprint, New York: Russell & Russell, 1963.

Yovell, Yoram. "From Mechanism to Metaphor—On Freud's Struggle with the Biology of the Mind." *Journal of The American Academy of Psychoanalysis* 25 (1997): 513–24.

# INDEX